THE TRIBE OF BLACK ULYSSES

WILLIAM P. JONES

The Tribe of

Black Ulysses

AFRICAN AMERICAN LUMBER WORKERS

IN THE JIM CROW SOUTH

UNIVERSITY OF ILLINOIS PRESS

URBANA AND CHICAGO

FRONTISPIECE: Logging crew, Greene Brothers
Lumber Company, Colly Swamp, N.C., 1948.
Courtesy of Ben Greene, Elizabethtown, N.C.

© 2005 by the Board of Trustees
of the University of Illinois
All rights reserved
Manufactured in the United States of America
∞This book is printed on acid-free paper.
I 2 3 4 5 C P 5 4 3 2 I

Library of Congress Cataloging-in-Publication Data
Jones, William Powell, 1970–
The tribe of black Ulysses : African American lumber workers in
the Jim Crow south / William Powell Jones.
p.   cm. — (The working class in American history)
Includes bibliographical references and index.
ISBN 0-252-02979-8 (Cloth : alk. paper)
ISBN 0-252-07229-4 (Paper : alk. paper)
 1. African American men—Southern States—Social conditions—
20th century. 2. Industries—Southern States—History—20th century.
3. Industrialization—Southern States—History—20th century.
4. Working class—Southern States—History—20th century. I. Title.
II. Series.
E185.92J66   2005
331.6'396073075'09034—dc22   2004018189

to my southern roots
Marjorie Pauline Kieser Wright
& William Powell Jones

Contents

Illustrations

Acknowledgments

This book would not have been possible without the openness and generosity of the people who shared their stories and experiences with me during my research. I am particularly indebted to Adel McDowell and Ben Greene in Elizabethtown, North Carolina; Willie Ginn and William Baily in Bogalusa, Louisiana; and Fletcher Curry and Ire Abrams in Chapman, Alabama. They not only shared their own memories but also helped me identify and track down others who spoke to me as well. My research was also facilitated by individuals who introduced me to people connected to the lumber industry in particular areas, suggested local archival sources, and provided me with office space and assistance during my travels. They include David Cecelski and F. W. Newton in North Carolina and Melinda Ettle and Marylyn G. Bateman in Louisiana. I also could not have completed these trips without the friendship and hospitality given by Karl and Emily Bader in Atlanta, Melinda and Bob Ettle in Franklinton, Steve Donahue and Tim Vining in Baton Rouge, and June Schneider in Washington, D.C.

I also appreciate the advice and assistance provided by librarians at the Southern Labor Archives, the Forest History Society, Perkins Library, the Southern Historical Collection, the Washington Parish Public Library, the Alabama Department of Archives and History, the National Archives, the Library of Congress, and the Walter Reuther Library. Nathaniel Green provided top-rate research assistance in Washington, and Jeff Place gave me access to the Smithsonian's collection of recorded music. Research was funded by a Ford Foundation Dissertation Fellowship for Minorities, a Smithsonian Graduate Student Fellowship at the National Museum of American History, a Minority Presence Fellowship for Doctoral Study at the University of North Carolina–Chapel Hill, an Oral History Research Stipend from the Southern Oral History Program at the University of North Carolina–Chapel Hill, an Archie Green Occupational Folklife Graduate Fellowship from the University of North Carolina–Chapel Hill, a George E. Mowry Research Award from the Department of History at the University of North Carolina–Chapel Hill, and an Institute of African American Research grant from the University of North Carolina–Chapel Hill. The Rutgers Center for Historical Analysis and the University of Wisconsin-Milwaukee College of Letters and Science supported the transformation of this project from a dissertation into a book.

From start to finish, Leon Fink and Jacquelyn Dowd Hall provided advice, encouragement, and (when needed) pressure that were critical to the completion of this project. Bob Korstad, Genna Rae McNeil, Peter Coclanis, Glenn Hinson, Richard Soloway, and Don Reid helped to frame the early stages of research and supported me as it developed. My efforts to analyze this material were aided immensely by conversations with Rachel O'Toole, Mark Healey, Rob Steinfield, Michelle Strong, Doina Harsanyi, Pete Daniel, Jerma Jackson, Adolph Reed, Alex Lichtenstein, Judith Stein, T. Dunbar Moodie, Gerald Horne, David Oshinsky, Steven Lawson, Toby Higbie, Dylan Penningroth, and Tom Klubock. Dave Anderson and Chris Endy read the entire manuscript as it developed and gave essential support and criticism throughout. Herman Bennett, Zachary Morgan, Paul Clemens, Peter Lau, Al Howard, Alison Isenberg, Jim Livingston, Eric Arnesen, Martha Biondi, Margo Anderson, Steve Meyer, Jasmine Alinder, and Tera Hunter provided close readings at later stages, as did participants in the "Industrial Environments" seminar at the Rutgers Center for Historical Analysis and the Newberry Library Labor History Seminar. Anonymous readers with *Labor History*, the *Journal of American History*, and *American Quarterly* helped me think through questions that were critical to the completion of this book. I am also grateful for the careful attention that this manuscript received from Laurie Matheson, Richard Wentworth, Angela Burton, Ann Youmans, David Montgomery, Joe W. Trotter, and an anonymous reader at the University of Illinois Press.

Finally and most importantly, I thank my family for the intellectual, spiritual, and financial resources that allowed me to complete this project. My partner Christina Ewig read this manuscript several times over the years, and her intellectual and political analysis informs every page. My son Gabriel lifted my spirits while I was writing and gave me better things to do when I could take time away. My brothers never told me I was crazy to spend so much time on this—even though I'm sure they thought I was. My parents gave me the interest in history, family, and social justice that inspired this project—as well as the intellectual training to complete it. This book is dedicated to their southern parents.

Introduction: Rethinking the Myth of Black Ulysses

Between 1870 and 1910, lumber grew faster and employed more workers than any other industry in the southern United States. The Atlantic and Gulf Coasts of the South, where lumber production was most intense, saw a rate of industrialization between 1880 and 1900 that was twice that of the mountains and three times that of the Piedmont, where the other important southern industries of mining and textiles developed. Southern lumber workers produced $185 million worth of lumber in 1900, twice the value of southern textile production and three times that of coal. Whereas other industrial employers marginalized or excluded black workers, African American men formed the majority of the southern lumber workforce. Eighty-three thousand black men worked in southern saw and planing mills in 1910, more than the entire number of southerners employed by cotton textiles and four times those employed in iron and steel. That number grew steadily until 1950, when roughly 180,000 black men toiled in saw or planing mills and logging operations, nearly all of them in the South. Before World War II, no other industry employed more African Americans.[1]

The Tribe of Black Ulysses tells the story of those black men and how they shaped the rural South in the first half of the twentieth century. At the nadir of the Jim Crow era, when white southerners used both law and terror to circumscribe African American social and political influence, black lumber workers retained a central role in the industrial transformation of the region. Early in the century, both black and white poor southerners fashioned southern labor markets by accepting lumber and other industrial work only as a seasonal supplement to farming. As black men conceded to lumber firms' demands for long-term employment in the 1920s, they retained influence by moving their families into sawmill villages and compelling their employers to adapt workplace and social policies to conform to their evolving social and cultural standards. Strengthened by New Deal labor regulations in the 1930s and supported by an expanding industrial union movement in the 1940s, these new communities presented a challenge to the social and political foundations of Jim Crow society.

In documenting black workers' influence in the lumber industry, I challenge readers to reconsider the relationship between African Americans and the history of economic and social change in the early-twentieth-century South. This book's title is a reformulation of a theory, first articulated by white sociologist Howard Odum in the 1920s, that understood black southerners as essentially incompatible with modernity. When individual black men entered the industrial workforce, according to Odum, they were forced to sever their ties to families and communities and to wander the South as outcasts, like Ulysses, the tragic hero of Greek myth. I propose an alternative interpretation that places Black Ulysses at the center of the story of modernization in the South. While they often left home in search of work, black lumber workers maintained ties to families and communities, initially returning to them between seasonal industrial employment and eventually bringing loved ones with them when they settled permanently in sawmill towns. Rather than developing outside of African American life, southern industrialization was in many ways defined by black lumber workers' struggles to establish new family and community relationships based on industrial wage work.[2]

Odum introduced Black Ulysses in a popular trilogy of novels published between 1928 and 1931, in which he called attention to a population that he believed was being victimized and pushed aside by the forces of modernization. Inspired by Alain Locke and other African American writers of the 1920s who argued that informed understanding of African American culture would be essential to progress in race relations, the sociologist refused to "sentimentalize the Negro" in ways that might detract from the damage that he believed was inflicted by racial oppression. Odum rejected the "minstrel types" that pervaded popular culture of the era and instead presented what he described as a "sort of untouched photograph" of the black men who toiled in sawmills, log camps, road gangs, and prisons of the rural South. He characterized those men as "Ramblin' minds," whose loose morals and weak connections to family and community stemmed from a shared background of "broken homes and family disorganization, open strife and struggle, wasted energies and resources in men, women, and children." To help readers empathize with the "finer points of humor, pathos, and poignancy" that he saw in black working-class culture, he tempered an otherwise tragic epic with lyrics of blues songs and romantic folk tales of "bad men" and "black sirens" who pursued "native quests for satisfaction, adventure and sex love" in worksites across the South. Black Ulysses, Odum contended, was "perhaps more representative of the Negro common man than any other."[3]

Selling more copies than any of his social scientific publications, Odum's Black Ulysses novels established the alienated working-class black man as a central figure in both fiction and nonfiction writing about the South in the 1930s. William Faulkner alluded to Black Ulysses in his 1932 novel *Light in August,* which featured the mixed-race Joe Christmas and other "young bachelors, or sawdust Casanovas" who wandered through Alabama and Mississippi sawmill towns selling moonshine whiskey and seducing young women. In 1933, folklorist John Lomax and his son Alan met Huddie Ledbetter, a black prisoner and blues musician who they repackaged and promoted to national and international audiences as "Leadbelly"; a lifelong criminal "who had no idea of money, the law or ethics and who was possessed of virtually no self-restraint." Ledbetter preferred

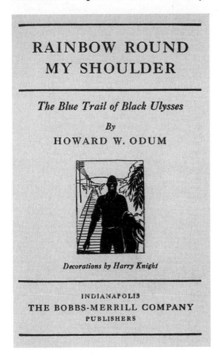

Photo 2. Frontispiece woodcut of Black Ulysses by Harry Knight in Howard W. Odum, *Rainbow 'round My Shoulder: The Blues Trail of Black Ulysses* (Indianapolis: Bobbs-Merrill Co., 1928).

to perform in a suit and bow tie, according to scholar Hazel Carby, but the Lomaxes convinced him to don overalls and a bandanna that more closely fit their image of a rural worker. They also emphasized his criminal record and violent temper, underscoring Odum's contention that African American manhood was personified by the southern working-class outlaw.[4]

Odum's depiction of pathological black working-class men did not go unchallenged, particularly among African American writers, but even his detractors accepted his central argument that racism had alienated black southerners from modernization. Anthropologist Zora Neale Hurston provided the sharpest critique of Odum in a series of short stories and novels based on her fieldwork in Florida sawmill towns in the late 1920s and early 1930s. The most influential of these was her 1935 publication *Mules and Men,* which adopted Odum's technique of combining descriptive prose with songs and stories that she claimed to have heard directly from African American mill workers. While Odum depicted Black Ulysses as damaged by modernization, however, Hurston portrayed black working-class southerners as heroic defenders of an alternative "folk" culture. Where Odum saw moral laxity and social pathology, Hurston discovered an alternative value system that she believed persisted only where African Americans were culturally isolated from whites. Both agreed that African Americans were essentially alienated by the process of modernization in the South, and that they could either resist or succumb to—but never influence—its development.[5]

A third variation on the myth of Black Ulysses emerged from African American writers such as E. Franklin Frazier, Richard Wright, and Langston Hughes, who accepted Odum's belief that industrialization debilitated black workers in the South but who saw the potential for liberation through migration to the North. Inspired by the proletarian literary movement of the 1930s, Frazier and the others argued that cultural breakdown associated with sawmill towns and logging camps in the rural South provided a necessary first step toward African Americans' assimilation into the multiethnic working-class culture that they believed to be emerging in the proletarian neighborhoods of the urban North. "Among the million Negroes who deserted the rural communities of the South," Frazier wrote in his notorious 1939 study *The Negro Family in the United States,* "there were thousands of men and women who cut themselves loose from family and friends and sought work and adventure as solitary wanderers from place to place. Some of the men had their first glimpse of the world beyond the plantation or farm when they worked in sawmills, turpentine camps, or on the roads," according to Frazier. "Some of the women had their first experience with city life when they went to a near-by town to work temporarily for a few dollars a month in domestic service." Freed from the "religious restraints imposed by rural churches" and the "censure of the elders for their 'sinful conduct,'" Frazier contended that "tribeless" men and women adapted quickly to the more egalitarian family styles of the urban proletariat. Because that "process of assimilation and acculturation will be limited by the extent to which the Negro becomes integrated into the economic organization and participates in the life of the community," however, the black sociologist predicted that those who remained in southern industrial towns would persist in a state of limbo between agricultural and industrial civilization. Frazier cited Odum's Black Ulysses as a "composite picture of the impulsive behavior of this group compressed in a single fictional character."[6]

With the increased visibility of African Americans in the industrial North during the 1940s, few scholars saw reason to question Odum's, Hurston's, and Frazier's pessimism about black workers' participation in the industrialization of the South. In his antimodern polemic *The Mind of the South*, W. J. Cash contended that southern blacks were too footloose—and southern whites too rooted in tradition—to embrace what he saw as the "dull and unvarying proletarian order" idealized by Frazier and other sociologists. Historian C. Vann Woodward challenged Cash in his influential 1951 study *The Origins of the New South*, showing that southern workers had in fact embraced industrialization and at times used economic change as a basis for reforming society. He also criticized Cash and other writers who based their claims for southern conservatism on generalizations about textile workers—who were nearly all white and who had in fact rejected repeated movements toward unionization and social reform. Even as he turned his attention to workers in interracial industries such as iron, steel, and tobacco, however, Woodward devoted very little attention to African Americans. He also continued an older tradition of centering the narrative of "southern labor" on the choice that white workers made between excluding black workers from the labor market or welcoming them into white-dominated unions.[7]

Ironically, even as scholars began to take seriously Woodward's criticism of southern exceptionalism, they did so in ways that often reinforced African Americans' exclusion from the narrative of southern industrialization. Authors of the groundbreaking 1987 study *Like a Family* set out initially to compare mostly white textile workers to interracial workforces in tobacco and furniture manufacturing. After those comparisons proved unwieldy, they turned instead to the question of how textile workers had reformed southern industry in ways that were over-

looked by historians preoccupied by unionization. In so doing, they produced a remarkable model of southern social history, one that proved
invaluable for scholars including myself who later took up their plan of
writing a racially inclusive southern labor history. *Like a Family*'s attention to family and community relations, as well as to the interactions
between economic, cultural, and political transformation allowed us to
see the wide intersections between the often segregated histories of black
and white working-class southerners. At the same time, however, *Like
a Family*'s singular focus on white textile workers did little to challenge
the impression that, as economic historian Gavin Wright wrote in 1986,
black lumber workers "did not build up either the sense of self-identity
or social visibility of the cotton mill people."[8]

The Tribe of Black Ulysses builds on and extends a body of literature—
much of it inspired by *Like a Family*—that has finally restored African
Americans to the narrative of southern industrialization. Tera Hunter's
study of Atlanta domestic workers demonstrates that even when black
women were excluded from industrial jobs they performed cleaning and
other household tasks that were critical to the emergence of the industrial New South. *Like a Family* coauthor Robert Korstad's study of tobacco
showed that black women also performed important industrial jobs, and
both Hunter and Korstad showed that black working-class women built
some of the most radical and transformative political movements in the
history of southern labor. Studies of unionization and political radicalism
among mostly male interracial workforces in docks, mines, and steel mills
also belied traditional images of quiescent and racially divided southern
workers. Even scholars of textile workers now recognize that African
Americans in fact lived and worked in cotton mill towns, and that their
presence in those communities and in the broader society led white workers to form racial identities that did not always preclude class-based alliances across the color line.[9]

While scholars provided a much richer portrait of working-class life
in the Jim Crow South, they have rarely generalized their insights to advance a coherent theory of black southerners' relationship to industrialization. Existing studies of the lumber industry focus almost exclusively
on the white minority of the workforce. Scholars of smaller interracial occupations such as mining, transportation, and tobacco processing have restricted their studies to specific cities and often to union campaigns, avoid-
ing broad regional and social-historical generalizations that remain
obligatory in studies of textile workers. Those who have generalized often turn back to theories very similar to those articulated by Odum, Frazier, and Hurston in the 1920s and 1930s. When Jacqueline Jones sought

to integrate the rural South into her study of the working poor, for example, she relied on reports by contemporaries of Odum who characterized industrial employment as an "assault" on African American traditions, one that "eroded family integrity," encouraged alcoholism and prostitution, and threatened black workers with a "slippery descent into peonage and convict labor." Ronald Lewis and Joe William Trotter echo Frazier when they describe black mining communities as "transitional" spaces in the broader trend toward African Americans' incorporation into the "proletarian synthesis." More often, scholars adopt Hurston's belief that African Americans were simply bypassed by industrialization in the South, often implying that exclusion placed them outside the otherwise progressive trends of modernization. Glenda Gilmore argues that black middle-class activism acquired a special significance in the early twentieth century because black workers were excluded "from participation in the South's industrial awakening." Leon Litwack writes that industrial employment allowed the white South to "pull itself up by its bootstraps," while black southerners found only a "fleeting" foothold in lumber and a few other industries before they "were forced back into agricultural labor."[10]

In the following chapters, I will demonstrate not only that black southerners had much more than a fleeting foothold in southern industry but also that industrial employment was seen by African Americans themselves as a basis for strengthening their families and communities. My theoretical premise grew out of an oral history project in eastern North Carolina in which older African Americans contradicted most written histories by telling me over and over how important lumber employment had been to the economic and social stability of their communities. The project was sponsored by the University of North Carolina's Southern Oral History Program (the same institution that sponsored research for *Like a Family*), and, being trained by scholars attuned to the "interpretive authority of ordinary people," I set out to test my informants' claims that industrial jobs helped them escape abusive relationships, build houses and buy consumer goods, and send their children to school. Memory, of course, can be deceiving, and I have not relinquished the historian's traditional responsibility to derive meaning from the various sources that compose the story that follows. One sawmill worker's claim that his employer was "a great asset to the black people," for example, must be considered in relation to the low wages and horrific conditions that characterized most African American employment in the Jim Crow South. I have corroborated oral history interviews with census and archival data, and I urge readers to keep in mind the racist terror, forced labor, and political disfranchisement that form the background against which *The Tribe of Black Ulysses* must be understood.[11]

As I expanded my focus beyond North Carolina, I found significant variations in the development of lumber towns, patterns that produced striking differences in the transformation of race and class relations in three distinct regions of southern lumber production. Large lumber companies moved to eastern North Carolina in the 1930s, rapidly transforming the region's economy from agriculture to industry and solidifying rigid race and class lines between black wage earners and white employers and landowners. More typical of early-twentieth-century lumber towns were those in southern Alabama, where the lumber industry developed in the 1880s. Because black and white Alabama lumber workers entered lumber employment on relatively equal standing, often working similar jobs for similar wages, they developed a remarkable degree of interracial cooperation by the 1930s and 1940s. A third pattern appeared in southeastern Louisiana, where the largest southern lumber companies began operating at the turn of the century but weathered timber shortages by diversifying into paper production in the 1930s. By granting white workers a monopoly on the well-paid and unionized paper mill jobs while restricting black workers to low-paid sawmill and logging jobs, managers encouraged economic and social distinctions between black and white workers and set the stage for protracted and often violent competition between these racially defined communities. Focusing on representative lumber towns in each of these states—Elizabethtown, North Carolina; Chapman, Alabama; and Bogalusa, Louisiana—illustrates how local variations in the industry complicated African Americans' efforts to move from farming to industrial wage work.

Despite local variations, black men in each of these regions made lumber work an essential component of their economic lives. In the first decades of the twentieth century, most black men viewed lumber work as a seasonal supplement—a way, as one Alabama sharecropper described it, "to make a speck if I could and then go back to my farm."[12] Rather than undermining traditional ways of life, industrial wages allowed many black men to accumulate livestock, farming equipment, and land that contributed to the goal of market independence that had defined many black men's aspirations since the Reconstruction and Populist eras. Only after World War I, when an agricultural depression rendered farming an increasingly unreliable occupation, did black men begin to accept lumber employment as a permanent and primary source of income. Even then, industrial wages allowed black men to establish households in sawmill towns and to contribute to schools, churches, and other institutional bases of what became southern proletarian societies. Hardly sources of despair and social breakdown, sawmill towns and logging camps provided thousands of black men with the economic foundation upon which they established new roles for themselves as husbands, fathers, and members of communities.

By creating proletarian communities in sawmill towns, African Americans played a central role in creating and transforming southern popular culture. Sawmill town saloons, or barrelhouses, were notorious for their rowdy, male-dominated environment, as well as for "barrelhouse blues," a piano style that gained a national audience in the expanding "race record" market of the 1920s. As women moved into sawmill town communities and as commercial culture became more accessible through phonographs and radio, however, working-class communities began to favor more mixed-gender and cosmopolitan musical styles such as swing. Historians have drawn a distinction between the "public" or "mainstream" culture dominated by whites and middle-class blacks, and the "private world" of working-class institutions, where, according to Robin D. G. Kelley, "one finds an essential component of Southern black working-class consciousness and politics in the Age of Jim Crow." Neither barrelhouses nor swing dances fit neatly into either category, however, since they were created by both African Americans and white employers and since both played important roles in shaping the mainstream of southern popular culture. Hardly a sanctuary from white oppression, black leisure culture became the terrain upon which class and racial tensions were fought out. If sawmill towns produced a "blues aesthetic," as Tera Hunter described the ethos that informed black cultural production, this was a style that attracted blacks and whites, workers and employers, and was never the property of black working people alone.[13]

Scholars who emphasize African American "private" expression assume that because black southerners were prevented from participation in "public" discourse they made home and community the primary focus of their cultural and political expression. They turned segregation, as Earl Lewis has written, into "congregation." While it may help us understand African American reactions to exclusion from electoral politics and segregation in public accommodations, this conception relies upon a rigid dichotomy between public and private spheres that cannot explain the extent to which African Americans influenced southern society in spite of Jim Crow. Unlike the slave and peasant societies from which such models were derived, the New South was a rapidly industrializing society, where black migration, literacy, and access to consumer markets provided a constant challenge to white or middle-class cultural supremacy. To relegate black working-class culture to a "hidden transcript," as James C. Scott proposes, is to describe Black Ulysses as Odum did: "Timeless and spaceless, a part of the nation and apart from it, wondering what it is all about."[14]

Perhaps the most significant difference between racial politics in the slave South and those of the post–Civil War New South was the replacement of a republican view of politics, which considered slaves to be the political dependents of their masters, with a liberal conception of citizenship that gave the state a primary and direct responsibility for regulating the lives of African Americans. While white supremacists succeeded in reserving that responsibility for southern state and local governments at the turn of the century, the expansion of the federal government in the 1930s complicated official efforts to manage black lives. This transformation was particularly important for black industrial workers, who unlike agricultural and domestic workers were subject to federal wage and hour laws designed to rescue the industrial economy from the Great Depression. Long before they gained voting rights, black industrial workers entered into debates over New Deal labor regulations and then used those policies to transform the distribution of wealth and power in their communities. By claiming citizenship rights stated by the Reconstruction amendments to the Constitution, these black workers played a role in "creating the modern South" that previous historians have attributed only to white textile workers.[15]

In addition to countering attempts to isolate them from state power, black workers' embrace of New Deal labor regulations also challenged the belief perpetuated by Odum and Frazier that Jim Crow had destroyed African American men's sense of responsibility to families and communities. When New Deal policy makers threatened to raise lumber wages above the starvation levels common at southern sawmills, many southern employers complained that since their workers were not heads of families they should not be expected to earn family wages. Invoking popular views of Black Ulysses, managers argued that lumber workers were "shiftless" and "irresponsible," and therefore that high wages would only encourage laziness and "mischief." So entrenched had these myths become in popular imagination by the mid-1930s that even some conservative African American activists agreed that "racial characteristics" justified the practice of paying lower wages to black workers. New Deal policy makers were skeptical of these arguments, however. Convinced that working-class participation in consumer markets provided a key to recovery from the Great Depression, and aware of African Americans' increasing importance as consumers, federal bureaucrats took seriously letters from lumber workers who argued that male breadwinning did indeed play an important role in the economies of black working-class households and communities. Those letters and lobbying from small but increasingly influential left wings of the National Urban League (NUL) and the National Association for the Advancement of Colored People (NAACP) convinced the Roosevelt administration to include black men within their policy of stimulating economic growth by bolstering male wage earning.[16]

By extending federal jurisdiction to black industrial workers, New Deal wage and hour laws furthered a transformation in black family and community relations that had been occurring since black men began seeking year-round lumber employment in the 1920s. Whereas previous generations of black men saw seasonal lumber work as supplementary to their cooperation with other members of farming families, in the 1930s lumber wages became the primary source of income for many African American families. Black women also shifted from agricultural work to work centered on the industrial setting of lumber towns. Many found independent sources of income through domestic wage work, taking in boarders and laundry, or operating stores, cafes, and saloons that catered to wage earners. Other women used male wages to enable them to restrict their labor to their own homes and families. Increased adult income allowed black children to withdraw from the labor market and increase their school attendance. Industrial wages provided an economic medium through which African Americans established new family and community models to replace those left behind in agricultural settings.[17]

In the late 1930s, as employers succeeded in limiting federal intervention in southern labor relations, black lumber workers turned to unions as critical allies in their struggle for a "family wage." Initially, national union leaders also accepted the myth of Black Ulysses, arguing that African Americans lacked the discipline and self-confidence to sustain a labor movement in the notoriously antiunion Jim Crow South. As black and white lumber workers began to organize themselves independently of established unions, however, and as civil rights organizations pressured unions to devote more resources toward recruiting black workers, both the American Federation of Labor (AFL) and the Congress of Industrial Organizations (CIO) started to support local unions in the southern lumber industry. As a result of unionization, wage increases that started in the 1930s continued until black lumber workers' wages approximated industrial wages in higher-paid northern industries. By the early 1950s, black lumber workers began to build houses, buy automobiles, and in other ways achieve a standard of living commonly associated with white working-class families of the same decade.[18]

While the lived experiences of black lumber workers often contradicted the theories of Odum and other writers who sought to analyze their
relationship to the industrial South, those experiences were nevertheless
deeply intertwined with the intellectual history of such analysis. Indeed
as historian Joan W. Scott points out, any effort to distinguish the experiences of oppressed peoples from the beliefs that rationalized their oppression runs the risk of reifying that system, or reproducing its terms. That
is why my account of black lumber workers' lives includes a "critical examination of the ideological system" that I call the myth of Black Ulysses. Federal regulations and union contracts lent strength to black men's
struggle for a family wage, but neither the government nor the labor movement was willing or able to ensure that lumber firms would continue to
employ black workers who no longer conformed to their expectations.
While New Deal bureaucrats and union leaders were willing to believe that
black men deserved wages that would support their families and communities, lumber company owners refused to think of their employees as
anything other than rootless and irresponsible. Starting with the success
of union campaigns in the late 1940s, southern firms began to abandon
lumber for less labor-intensive paper production and, increasingly in the
1950s, to shut down production completely. Government officials coun-
tenanced the defeat of black men's half-century-long struggle to redefine
their families and communities in the 1960s and 1970s when they failed
to ensure a place for well-paid black workers in the high-tech and service
industries that replaced lumber and textiles as the staples of southern
economies.[19]

An irony of the decline of the southern lumber industry is that the
loss of black industrial jobs allowed Odum and Frazier's descriptions of
Black Ulysses to prevail in subsequent writing about black working-class
southerners. Because civil rights activism was most visible in urban,
middle-class communities, few scholars questioned Odum's portrait of
powerless and defeated black workers in the rural South. Richard Kluger
wrote in 1977, for example, that economically and educationally privileged African Americans initiated the movement while "the black masses
were still ignorant of their rights, for the most part." Such claims have
been thoroughly discredited by Charles Payne and other scholars who
demonstrated that working-class African Americans were in fact early
and often the only supporters of civil rights activism in both urban and
rural communities. Nevertheless, revisionists write against the grain of
a literature deeply informed by the myth of Black Ulysses.[20]

As they rediscovered a history of black working-class activism in
northern cities, scholars also adopted Frazier's clarification that Black

Ulysses was a transitional character, whose pathologies would erode with assimilation into the urban industrial proletariat. Even this narrative retained a tragic epilogue, however, as deindustrialization in the North robbed black men of the relatively high wages and steady employment that may have allowed them to establish the male-breadwinner households idealized by Frazier. In the 1960s, scholars and policy makers revived the myth of Black Ulysses—"the abandoned mothers, the roving men, the sexually experienced youth," to quote sociologist Nathan Glazer—as a medium for calling attention to the damage inflicted by racial oppression. Initially, liberals hoped that imagery would lend support for education and job creation programs aimed at supporting male breadwinning in black communities. When those programs proved insufficient to counteract the crisis generated by deindustrialization of urban areas and the shifting of resources toward suburbs, similar imagery served to justify conservative claims that racial inequalities resulted from cultural pathologies that were only exacerbated by government aid. Illustrating the degree to which contemporary analysis of black poverty remains rooted in the myth of Black Ulysses, historian Jacqueline Jones characterizes rural southern wage earners as prototypical of "America's Underclass."[21]

Returning to the historical context in which this myth first emerged, *The Tribe of Black Ulysses* provides a perspective that may help us transcend the combination of romanticism and fatalism that informs much analysis of racial inequality. The early twentieth century brought a tumultuous economic transformation to the South, as the collapse of agriculture destroyed an economic sector in which both black and white families had struggled to establish a modicum of economic and social security during the previous fifty years. As with the shrinking of urban industrial employment later in the twentieth century, that transformation threatened to plunge an already impoverished African American population into crisis, particularly as white workers, employers, and policy makers conspired to shut black workers out of jobs that may have replaced those lost to the transformation. Without minimizing the hardship caused by those restrictions, the story that follows shows that African Americans retained the ability to negotiate and at times even determine the direction of economic transformation in the early-twentieth-century South.

Black men's initial resistance to proletarianization through seasonal employment before World War I belied their image as helpless victims of modernization. Their efforts to establish themselves as breadwinners through lumber jobs in the 1920s and 1930s also demonstrated an ability to embrace new opportunities afforded by industrialization and to adjust their values and aspirations to fit a changing economic and social reality. At the same time, federal labor legislation and support from established labor and civil rights organizations proved critical in forcing employers to recognize and at times even concede to black men's claims to a family wage. The fact that black workers ultimately failed to maintain those claims should not lead us to accept the premise that their defeat was preordained. Indeed, the extent to which they succeeded demonstrates the great possibilities that arise when governments and social movements lend political support to the social and economic aspirations of working people.

1 Remaking a Southern Lumber Mill World

When George Williams joined the International Union of Timber Workers (IUTW) in 1919, he risked everything that he had worked for since moving to Bogalusa, Louisiana, twelve years earlier. Born in the decade before the Civil War, Williams belonged to a generation of black men who believed that property ownership formed the sole basis for economic and social security. That goal motivated former slaves to claim rights to land during the war and Reconstruction, and it formed the common ground upon which biracial Republican and Populist political movements rose and fell in the 1880s and 1890s. It also led Williams and hundreds of other black and white men to settle near Bogalusa, where they worked "off and on" for the Great Southern Lumber Company after it erected one of the region's largest sawmills in 1907. These men did not view their industrial jobs as their primary occupation. Rather, they thought of them as "public work," through which they earned the cash necessary to sustain their private lives as family farmers. Viewing wage work through the lens of nineteenth-century republicanism, they purchased land close enough to the company town that they could take industrial jobs without relinquishing the independence that they associated with farming. By 1919, Williams had accumulated "something like sixteen hundred dollars worth of household goods, and a very large house." Sol Dacus, who was elected president of the Bogalusa IUTW, claimed ownership of $3,500 worth of land and livestock as well as $1,300 worth of War Saving Stamps.[1]

It was not a quest for landed independence that impelled nearly eight hundred younger black men to follow Dacus and Williams into the timber workers' union in 1919. Earlier that year, Great Southern had threatened to lower wages just as wartime inflation began to raise prices in the region. Building on a wave of radical unionism in southern sawmills before the war, and emboldened by the unionization of nearly 70,000 West Coast sawmill workers, the American Federation of Labor (AFL) supported organization among white craft workers and eventually extended union membership to black and white unskilled laborers in Bogalusa. According to Mary White Ovington, a white socialist who was in Louisiana for a meeting of the National Association for the Advancement of Colored People (NAACP), southern lumber workers had even more potential for organization than their West Coast counterparts because "the western timber worker is usually single while the southern supports a wife and child." Aged sixty-five and fifty-five, respectively, Williams and Dacus had long supported their families by supplementing agriculture with industrial wage work. Rising land prices and falling agricultural profits had driven many younger men into complete reliance upon wage work, however. By 1919 even many white workers defended black men's demand that the Great Southern Lumber Company pay them enough to support their families. According to Ovington, this brief moment of interracial cooperation "marked, let us dare to hope, the turning point in the history of southern labor."[2]

The 1919 union drive failed to usher in an era of interracial unionism in the South, but it did mark a transition between two systems of labor relations in the region. Before Ovington's article reached print, Great Southern dashed her hopes by recruiting an armed militia that killed three union officers, drove hundreds of their supporters out of town, and fueled a wave of racist and antiunion violence that devastated African American communities from Brownsville, Texas, to Rosewood, Florida, between 1919 and 1923. Even as they destroyed the Bogalusa union movement, however, company managers conceded to workers' demands for a family wage. General manager William Sullivan threatened to close the mill permanently following the union drive, but he reopened it in 1920 with a new commitment to what he termed "industrial permanency." Promising that "unless it is absolutely inevitable, we will not lay off men," Great Southern's managers pledged to transform their company town into a "healthful place" for a "man of family" to settle. The town was to be clearly segregated, and workers and managers would rarely agree on what constituted "healthful" conditions or even a "man of family." Nevertheless, following World War I, increasing numbers of southern lumber workers would accept employment on the assumption that it would serve as their only basis for supporting their families and communities. Whereas Williams and Dacus had viewed lumber jobs as supplemental to farming, younger generations would look to industrial employment as their most important and often sole source of support for their families and communities.[3]

"Cut-Out-and-Get-Out"

The lumber industry emerged on the geographic and political peripheries of the South. Some of the nation's richest pine forests grew naturally in a wide diagonal belt that stretched between the Appalachian Mountains and the Atlantic and Gulf Coasts, from southern Pennsylvania to eastern Texas. Within this belt a narrower swath produced longleaf pine, the dense but slow-growing wood most valued by lumber manufacturers and builders. Due to the concentration of prize timber in the lowlands, and the clearing of shortleaf pine in the plantation and Piedmont regions, southerners referred to the coastal plains of the Carolinas, Georgia, Florida, Alabama, Mississippi, Louisiana, and Texas as the "pine belt" or "piney woods." Between 1900 and 1949, this region accounted for roughly one-third of the lumber produced in the United States.[4]

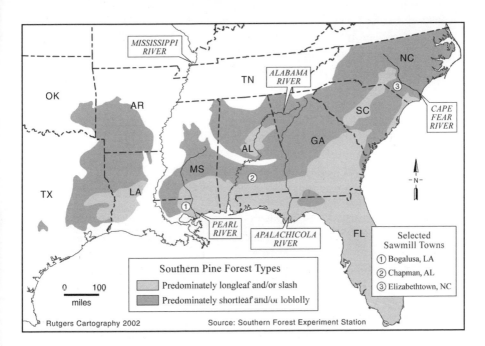

Figure 1. Map of southern pine region.

In a region dominated by plantation agriculture, southern lumbermen adapted their production strategies to meet the demands of an agricultural economy. Before the Civil War, few southern landowners saw enough profit in lumber production to invest in the logging and milling equipment necessary for market production. Even after emancipation shifted the basis of wealth in the region from ownership of slaves to ownership and improvement of land, southern industrialists lacked the capital, technology, and political influence necessary to compete with landlords for a steady supply of labor. Instead industrialists followed the ebbs and flows of the agricultural sector, employing labor primarily between the planting and harvesting seasons when labor costs were lower.[5]

Lumber firms were aided in this arrangement by the South's seemingly endless supply of timber. Lumber firms had overlooked southern forests during the northeastern and Great Lakes logging booms of the mid-nineteenth century, and by 1880 these forests contained twice as much pine as the rest of the United States. Reconstruction-era homestead laws sought to reserve abandoned plantation lands for small farmers and protected them from speculation by lumber firms and railroads. In 1877, the defeat of Reconstruction weakened homestead laws that reserved public lands for poor farmers, unleashing speculators in a buying frenzy that led one Forest Service authority to wonder whether "any parallel exists of such enormous capitalization of a natural resource." Five southern states privatized 5.5 million acres of public forestland before Congress revived homestead laws in 1888. In the interim, more than two-thirds of that land went to lumber firms based in Illinois, Michigan, and Wisconsin. Much of the remaining third went to southern-owned companies.[6]

The availability of cheap timber facilitated a wasteful "cut-out-and-get-out" strategy that lumber companies developed to overcome other impediments to southern production. Southern tax codes typically classified unused land at the same rate as productive land, discouraging firms from holding forests in speculation. Southern lumber companies were typically poorly capitalized collaborations between northern investors and New South entrepreneurs, and rather than purchase timberland outright, companies often bought it on loan, cleared it rapidly, and sold the land before interest and taxes accumulated. Firms also controlled costs by extracting only the most valuable, easily accessible timber, leading one critic to describe the four decades following Reconstruction as the "cream skimming" years of southern lumber production.[7]

Industrial wage employment in the South emerged in tandem with the rhythms of the region's agricultural sector. Seasonal bursts of production, typically running around the clock for a few weeks at a time, allowed

Photo 3. "Flatheads" logging with mules before introduction of steam skidders at Greene Brothers Lumber Company, Lewiston, Ala., 1920s. Courtesy of Ben Greene, Elizabethtown, N.C.

industrial firms to employ large numbers of men who were reluctant to abandon their family farms or sharecropping plots. "Public work," as both black and white farmers called their off-season wage employment, provided a convenient source of quick cash that most often went toward strengthening their position as independent farmers. Alabama sharecropper Ned Cobb, for example, sought sawmill work with specific goals in mind, such as financing his wedding, buying a mule, or as he put it, "to make a speck if I could and then go back to my farm." Asked why he rejected offers of long-term lumber employment, Cobb replied, "I didn't know definitely at the time 'bout what the sawmills would bring me."[8]

Economists have labeled such a relationship "articulation" to describe the process whereby agricultural and industrial economies supplement each other. This concept has been developed most thoroughly in the cases of southern and western Africa, where mining and manufacturing sectors employed peasant laborers without forcing them to move permanently into industrial towns and cities. This arrangement provided workers with the cash income that was critical to their ability to maintain family farms, but it also freed employers from the responsibility of providing steady income, decent housing, and other social wages that would have been necessary to support working-class families and communities. In the United States, that freedom allowed southern lumber firms to emerge as the largest and most profitable enterprises in what became known as the New South. Sawmills produced 16 percent of southern manufacturing value in 1900, and they paid an equal portion of the region's manufacturing wages. Between 1870 and 1910 lumber employed roughly twice as many southern workers as textiles, the region's next largest industrial employer. Despite their first allegiance to farming, southern workers produced nearly forty percent of the value added through lumber manufacturing in the United States between 1910 and 1930.[9]

As a result of this growth, lumber emerged as the most important employer for black men looking for alternatives to agriculture in the early twentieth century. A third of all black workers remained in agriculture in 1930, but a steady number of them abandoned farming for what they saw as more lucrative and personally satisfying work. For black women, such jobs were most readily available in domestic and personal service sectors, which employed more than a million black women in 1930. Black men preferred manufacturing and transportation, and by 1930 those two sectors employed almost as many black men as did agriculture. One hundred

Photo 4. "Fellers" using crosscut saw, Greene Brothers Lumber Company, Lewiston, Ala., 1920s. Courtesy of Ben Greene, Elizabethtown, N.C.

seventy thousand black men worked for railroads and railroad repair shops, jobs that were similar to lumber work in terms of wages and working conditions. Another seventy-five thousand found comparable employment in mining, primarily coal (table 1). The vast majority of black men who left agriculture ended up in manufacturing, and the plurality of these men worked in lumber. Black men held roughly 60 percent of sawmill and planing mill jobs in the South between 1890 and 1930. For the first half of the century, southern lumber was the largest employer of African American factory workers in the United States (tables 2 and 3).[10]

Black men were so successful at combining agricultural and industrial work that southern industrialists sometimes took desperate measures, such as using convict labor, to force them into long-term employment. Convict leasing is often cited as a cultural legacy of slavery, but as labor historian Alexander Lichtenstein has shown, the practice represented a response to black southerners' ability to negotiate their employment options in the New South. Rather than attempting to restore antebellum labor relations, employers hoped that forced labor under the convict system would accustom black workers to industrial discipline. The Alabama prison system leased nearly five hundred of its convicts to sawmill and turpentine producers in 1910, and according to a foreman at Dunham Lumber Company, the practice was critical to lumber production in the

Table 1. Black Gainful Workers Ten Years Old and Over, by Sector and Gender, for the United States, 1930

Sector	Total	Male	Female
All sectors	5,503,535	3,662,893	1,840,642
Agriculture	1,987,839	1,492,555	495,284
Domestic and personal service	1,576,205	423,645	1,152,560
Manufacturing and mechanical industries	1,024,656	923,586	101,070
Transportation and communication	397,645	395,437	2,208
Trade	183,809	169,241	14,568
Professional service	135,925	72,898	63,027
Extraction of minerals	74,972	74,910	53
Public service (not elsewhere classified)	50,203	49,273	930
Clerical occupations	40,549	29,687	10,862
Forestry and fishing	31,732	31,652	80

Source: U.S. Bureau of the Census, *Negroes in the United States, 1920–32:* 310–72.

Table 2. Employment in Leading (>20,000 workers) Southern Manufacturing Industries, 1910, 1930

Industry	Employment	Percent of U.S. Employment
1910		
Lumber and timber products	304,093	43.8
Cotton goods	145,589	38.4
Car and general shop construction by steam railroad companies	49,499	17.5
Turpentine and resin	39,511	100.0
Tobacco manufactures	31,578	18.9
Foundry and machine shop products	23,313	4.3
1930		
Cotton goods	269,991	63.5
Lumber and timber products	241,446	44.7
Car and general shop construction by steam railroad companies	69,803	18.9
Hosiery and knit goods	53,502	25.7
Turpentine and resin	40,157	100.0
Tobacco manufactures	37,000	31.9
Furniture	32,487	16.8
Printing and publishing	25,129	8.9
Foundry and machine shop products	21,986	4.8

Source: Gavin Wright, *Old South, New South: Revolutions in the Southern Economy since the Civil War* (New York: Basic Books, 1986), 160–61.

state, "especially in farming season" when free workers often abandoned sawmill work. Even Scarlett O'Hara, the protagonist in Margaret Mitchell's best-selling 1936 novel *Gone with the Wind*, contracted African American prisoners to work in her sawmill after the Civil War. "What she did and why she did it were typical of large numbers of resourceful Southerners," a spokesman for the Southern Pine Association (SPA) noted approvingly.[11]

After most southern states banned convict leasing in the first decade of the twentieth century, southern lumber firms attempted to secure reliable sources of labor through debt peonage. A Florida ship captain complained in 1921 that local sheriffs routinely removed black sailors from his vessel and delivered each of them as "a bonded prisoner" to nearby sawmills, mines, and plantations to work "at a starvation wage." As late as 1951, a Georgia attorney testified before the U.S. Senate that debt peonage was still "prevalent" in his home state and that "sawmill

Table 3. Black Gainful Workers Ten Years Old and Over in Leading
(>20,000 workers) Manufacturing and Mechanical Industries by
Occupation and Gender, for the United States, 1930

Occupation	Total	Male	Female
Building industry	181,423	181,173	250
Saw and planing mills	113,862	112,264	1,508
Blast furnaces and steel rolling mills	52,956	52,625	331
Other iron and steel and machinery factories	41,618	40,833	785
Other miscellaneous manufacturing industries	34,394	31,255	3,130
Cigar and tobacco factories	34,301	15,789	18,512
Turpentine farms and distilleries	32,683	32,402	281
Other not specified manufacturing industries	31,600	24,887	6,713
Independent hand trades	27,530	6,565	20,965
Automobile factories	25,895	25,598	297

Source: U.S. Bureau of the Census, *Negroes in the United States, 1920–32*, 337–59.

people—and I think they are the worst offenders I know of—get Negroes in debt to them purposely." The following year, a North Carolina union organizer complained of a judge who routinely bonded prisoners to the manager of a local sawmill in which the judge was also a stockholder.[12]

Mill owners also attempted to exploit other sources of labor, such as hiring immigrants, who could not so easily move back and forth between farm and factory. The Jackson Lumber Company lured more than a hundred European immigrants with promises of high wages and fair treatment to their Lockheart, Alabama, sawmill. In a trial that inspired that state's antipeonage movement in 1906, five German immigrants described being beaten, treated "worse than dogs," and forced to work like "white slaves" at the Lockhart mill. The W. T. Smith Lumber Company paid the New Jersey–based International Labor Exchange $500 to recruit twenty-five men to their operation at Chapman, Alabama, in 1905. Assuming that familial responsibilities would make employees more dependable, the recruiting service guaranteed the immigrants to be "sober, steady, industrious, aged from 30 to 40 years, and with families." The new employees expected to be paid one dollar a day in addition to board. Indicating that such arrangements did not offer a viable alternative to hiring local sources, W. T. Smith did not repeat the deal in the future.[13]

For southern lumber companies, neither forced nor immigrant labor provided a viable alternative to recruiting from agricultural labor markets. Convict contracts made employers responsible for escapes, strikes, and sabotage, and the need to counter progressive reform campaigns rendered leasing convicts as expensive as free labor. Peonage shifted these burdens to state law enforcement agencies, but officials were more likely to work prisoners on roads and other public works than to lease them to private enterprises. Immigrant labor contracts were expensive, and immigrants abandoned inhospitable workplaces as quickly as did local farmers. Eventually, post–World War I era immigration restrictions cut off this alternative entirely.[14]

The war also opened up northern industries to southern black workers, pushing the South's already unstable labor regime into a severe crisis. The Great Migration out of the South spelled the collapse of the seasonal labor system upon which southern mill owners had relied since the 1880s. Resistance to full-time wage employment had grown out of black men's belief that they could establish their economic independence through farming. The case of Alabama provides an instructive example. While lumber employment provided many Alabamans with access to land, most black farmers could afford only infertile lands on the fringes of the plantation "Black Belt" and coastal "piney woods" region. When agricultural prices collapsed after 1910, according to scholar Horace Mann Bond, "these small owners on unfruitful land speedily succumbed to the general decadence" of southern agriculture. Arthur Goodlett, whose father worked at a southern Alabama sawmill, claimed to have helped nearly a thousand African Americans leave the state between 1917 and 1921. Migration was most intense during fall months "after the crops had been reaped" and when local farmers were most likely to seek "public work" in the mills. Eight percent of Alabama's black population moved to the North in 1916 alone. One third of those who migrated between 1865 and 1920 did so between 1916 and 1918. A survey of black migrants living in Chicago in 1919 found that 20 percent of the men had worked in a sawmill before leaving the South.[15]

By 1919, federal investigators reported a "serious labor shortage" in the industry, finding 17 percent of all southern lumber jobs unfilled. Southern Pine Association officials attributed the shortfall to northern "labor agents . . . actively at work among the sawmills and logging camps." Hoping to counter the rumors spread by those who "organize the Negroes to go north," the SPA sent its own agents to the "Negro section of Chicago," where they endeavored to "show colored workmen that it is to their best interest to return and to remain in the South." The association also recommended that members support the *Negro Advocate,* an industry publication that industry leaders hoped would "keep the colored laborers of the South satisfied with their conditions, . . . advise against exodus of neighbors, . . . and elevate their morals."[16]

Even more alarming for southern employers than the Great Migration was the surge in union activity among black workers during World War I. Because southern men accepted lumber jobs only temporarily, they provided sporadic but militant support for unionization before the war. The Knights of Labor supported a series of biracial sawmill strikes on the Gulf Coast in the 1890s, but local assemblies disappeared quickly after management met their initial demands. The United Brotherhood of Carpenters and Joiners maintained a more consistent presence in southern sawmills, but it restricted membership to the tiny number of skilled craftsmen—carpenters, machinists, and lumberjacks—who relied solely on lumber wages. By controlling access to certain skills and by migrating among several employers, the members of the carpenters' union were able to demand "living wages" that distinguished them from the majority of southern lumber workers. The Brotherhood of Timber Workers, which appeared in 1911, represented an alternative to the Carpenters. The Brotherhood rejected the craft model and organized as many as twenty thousand skilled and seasonal workers in Texas and Louisiana by 1913, when it affiliated with the anarchist Industrial Workers of the World. According to a leader of the union, it was formed by skilled "lumberjacks" and "farmers" who sought seasonal employment in sawmills and logging operations. Even the carpenters union began organizing seasonal workers after Great Southern Lumber Company began replacing unionized craftsmen with "unskilled" African Americans in Bogalusa.[17]

Southern mill owners tolerated unionization among craftsmen, but they viewed unionization of their mostly African American common laborers as a threat to the very foundations of Jim Crow society. The Southern Lumber Operators' Association was created in 1906 "to resist *any* encroachment of organized labor" (emphasis in original). Southern mill owners created the less-militant Southern Pine Association (SPA) in 1914 in order to dispel criticism about antiunion violence and to focus more squarely on promoting their products. The resurgence of union activity during World War I pushed the SPA toward antiunion activism, though. By 1917 its president declared, "The labor of the South is very largely black labor, and unless we want to go back to the . . . Reconstruction period, we must avoid organization of these men." In 1919 the SPA hired detectives to investigate unionization in member sawmills and then coordinated a regional effort to destroy the AFL's International Union of Timber Workers. Following Great Southern's expulsion of union supporters from Bogalusa, firms in Florida and Mississippi halted union activity among common laborers by dragging organizers off trains, beating them, and promising to "kill everybody connected with all the unions in the world." AFL leaders requested federal protection for their organizers in the South, but the Department of Labor, conceding its weakness in the face of southern white supremacy, expressed doubts "as to what can be accomplished in Southern lumber camps having a large percentage of colored employees."[18]

Antiunion violence in southern sawmills fueled the wave of racist terror that swept through the South and the rest of the nation between 1919 and 1923. During the "Red Summer" of 1919, local officials in Elaine, Arkansas, responded to a union drive among local black sharecroppers by burning the church in which they met, shooting scores of union members, executing twelve other members, and imprisoning most of the others. Other acts of defiance inspired white mobs to burn black communities to the ground in twenty-five other cities. The number of lynchings peaked in 1919. One of those lynchings occurred in Bogalusa, one day before a biracial Labor Day parade was scheduled to take place. The general manager of the Bogalusa mill took advantage of the climate created by racist hysteria, warning that organization of "the darkies would . . . cause a race riot." The terror finally culminated in 1923 with a massacre in the Florida lumber town of Rosewood.[19]

The Rosewood massacre epitomized the ways in which southern lumber firms exploited racist terror in order to regain control over African American workers following World War I. Rosewood was adjacent to Sumner, a company town operated by Cummer and Sons Lumber Company on Florida's Gulf Coast. Like Great Southern, Cummer and Sons claimed to have lost control over local white supremacists who killed and terrorized company employees. The Rosewood massacre began after a white woman claimed to have been raped in Sumner, however, and managers did nothing to prevent a local mob from lynching a black man in the mostly black town of Rosewood. Rumors spread that Rosewood residents were arming themselves to prevent a second lynching, and mill superintendent Henry Andrews organized an armed posse to investigate the incident. He was met in Rosewood by a former "quarter boss," a white security officer who had been fired after repeated complaints from black workers. Company officials do not seem to have participated in the gunfight that broke out that evening, but the company commissary sold guns and ammunition to the members of the white mob who rushed into Sumner, bragging about how "they were shooting the whole town [of Rosewood] up, setting fire to houses, shooting people that ran out, just shooting everything they could, which was more or less the elderly men and women." Only after word spread that the mob was threatening to burn the company-owned "colored quarters" in Sumner did manager W. H. Pillsbury organize an armed group to defend the line between the two towns.[20]

Cummer and Sons used the Rosewood massacre as an opportunity to extend its influence over African Americans who previously lived outside of company control. Rosewood had been a classic "cut-out-and-get-out" community, organized by black and white families who established farms close to the company town of Sumner. Seven hundred people lived in Rosewood by 1910, a quarter of them white, and they earned a relatively comfortable living by combining family farming and sawmill work. When Cummer and Sons approached the end of its timber supply around 1920, company managers prepared to "get out" by establishing a second mill a hundred miles away in Lacoochee, Florida. Workers began to leave Rosewood as production slowed in Sumner, leaving a core of thirty black families and one white store owner by 1923. As one white resident recalled, those who remained were "high-type people" who "worked hard and seemed to do fairly well for themselves." Such independence may have allowed black Rosewood residents to remain in town even after the lumber company moved, but it also attracted the anger of white supremacists who resented any indications of black success. Having turned a blind eye to the destruction of their employees' property, Cummer and Sons managers arranged for a train to drive through the swamps, picking up survivors of the Rosewood massacre and offering them housing and employment in the brand new "colored quarters" in Lacoochee.[21]

Southern lumber firms could not afford to allow racist terrorists to deprive them of black labor. That is the reason Cummer and Sons barred the Ku Klux Klan from meeting in Sumner and why firms such as W. T. Smith Lumber Company likewise attempted to suppress the white supremacist organization in Butler County, Alabama, in the 1920s. Indeed, the destruction of Rosewood was most likely facilitated by the relinquishing of company control over Sumner after 1920. Reflecting on Great Southern's support for antiunion violence in Bogalusa, historian Horace Mann Bond observed that the mill's general manager was not "averse to violence, where the interests of his realm seemed to demand it." Following the 1919 lynching in Bogalusa, Louisiana, Great Southern imposed "necessary control" over the white supremacists in the area, who Bond called "local rebels." In words that would describe any of the largest southern lumbermen, Bond explained that "Sullivan was an autocrat; ruthless, sometimes whimsical, but always supreme, and lynchings were no part of the program of the process of civilization which he inaugurated in the Parish."[22]

Sullivan's civilizing efforts were adopted by other self-styled "Progressive Lumbermen" throughout the South in the 1920s and 1930s who began to consider more paternalistic methods of generating employee loyalty through the provision of "better housing and living conditions for their colored laborers, increased school facilities, fair wages and protection for the Negroes against unscrupulous officers of the law." In 1919, the owner of the W. T. Smith Lumber Company donated several hundred dollars to local "evangelical work," a "Negro school," and toward "encouraging gardening by employees." Such community improvements were needed if management was to recruit the respectable workers it sought. A 1921 federal report on African American industrial employment claimed that "floaters" and "crap-shooters" predominated among southern sawmill workers, because "respectable workers and their families" refused to live in the typical "quarters provided for logging and mill camps." The authors highlighted an exception to that rule, however, praising one employer who created a "real community" in his company town and "stimulated local pride in it." After hearing how that employer "spoke of his success in getting and holding labor of a splendid class in his little town," the investigators hoped other lumbermen would take a similar interest in the "development of community life in their camps, with better housing and family settlements."[23]

During the 1920s, most mill owners maintained that the only way to secure labor from a black man was to "keep him broke," but an influential minority of owners claimed that "the time has arrived for a more enlightened program" of labor recruitment. "We have tried to make [the sawmill town] a more liveable place," one mill owner reported to a 1926 meeting of the SPA. "We have worked with an idea of making a more contented crew, and I believe we have all accomplished a great deal along that line." A Texas lumberman pointed out to the same meeting that improved living conditions had decreased "movement" and "agitation" among his employees, and that it had the additional benefit of mitigating "friction between white and colored labor." Reversing the older orthodoxy that southern workers were too inefficient to justify investment in community improvements, a Department of Labor official pointed out that "it is unreasonable to expect one hundred percent efficiency from a man who is obliged to sleep in a public park, in a sub-basement, in a bathtub, or in a ten-by-twelve foot room with half a dozen other men."[24]

Those employers who did not alter their recruiting tactics benefited from a broader shift toward industrial employment in the region. The number of southern industrial workers rose by 4 percent between 1910 and 1920, while agricultural employment declined by 10 percent. The number of southern manufacturing workers again increased by 9 percent during the next decade, while northern industrial employment actually declined. Increases were most dramatic in southern lumber and textiles, each of which employed over 200,000 workers by 1927, at which time the South manufactured 40 percent of the nation's lumber and more than 50 percent of its cotton products. As they abandoned strong-arm tactics of the war era, southern lumber firms reestablished themselves as leaders in the industrialization of the region. This transition was facilitated by a stabilization of labor relations, but it also required new tactics for procuring raw materials. As in the "cut-out-and-get-out" era, labor recruitment and production strategies evolved in tandem following World War I.[25]

The "Cream Skimming Years" Come to an End

In addition to relying on cheap, seasonal labor, lumber managers' "cut-out-and-get-out" strategy also depended upon a cheap and seemingly endless supply of raw material. By 1920 the timber supply no longer looked endless. "There has been so much capitalistic exploitation of southern forests," one mill owner observed early in the twentieth century, "that in another decade the southern forest land will be barren." More than 150 million acres of forest were leveled between 1880 and 1920, primarily the thickest, most valuable, and easily accessible stands of timber. SPA members had debated the possibility of reforestation since 1914, but few saw it as a viable and productive strategy. Tree farming would have required fire management projects and changes in tax laws that were impossible to secure without considerable lobbying efforts. Furthermore, tree farming required additional capital to buy less wasteful logging and milling equipment and a workforce that was stable enough to learn how to operate it.[26]

Despite their reservations, Southern lumbermen's support for reforestation grew with the victory of a conservative movement within the U.S. Forest Service. In 1920, William B. Greeley replaced Gifford Pinchot, a foe of the SPA, as chief of the Forest Service. The SPA had criticized Pinchot's "radical" proposals for government oversight of the nation's disappearing timberlands, but southern lumbermen were enthusiastic about Greeley's "cooperative" strategies to provide federal tax incentives and fire protection services to support private reforestation. Alabama lumberman John Kaul invited Greeley to tour his company town in 1920, and the chief forester applauded the "excellent" results that Kaul had achieved in forests that had been "lumbered conservatively" in previous years. He also recommended a new French turpentining technique, "which can be done for twenty to thirty years without reducing growth of trees." Recognizing that productive strategies depended upon the ability to secure labor, Greeley noted that tests in Florida had shown good yields and had demonstrated that "its use by the average negro laborer is practicable."[27]

SPA president A. L. Clark endorsed Greeley's "cooperative" strategy in his 1921 presidential address, initiating a relationship between southern firms and federal forest management programs that would extend through the New Deal era. The SPA lobbied for a 1925 conservation act that funded state and federal fire prevention programs without limiting logging. The SPA also supported a 1928 bill that funded a national network of forest and range experiment stations to study forest resources and recommend uses for wood. While SPA members decried New Deal labor reforms in the 1930s, they limited their opposition in exchange for the strong conservation and marketing programs included in the legislation. The SPA also worked closely with the Civilian Conservation Corps, the New Deal job creation program that built logging roads and fire towers in both private and public forests. The SPA continued to support federal forest protection measures even after most southern lumbermen supported a movement to abolish other New Deal programs in the late 1930s.[28]

Cooperation with state and federal governments helped southern lumber owners to absorb some costs involved in the shift from "cut-out-and-get-out" to conservation in the 1920s and 1930s. Several southern states revised their tax codes to shelter timber land that was being held for regrowth. Greeley assured southern lumbermen that "too much emphasis should not be laid upon the matter of accessibility of second growth timber," since both state and federal governments helped firms offset the costs of harvesting thinner and more remote timber stands. By converting from log trains to trucks, mills took advantage of state-funded "good roads" initiatives that used unpaid, mostly African American, convicts to extend and improve southern highways. Federal forestry experts developed wood treatment processes that allowed firms to substitute depleted cypress and longleaf pine supplies with less weather-resistant shortleaf pine. Machinery developed during the mobilization for World War I was converted to peacetime use as overhead skidders that extracted large trees without damaging new growth below them. Military-grade steel created thinner saw blades, reducing the amount of wood that was ground into sawdust.[29]

Southern lumber companies that emerged as the industry's leaders after World War I were those that most successfully embraced the conservation movement. Great Southern Lumber Company, which operated what

It claimed was the "world's largest sawmill" in Bogalusa, Louisiana, first began farming and managing forests in the early 1920s. Discovering that second growth timber matured too slowly to sustain regular harvesting for lumber, Great Southern also began to diversify into paper production. While lumber would remain an important part of Great Southern's operations, its paper factories increasingly employed a larger percentage of its workforce. The Chapman, Alabama-based W. T. Smith also pioneered the application of conservation techniques to southern lumber production. Rather than seeking alternatives to large-scale production, W. T. Smith developed smaller sawmills that it dispersed throughout the local countryside to take advantage of thinning and second growth forests. Another strategy that lumber owners pursued was to find stands of virgin forest. The Greene Brothers Lumber Company adopted new technologies to survive the timber shortage of the 1920s, but it also adjusted by moving its operations from Alabama into previously untapped forests surrounding Elizabethtown, North Carolina. These three company towns—Bogalusa, Chapman, and Elizabethtown—not only illustrate the different strategies that lumber managers used to surmount the lumber shortage but provide a comparative perspective to analyze the impact of southern lumber production on race and class relations in the rural South.

Bogalusa, Louisiana

When brothers Frank and Charles Goodyear began construction of their company town of Bogalusa in 1905, they hoped it would become the "Magic City" of the "cut-out-and-get-out" era. Having depleted the timber surrounding three other company towns in western Pennsylvania, the Goodyear Lumber Company purchased 130,000 acres in southern Louisiana and Mississippi between 1880 and 1905. They sent William H. Sullivan to supervise construction of the "World's Greatest Lumber Plant" in Louisiana just south of the Mississippi border and to surround it with a "New South City of Destiny" named for the nearby Bogue Lusa Creek. They also ordered construction of the New Orleans and Great Northern Railroad (NOGN), which ran through Bogalusa between New Orleans and Jackson, Mississippi. The state of Louisiana chartered the entire operation—mill, town, and railroad—under the ownership of the Great Southern Lumber Company.[30]

While Bogalusa's scale gave it an appearance of permanence, Great Southern followed the "cut-out-and-get-out" practice of purchasing enough timber to support its operation for a fixed period of time. With nearly 200,000 logs entering the Bogalusa mill every month, Goodyear Lumber

Photo 5. Sawmill, Great Southern Lumber Company, Bogalusa, La., n.d.
Courtesy of Louisiana State University Special Collections, Baton Rouge, La.

Company calculated that their "Green Empire" contained 7 billion board feet of lumber, enough to sustain twenty years of production. To consume the enormous volume of timber that the company acquired, Sullivan extended three logging railroads six miles into the surrounding forests where management established logging camps. Mammoth steam skidders operated in each of the outlying camps, loading entire trees onto trains that carried them to a twenty-seven-acre millpond in Bogalusa. "Haul-ups" 280 feet high lifted logs into the mill, where four eight-foot band saws devoured seventy-foot logs at a rate of one every six minutes. Operating around the clock, Great Southern's 3,000 employees turned sixty acres of timber into a million board feet of lumber every day.[31]

Great Southern's thirst for labor lent a fleeting sense of stability to the local farm economy. Horace Mann Bond noted the relatively high number of black landowners in Washington Parish, which surrounds Bogalusa, in 1933, and credited that to black farmers' ability to earn cash wages at Great Southern. Historian Adam Fairclough found a "remarkable" level of economic parity between black and white farmers in Washington Parish, a measure of black farmers' ability to accumulate property through industrial wage work. "If the census had not classified people according to race it would have been impossible to tell black and white

Photo 6. Skidder crew posing with managers, Great Southern Lumber Company, Bogalusa, La., ca. 1931. Courtesy of Louisiana State University Special Collections, Baton Rouge, La.

families apart," Fairclough wrote in regards to the years between 1870 and 1920. By settling near Bogalusa, both black and white families were able to maintain family farms while continuing to send their young men periodically into wage work.[32]

Black and white workers seem to have used wage employment to establish independent communities near Bogalusa. Richardsontown, which was incorporated into Bogalusa in 1914, was named for the farmer who sold plots to white workers who settled there in 1908. Likewise, Poplas Quarters began as a community of black workers who bought land just beyond the town's northeastern border. Northwestern Bogalusa began as a patchwork of Italian immigrant and native-born white homesteads, all lying outside of company property. Such strategies allowed Sol Dacus, George Williams, and other men of their generation to maintain a level of autonomy through seasonal industrial employment. Bond noted that only the most successful black families were able to survive in Washington Parish without sending men to seek work in "the industrial city of Bogalusa, which has recruited all of its four thousand Negroes from the surrounding countryside within the last thirty years."[33]

For a time, local farmers persisted by buying up cut-over land from local lumber companies during the "cut-out-and-get-out" era, a practice first pioneered by Great Lakes lumber firms in the 1880s. But attempts to farm cut-over lands only "heaped tragedy upon tragedy" for those farmers who lacked the resources to clear and fertilize them. "With the exception of coarse wiregrass, nothing remained on the barren rolling hills save the tops and stumps" of felled trees, historian Jerry L. Merrick wrote of Great Southern's early operations. The firm even established a demonstration farm in 1912 in an attempt to sell its cut-over land to local farmers but could not avoid the fact that logging leaves lands in poor condition. Trees sequester large amounts of nutrients from forest soils in their wood and take them along when they are hauled to the mill. In addition, early skidders dragged logs across the forest floor, scraping off the topsoil and crushing young growth. Loggers cut trees several feet above the ground and left tree tops and branches where they fell. While it provided local farmers with cheap land, "cut-out-and-get-out" eventually proved an unsustainable method of agricultural development.[34]

In addition, even Great Southern's timber holdings were not infinite. At the first signs of dwindling resources, lumber companies explored their options overseas. Charles Goodyear surveyed pine forests on the Caribbean coast of Nicaragua in cooperation with New Orleans–based United

Photo 7. Skidder crew with log pond and sawmill in background, Great Southern Lumber Company, Bogalusa, La., 1938. Courtesy of Louisiana State University Special Collections, Baton Rouge, La.

Fruit Company, but decided that the timber was too small and full of pitch for sale in U.S. markets. William Sullivan toured an experimental tree farm in France during World War I, and he became an ardent supporter of conservation at home after touring forests managed by Louisiana lumberman Henry Hartner, the "father of forestry in the South." Sullivan announced upon his return to Bogalusa that Great Southern would place 175,000 acres under reforestation in 1920. The state of Louisiana supported his plans by granting the company a tax exemption to those lands in 1922. "It is almost impossible to over-estimate the importance of the change of outlook of this influential firm," business historian James E. Fickle has written of Great Southern's conversion to conservation. Commenting on the firm's pioneering role in the conservation movement, William Greeley dubbed Bogalusa the "Mecca of American foresters."[35]

Even as he proclaimed that "reforestation is a basis for the industrial permanency of Bogalusa," Sullivan diversified Great Southern's operation, a move that allowed the company to prosper under its new conservation regime. To "fill the gap of a few years until the reforested timbers would be ready to be manufactured," the firm acquired redwoods from forests that it had purchased in California. Great Southern also planted several thousand acres of fast-growing tung trees, which produced the oil used to manufacture paint. The most successful diversification project was the opening in 1918 of Bogalusa Paper Company, a semi-independent subsidiary of which Sullivan acted as a vice president. Using the Kraft process first developed for southern pine in 1909, Sullivan predicted that paper production would eventually replace lumber as the basis for Bogalusa's economic health. "No permanent city can be built around a saw mill," Great Southern proclaimed in the early 1920s, "but it can be built permanently around a paper manufacturing center."[36]

Great Southern adopted "cut-out-and-get-out" when it established its huge sawmill at Bogalusa but adjusted that strategy in the face of labor unrest and timber shortages in the following decade. An important part of that adjustment entailed diversification into paper production, which decreased the firm's need for both cheap timber and cheap labor. Despite managers' claims that paper would sustain the firm, however, lumber production continued to employ large numbers of low-wage, mostly African American workers in Bogalusa. To maintain that production, the firm instituted a parallel policy based on timber conservation and the recruitment of a reliable and stable supply of workers. As we will see in further chapters, that strategy lay the basis for a new relationship between southern lumber firms and the African American men who continued to compose the majority of their workforce.

Chapman, Alabama

Some attributed the "cut-out-and-get-out" strategy to northern inves-tors such as the Goodyears, but brothers Greeley and Joe McGowin, who were natives of Alabama and sons of a Confederate veteran, paid little attention to sustainability at their W. T. Smith Lumber Company in Chap-man, Alabama. The brothers purchased the lumber company from its namesake in 1905. The dictates of the "cut-out-and-get-out" strategy may explain why the McGowins retained the names that previous owners had given to the company and the town and waited twenty years before build-ing a home for themselves in Chapman. "This was a cut-out-and-get-out industry in basic truth," Greeley McGowin's son Earl explained. His fa-ther never "planned more than eight years ahead."[37]

Like most southern industrialists, the McGowins lacked ready cap-ital, and for that reason they situated their operation along an existing rail line and purchased timber in small parcels. The town of Chapman lay on the Louisville and Nashville Railroad (L&N), the most aggressive of the lines that promoted industrialization in the New South. After es-tablishing Birmingham as Alabama's "Magic City" in the 1870s, the L&N attracted the business of aspiring lumbermen by chartering depots and selling timberland along its southern Alabama line. The McGowins were unable to purchase thousands of acres up front as the Goodyears had done in Bogalusa, so they bought timber as needed, starting with plots on the L&N near Chapman and nearby Greenville. In 1906 they purchased the Dunham Lumber Company, six miles to the south on the L&N line. Only after establishing themselves as leaders in the state's lumber industry did they begin constructing their own rail lines and purchasing larger tracts of land away from the L&N's main line.[38]

Uncertain how long they would operate in Chapman, the McGow-ins saw little reason to improve their company town. "Chapman had the reputation of being the worst place on the L&N line," recalled a worker who moved there in 1908. The town, located at the bottom of a shallow, wide valley, had poor drainage and even a slight rain flooded the streets with muddy water for days at a time. "When I first came here it was just a mud hole," said another worker. "Every time the creek would get up those of us who lived across it couldn't get to work." Jesse Brown, who lived in Chapman while his father worked for W. T. Smith in 1904, described the unhealthy conditions created by standing water in a region ravaged by malaria. "We had no protection from mosquitoes or flies," Brown recalled, "and every member of our family was sick when we left."[39]

Given the conditions the McGowins provided at Chapman, it is not surprising that few workers—black or white—sought long-term employment from W. T. Smith. White worker Jesse Brown's father left Chapman as soon as he could afford to buy a farm. Black worker Roy Gandy's grandfather moved from the Carolinas to work at a turpentine company near Chapman, but he quit soon after purchasing two forty-acre homesteads. Such forays into "public work" were critical to the "remarkable increase in Negro land ownership" that Horace Mann Bond observed in Alabama between 1880 and 1910, and it allowed even larger numbers of poor whites to become landowners in the state.[40]

While the McGowins remained skeptical of the reforestation strategies adopted by Great Southern in the 1920s, they found other methods to sustain production beyond the projected limits of their available timber supply. Originally operating sawmills and planing mills in Chapman and Dunham, the W. T. Smith began diversifying its operations, including the manufacturing of veneer, shingles, and barrel staves at both locations. W. T. Smith and several other southern pine firms hired black women to assemble wooden boxes during World War I. Over the next ten years, they continued to expand production to include six sawmills located in Chapman, Greenville, Dunham, and Linden, and logging camps at Dunham, Crenshaw, and McKenzie. Employees assembled boxes in Chapman and distilled turpentine in Chapman and McKenzie.[41]

W. T. Smith extended the life span of its original holdings through diversification, but the firm achieved stability only by gaining access to new supplies of timber. The McGowins purchased the Empire Lumber Company in 1914 and established a timber holding company that bought four additional firms between 1921 and 1929. These investments put the McGowins in control of more than 140,000 acres of timber in southern Alabama and northwest Florida, accounting for an annual production of 70 million board feet throughout the 1920s.[42]

Use of these new timber stands required that the McGowins expend a considerable investment in new logging and milling technology. The firms that W. T. Smith purchased in the 1920s were traditional "cut-out-and-get-out" operations by the industry's standards, which meant that their timber holdings were too thin to sustain a large mill. In their first move towards stability, the McGowins began constructing their own rail lines. Starting with a branch line off the L&N near McKenzie in 1916, the firm constructed more than one hundred miles of rail before 1930. Using a combination of trains and trucks, they were able to transport logs cheaply from dispersed forests to centralized mill locations. Greeley McGowin's son Julian invented a portable sawmill that, in addition to allowing them to exploit outlying forests, won the firm credit from *The Southern Lumberman* for pioneering a "new era in the better and more economical manufacture of lumber by small mills."[43]

The journal's enthusiasm for McGowin's invention reflected a history of conflict between owners of large mills and poor farmers who used portable "peckerwood" or "ground" mills to clear land and supplement their income. Industrial producers blamed these mills for flooding southern markets with cheap, low-quality lumber, and they invented the slur "peckerwood," which became synonymous with "redneck" as a derogatory label for poor white farmers. Julian's invention, which he developed in cooperation with "several of the country's largest sawmill machinery manufacturers," was small enough to compete with peckerwoods but also fast and stable enough to produce market-grade lumber. While peckerwoods were often mounted on the backs of trucks, the new "small mills" had to be disassembled and transported in several pieces from one site to another.[44]

The new technology meant that the site could support a permanent mill, and so Greeley McGowin's sons launched an "ambitious modernization program" in Chapman. Alabama built a new state highway through Chapman in 1931, improving the town's drainage in the process. The com-

Photo 8. Primitive "peckerwood" or "ground" sawmill, Francis Marion/ Sumpter National Forests, South Carolina. Courtesy of USDA Forest Service Collection, Avery Research Center, Charleston, S.C.

pany followed by removing vast piles of sawdust from the mill grounds and doing "everything possible to present an attractive view of the plant" from the new highway. After family patriarch Greeley died in 1934, his sons vigorously pursued their modernization project, paving Chapman's streets, rebuilding the main sawmill, and transforming their company town into "one of the finest of its sort east of the Mississippi." They also invited the New Deal Civilian Conservation Corps to establish a camp on company land and used its fire prevention and transportation projects to begin reforestation. By 1947, the company boasted that Chapman consisted of 250 homes, two schools, several churches, a community house, a hotel, and "many other factors that make up a modern industrial town."[45]

As Great Southern had done in Bogalusa, W. T. Smith relied upon black men to aid its transition toward sustainable production in Chapman. The number of black-owned farms decreased by 7 percent in Alabama in the 1920s, and the value of those farms fell by 14 percent. Although white farmers faced similar difficulties during that period, they enjoyed access to textile jobs or skilled trades in iron, rail, and other industries that were closed to African Americans. Reforestation also eliminated a significant avenue toward land ownership for many black men in southern Alabama, as cut-over lands were replanted rather than sold to poor farmers. Facing the mass migration of their former seasonal laborers from the region, the McGowins' expanded and diversified company offered a reliable alternative to family farming.[46]

Elizabethtown, North Carolina

The Greene Brothers Lumber Company offers a third example of the shift from "cut-out-and-get-out" to sustainable production. Whereas Sullivan and the McGowins played leadership roles in that transition, the Greenes followed the others' lead when they reentered the lumber industry after a brief retirement in the 1920s. Alvin and Cecil Greene opened their first sawmill on the Alabama plantation owned by their father, a Confederate veteran. They began buying and cutting timber and selling timberlands in southern Alabama and in 1915 acquired a planing mill and drying kiln in Lewiston, about 150 miles east of Chapman. Buying logs and unfinished boards from local groundmills, the brothers sold enough lumber during World War I to retire to Atlanta, where they built two homes and lived off their stock investments. The 1929 stock market crash forced them back into business, first selling automobiles and then opening a sawmill in Beach Island, North Carolina.[47]

Opening a large mill in eastern North Carolina required the Greenes to adopt technology developed in other regions that allowed them to exploit thin timber stands. The Carolina coast had been logged since colonial times, and industrial sawmills had begun abandoning the area earlier in the twentieth century. As the McGowins had done in southern Alabama, the Greenes used trucks to reach timber that was too thinly spaced to be logged by train. The state of North Carolina aided that transition by investing $200 million in its highway system between 1920 and 1936. The Civilian Conservation Corps established several camps in the region as well, carving logging roads into state forest lands and erecting a fire prevention infrastructure that facilitated the growth of new timber. "Once famous for its vast stands of longleaf pine," according to J. W. Cruikshank, eastern North Carolina, under the Greenes' initiative, entered a new era of lumber production based upon the shortleaf and cypress that remained scattered in coastal swamps and tidewaters.[48]

Convinced that roads and reforestation gave them an unlimited supply of timber, the Greenes established what they believed would be a permanent sawmill in Elizabethtown, the seat of Bladen County in eastern North Carolina. They purchased twelve thousand acres of cypress and pine forest in nearby Colly Swamp and an additional eight thousand acres in small plots scattered throughout neighboring Columbus and Robeson Counties. Investing far more in technology and infrastructure than a "cut-out-and-get-out" operation could have afforded, the Greenes diverted water from the Cape Fear river into a hydroelectric generating plant and installed electric conveyors and hydraulic "shotgun feeds" to move logs through several sets of saws. The acquisition of an electric drying kiln and planer allowed them to purchase green and poorly cut lumber off the open market, supplementing their timber holdings with wood they acquired from local farmers and independent loggers. The Greenes' expansion strategy was reflected in their production numbers. Their Elizabethtown mill produced twenty million board feet annually by 1940, and between 1937 and 1951, the three counties surrounding the town accounted for one third of all lumber produced in North Carolina.[49]

The Greene Brothers could not have maintained those levels of production without an experienced and reliable workforce. It was fairly common for southern lumber firms to recruit skilled white workers from other towns and even other parts of the country when opening new mills. Cecil Greene hired his former superintendent Robert Beasley and foreman John Al, who agreed to abandon jobs that they had secured after the Lewiston, Alabama, mill closed. Beasley also convinced his brother, a skilled sawyer, and John Daniel, a lumber grader, to move to Elizabethtown, along with a logging foreman from Charleston, South Carolina,

Photo 9. Skidder crew posing with A. H. Greene, Greene Brothers Lumber Company, Colly Swamp, N.C., 1948. Courtesy of Ben Greene, Elizabethtown, N.C.

with twenty-five years' experience in the industry. Along with these skilled workers, the Greenes found that they also had to recruit "semiskilled" and "unskilled" workers from out of state, rather than from local labor markets as was typical for the industry. "There weren't many people in North Carolina with experience in a large mill," Cecil Greene's son Ben explained. Frustrated by the increased accidents, broken machinery, and miscut lumber produced by novices, the Greenes sent Beasley and Al to recruit their former employees who still lived near Lewiston.[50]

Facing the same economic hardships that led other rural southerners to settle in Chapman and Bogalusa, scores of black men accepted the Greenes' offer to move to eastern North Carolina. To encourage long-term employment, the firm sent trucks to move these workers' entire families from Alabama and other states. Unlike their competitors who established biracial company towns early in the century, the Greenes were forced to adapt to patterns of racial segregation that were already well established in Elizabethtown. African Americans were not allowed to live within town limits, for example, and they could not shop in local stores. For that reason, the firm settled black workers in "colored quarters" on company property beyond the town limits and operated a store and a medical clinic out of the company offices. These measures increased the company's control over black workers' everyday lives, but they also demonstrated the extent to which the firm relied upon the experience of those workers. The firm continued to classify African American workers as either "unskilled" or "semiskilled," but Ben Greene recalled, "The really skilled guys in the mill were black."[51]

Conclusion

Between 1920 and 1930, workers and employers in the southern lumber industry took part in a broad transformation of production strategies. Facing a shortage of timber, leading lumber firms rejected the wasteful "cut-out-and-get-out" strategy of the late nineteenth century for a more sustainable policy of conservation and reforestation. Great Southern, W. T. Smith, and Greene Brothers emerged as the most successful pratictioners of this new approach to lumber production in the South. Through diversification, decentralization, and migration, they extended their productive lives well beyond the years that most southern lumbermen predicted they would have early in the century.

In making this transition, these three companies were also responding to a change initiated by southern men who looked to industrial wage employment as one alternative to the region's failing agricultural sector. The firms survived because they convinced large numbers of African American men to accept permanent jobs in their sawmills and logging operations. Abandoning the quest for land that had motivated earlier generations, black men who grew up in the 1910s and 1920s settled in sawmill towns and relied upon industrial wage work as their sole means of supporting their families. In so doing, they provided a reliable and experienced supply of labor that was critical to the continued profitability of the southern lumber industry.

2 Black Families between Farm and Factory

The recollections of black men who accepted permanent industrial work in the 1920s and 1930s are filled with allusions to emancipation. In a 1996 interview, Orie Tyson recalled that he abandoned his parents' sharecropping plot in the early 1930s because it too closely resembled "slavery time." Asked to elaborate, he stated, "The white folks whooped the black folks, and I didn't want them knocking on me." R. C. Rudolph described his family's escape from an Alabama plantation in the late 1930s in terms that could have described a ride on the Underground Railroad. "They would hang you Lowndes County in a minute," he recalled in 1998. Rather than live under such a violent regime, Rudolph's father packed his wife and six sons in a wagon, greased the wheels to prevent squeaking, and "slipped off" under cover of night. These anecdotes support the findings of sociologist Charles S. Johnson, who surveyed the "occupational outlook" of young African Americans in the rural South in 1941. Most of his subjects had originally expected to spend their entire lives working in agriculture, but they expressed "little desire to remain there." When given the opportunity, these young southerners invariably looked to industrial employment as an escape from what Johnson described as the low "status and drudgery of farming."[1]

Particularly striking about these accounts is their stark contrast with the observations of contemporary scholars and social reformers who studied black men's movement into southern industrial employment in the 1920s and 1930s. As historian Victoria Wolcott has written, scholarly attention to black southerners arose in response to the Great Migration of African Americans into northern cities. Despite the fact that many migrants had worked in industry and lived in cities before leaving the South, black and white middle-class reformers often emphasized their "backward" and "backwoods" character in contrast to the "sophisticated" behavior of native black northerners. Forester B. Washington, who led the Detroit Urban League's efforts to assimilate migrants in the 1910s, oversaw the creation of Atlanta University's school of social work in the 1920s. In a 1928 article, he argued that southern industrial employment was "at the same time at the root of the migration of the Negro and of much of the social pathology that has grown out of it." His conclusions were echoed two years later by historian Carter G. Woodson, who attributed "present-day troubles" such as alcoholism and sexual promiscuity among rural African Americans to "a natural consequence of passing through a transition period." Those studies informed Howard Odum's portrait of Black Ulysses, which depicted industrialization as destructive to African American family life in the South.[2]

Middle-class writers and reformers expressed condescension toward working-class southerners, but their writings also reflected a genuine concern for a perceived breakdown of African American family and community life in the rural South. Scholars often assumed that men's enthusiasm for industrial employment reflected their desire to escape their family responsibilities and the moral constraints of their agricultural homes. Despite the scholarly tendency to assume that rural industrial workers wandered perpetually—"without anchor" as Odum described Black Ulysses—most men viewed industrial employment as a means to strengthen their roles as husbands and fathers. Observers often overlooked the fact that lumber workers typically accepted industrial employment only temporarily and that they returned to agricultural communities when that employment ended. Rather than sever family ties when they accepted long-term lumber employment in the 1920s and 1930s, men frequently brought their families with them or established families within the black working-class communities that appeared in southern mill towns following World War I.[3]

As with emancipation two generations earlier, movement from agricultural to industrial employment involved a renegotiation of relationships not just between black men and their employers but also among black men and women. Historians once viewed sharecropping as a cynical trick by which plantation owners revived slavery under a different name. More recent research has revealed, however, that the sharecropping system emerged out of negotiation between plantation owners who wanted to secure a reliable source of labor and freed people who were determined to establish some sovereignty over their families' lives and their labor. That negotiation involved a second negotiation within black families themselves, resulting in a relatively egalitarian "family wage system" in which men, women, and children worked in close proximity and often performed the same tasks. This system remained largely intact early in the twentieth century even as individual men periodically left the farm to seek seasonal wage work. As they began to accept long-term industrial employment, and particularly as they began to establish households in industrial towns, black men were forced to renegotiate their responsibilities to families and communities as well as to their employers.[4]

Observation of this negotiation was at the root of reformers' fear that rural industrialization contributed to the breakdown of black family and community life. "Among the million Negroes who deserted the rural communities of the South, there were thousands of men and women who cut themselves loose from family and friends and sought work and adventure as solitary wanderers from place to place," black sociologist E. Franklin Frazier wrote in 1939. "Some of the men had their first glance of the world beyond the plantation or farm when they worked in sawmills, turpentine camps, or on the roads." Frazier noted correctly that industrial employment drew men away from agricultural communities, but he overlooked the opportunities that those jobs provided to men who confronted the agricultural crisis that plagued the South in the 1920s and 1930s. Previous generations of black southerners had defined manhood by the ability to establish an independent family farm through either sharecropping or, for a lucky few, independent land ownership. As family farming became less viable, men turned to lumber and other forms of industrial employment, first as a supplemental wage and then as a permanent replacement for family farming. Rather than removing them from family and community responsibilities, industrial employment provided a new basis upon which they could define their roles as men.[5]

Of "Family Men" and "Sawdust Casanovas"

Compared to the social breakdown thesis advanced by social scientists in the 1920s and 1930s, William Faulkner's novel *Light in August* contained a more accurate portrayal of southern lumber workers' family and social lives during that era. Using the trope of unattached young men popularized by Odum and other writers, Faulkner centered his story around Joe Christmas, a psychologically troubled young mulatto who wandered through the sawmill towns of southern Alabama and Mississippi seducing young women and selling moonshine whiskey. He clarified, however, that "young bachelors, or sawdust Casanovas anyway, were even fewer in number than families" in those towns. Men like Christmas lent drama to his story, but Faulkner knew that it was the "family men" who set the pace of social life:

> Some of them were young and they drank and gambled on Saturday night, and even went to Memphis now and then. Yet on Monday morning they came quietly and soberly to work, in clean overalls and clean shirts, waiting quietly until the whistle blew and then going quietly to work, as though there were still something of sabbath in the overlingering air which established a tenet that, no matter what a man had done with his sabbath, to come quiet and clean to work on Monday morning was no more than seemly and right to do.[6]

Faulkner described the 1930s, but even in 1900, according to historian Vernon Jensen, "The southern lumber industry did not produce a homeless migratory class." Jensen was responding to a common complaint among southern mill owners that both black and white men refused to accept permanent employment. Because those men tended to arrive in mill towns without families and because they often left without notice, one trade journal described southern lumber workers as "hoboes" who darted "around the countryside like a bat at dusk." He also compared southern workers to the mostly single, European immigrants who worked in northwestern and Great Lakes lumber regions. Studying the 1900 census, however, Jensen noted a "conspicuous difference" between northern and southern workers in the "predominance of family men" among southern lumber workers. Married men outnumbered single men in the South, whereas their northern counterparts were twice as likely to be single as married. Those figures remained fairly constant through 1910, when married men accounted for 52 percent of all southern lumber workers (table 4).[7]

It is true that black lumber workers were slightly less likely to be married than either white lumber workers or the southern population as a whole. In 1910, southern men displayed slightly higher marriage rates than their counterparts in other regions, due in part to the large rural population in the region. The marriage rate for men over fifteen was 63 percent in the South compared to 60 for the country as a whole. African Americans were concentrated in the South and in agriculture, and they

Table 4. Marital Status of Male Sawmill and Logging Workers in South, by Race; and Marital Status of All Men in United States, by Race, 1910

| Marital Status | Race South (Total Cases)[a] | | | United States[b] | |
	Black	White	Total	Black	Total
Ever married[c]	58.6% (368)	63.3% (527)	61.0% (896)	64.0%	70.0%
Never married	41.4 (260)	36.7 (306)	39.0 (574)	35.4	29.7

a. Numbers for workers other than black or white workers were too small for comparison. Out of 1,470 cases in 1910, two were American Indian and seven marked "other."

b. U.S. figures are for males fifteen years of age and older.

c. Includes married with spouse present, married with spouse absent, widowed, and divorced. U.S. totals do not include people whose marital condition was not reported, which is why combined totals do not equal 100 percent.

Source: 1910 general sample (1-in-250 national random sample of the population), Steven Ruggles, Matthew Sobek, Trent Alexander, Catherine A. Fitch, Ronald Goeken, Patricia Kelly Hall, Miriam King, and Chad Ronnander, *Integrated Public Use Microdata Series: Version 3.0* [Machine-readable database] (Minneapolis: Minnesota Population Center, 2004) <http://www.ipums.org>; "Abstract of the Census–Population," *Thirteenth Census of the United States, 1910*, 146–55.

showed correspondingly high rates of marriage. Sixty-four percent of adult black men were married in 1910. From this perspective, the relatively high rates of single men among southern sawmill workers appear to support Jensen's contention that such work attracted "self-contented and strongly individualistic" men who could not "hold themselves down to continuous routine work."[8]

But when we consider the relationship between industrial and agricultural employment in the early-twentieth-century South, it becomes clear that both black and white men's employment decisions were motivated by their acceptance, not rejection, of family and community responsibilities. Before World War I, the majority of black and white southerners viewed industrial wage work as a temporary means to achieve their long-term goal of family farming. They sought such "public work" as young men and hoped to abandon it after purchasing equipment, a house, or land that would ensure their economic independence. The exceptions to that rule were white men who gained employment in craft or managerial positions. These "skilled" workers earned significantly more than laborers, and therefore were able to remain in lumber jobs after they married and started a family. Because black men were almost entirely excluded from these positions, they were even more likely than whites to leave lumber jobs near the time that they married.

The pattern of black men leaving industrial employment near the

time they got married can be seen in table 5, which shows that when occupational status is accounted for, black and white lumber workers showed
almost identical marriage rates in 1910. Marriage rates for "skilled" and
"semiskilled" black workers were even higher than those for whites, although the numbers of black workers in these categories are too low for a
reliable comparison. Figure 2 shows that most southern lumber workers
were between fifteen and forty years old in 1910, but that employment
in the industry declined steadily after the age of twenty-five. The single men were almost entirely under the age of thirty; nearly all the men
who stayed in the industry beyond that age were married. The impact
of black men's exclusion from higher-paid positions is illustrated in the
difference between black and white men's employment in later years.
Married white men stayed in the industry because they attained jobs
that paid a "family wage." Black men's exclusion from such jobs—and
not some biological or cultural pathology—explains the "large labor
turnover" that plagued southern mills before the 1920s. As one employer explained, this problem was "true principally among the Negroes or
common laborers."[9]

Reliance upon farm labor may have freed employers from responsibility for their workers' families, but it also meant that workers were
motivated by fast rather than steady income. As one Florida mill owner
complained, "The great trouble here is to get hands who will stay any
length of time. It is no trouble to get hands who will work a week or two

Table 5. Percent Married of Male Sawmill and Logging Workers in
South, by Race and Occupational Class, 1910, 1940

| | Percent Married[a] (Total Cases) | |
	1910	1940
Black		
Craftsman	100 (3)	84.2 (6)
Operative	68.5 (73)	83.4 (181)
Laborer	56.5 (540)	71.4 (1,116)
White		
Craftsman	77.4 (84)	89.8 (167)
Operative	65.8 (190)	77.9 (457)
Laborer	55.8 (437)	63.7 (1,086)

a. Includes married with spouse present, married with spouse absent, widowed, and divorced.

Source: 1910 general sample (1-in-250 national random sample of the population), Steven Ruggles, Matthew Sobek, Trent Alexander, Catherine A. Fitch,
Ronald Goeken, Patricia Kelly Hall, Miriam King, and Chad Ronnander, *Integrated Public Use Microdata Series: Version 3.0* [Machine-readable database]
(Minneapolis: Minnesota Population Center, 2004) <http://www.ipums.org>.

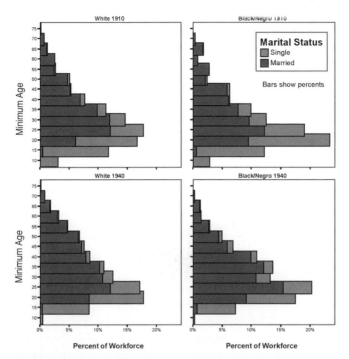

Figure 2. Age Distribution of Sawmill and Logging Workers in South, by Race and Marital Status, 1910, 1940

Source: 1910 general sample (1-in-250 national random sample of the population) and 1940 general sample (1-in-100 national random sample of the population), Steven Ruggles, Matthew Sobek, Trent Alexander, Catherine A. Fitch, Ronald Goeken, Patricia Kelly Hall, Miriam King, and Chad Ronnander, *Integrated Public Use Microdata Series: Version 3.0* [Machine-readable database]. (Minneapolis: Minnesota Population Center, 2004), <http://www.ipums.org>.

to get a little corn or meat, but it is very hard to get those who will remain over two months." Workers abandoned jobs without notice to attend to emergencies at home and seldom kept lumber jobs long enough to acquire specific skills. This forced firms to retain primitive production techniques that could be learned quickly and maintained in the face of rapid labor turnover. For example, logging crews depended upon mule and ox-drawn carts, familiar tools for a farmer, well into the 1920s. Even after larger companies introduced mechanical steam skidders and log trains in the 1890s, employers voiced frustration at not being able to retain workers long enough to train them. "Just about the time I get a man thoroughly acquainted with his duties he wants to go home, which is very vexatious," wrote the Florida employer.[10]

Remaking Black Manhood

What changed in the 1920s was not so much black men's attitude toward family as the type of work that they believed best suited their social and familial responsibilities. Although farm wages rose slightly during the war, they fell rapidly afterward, decreasing the possibility that young men could eventually support themselves and their families through farming. In addition, postwar inflation of land and livestock prices rendered farm ownership nearly impossible for black men. Black farm ownership, which had increased before World War I, fell dramatically in the 1920s. Faced with what seemed to be a permanent agricultural crisis, increasing numbers of black men decided that industrial employment offered a more reliable source of income. By 1930, one in four employed black men held a manufacturing job. White southerners also abandoned farming during World War I, but they had more alternatives than African Americans for employment outside of agriculture. Young white men continued to take common lumber jobs after the war, but many possessed the realistic expectation that they would advance into the higher-paid and more stable "skilled" positions that were reserved for them by both unions and employers. Many whites also found work in textile mills, where wages outpaced those in lumber and where blacks were almost entirely excluded. Other whites continued to use their wages from industrial employment to buy land and retire from "public work" to return to family farming, where they enjoyed greater access to loans and agricultural markets than did blacks.[11]

A notoriously unreliable occupation during the "cut-out-and-get-out" era, in the 1930s and 1940s lumber employment became more stable than any other southern industry. A majority of southern pine managers surveyed in 1933 reported that nearly all of their "normally employed" workers had "remained in the community" since 1929. Even among those who were laid off during that period, most found temporary employment nearby, in farming, packing, canning, or relief work, so that they could continue to find "staggered employment" in the mills. Only in the "few cases where mills have shut down completely" did managers report that workers left their mill towns.[12]

Available census figures and state reports reveal black and white lumber workers' increasing commitment to industrial employment. By 1934, only 4 percent of black lumber workers "either owned or rented" a farm. Although white lumber workers were twice as likely to maintain that tradition, farmers were a tiny minority even among that privileged group. The 1940 census, for example, revealed that only 33 percent of

southern lumber workers had lived on a farm in 1935. In contrast to car
lier decades, when black men were more likely than whites to oscillate
between farm and factory, black sawmill workers had one of the lowest
turnover rates for southern industrial workers by the 1940s. Nearly 60
percent of black lumber workers in 1940 had worked in industry five years
earlier, compared to just over 50 percent of whites. A study by the Alabama Department of Industrial Relations showed that overall lumber
employment in that state fluctuated by just 7 percent over the course of
1949, compared to 10 percent for all industries combined and over 10
percent in textiles.[13]

Industrial employment, contrary to the fears expressed by contemporary scholars and reformers, seems to have sustained nuclear families
among both black and white lumber workers in the rural South. By 1926,
67 percent of workers in the region's largest mills were married, and that
figure rose to 75 percent by 1933. This trend was most dramatic among
black men, whose marriage rates jumped from 60 to nearly 75 percent
during this period. By 1940, black mill workers were slightly more likely than whites to be married (figure 4). That black men remained slightly younger as a group than white men also suggests that they were mar-
rying at an earlier age (figure 3). To be sure, black men remained more
likely than whites to be widowed or to live separately from their wives,
as they had been in 1910, but these figures remained nominal in comparison to the vast majority of married couples who shared the same
household. Compared to 1910, when black men were more likely than
whites to leave industrial work when they reached middle age, by 1940,
both groups of men displayed similar rates of employment across age and
marital status.[14]

As these figures make clear, black men did not abandon family life
when they moved from agriculture into industrial work. Instead, they
adjusted their relationships with wives and children to fit a new economic context. Interviews with black men who worked in the southern lumber industry in the 1930s and 1940s indicate that previous generations of black men associated manhood with the control of land. They
measured personal success by one's ability to climb the agricultural
ladder from sharecropping to renting and, for a significant minority, land
ownership. Even among those who remained sharecroppers their entire
lives, most considered family farming a more suitable and manly occupation than industrial wage work. When the ability to remain on the
land became increasingly difficult after World War I, black men faced
hard choices. Some black men certainly abandoned their families and
succumbed to socially pathological behavior, but as is evident from

Table 6. Marital Status of Male Sawmill and Logging Workers in South, by Race, 1940

Marital Status	Race (Total Cases)		
	Black	White	Total[a]
Ever married[b]	73.2% (1,001)	72.8% (1,501)	73.0% (2,510)
Never married	26.8 (367)	27.2 (560)	27.0 (928)

 a. Numbers for workers other than black or white were too small for comparison. Out of 3,438 cases, eight were American Indian and one Chinese.
 b. Includes married with spouse present, married with spouse absent, widowed, and divorced. U.S. totals do not include people whose marital condition was not reported, which is why combined totals do not equal 100 percent.
 Source: 1910 general sample (1–in-250 national random sample of the population), Steven Ruggles, Matthew Sobek, Trent Alexander, Catherine A. Fitch, Ronald Goeken, Patricia Kelly Hall, Miriam King, and Chad Ronnander, *Integrated Public Use Microdata Series: Version 3.0* [Machine-readable database] (Minneapolis: Minnesota Population Center, 2004) <http://www.ipums.org>; "Abstract of the Census_Population," *Thirteenth Census of the United States, 1910*, 146–55.

census figures, the majority of them adjusted their idea of manhood to meet a new reality. The black man who came of age in the 1930s increasingly measured his manhood by his ability to earn a cash wage that allowed him to support his family in some comfort.[15]

Black men's new gender consciousness attested to the changing significance of male wage earning in the rural South during the first half of the twentieth century. Dewitt Brumfield and Lemalie Holmes, who worked for the Great Southern Lumber Company through the 1930s and 1940s, recalled that their fathers and grandfathers had also worked in sawmills in southern Mississippi in the 1920s. What differentiated their work experiences from earlier generations was that they intended to remain in the mill, while older men used sawmill wages to purchase land. Brumfield's grandfather was a landowner who passed on forty-acre plots to each of his children, which allowed them to avoid sharecropping. Holmes recalled proudly that land ownership gave his father's generation a level of independence from white employers. Thus the previous generations of black men who came of age between Reconstruction and World War I accepted sawmill work as a temporary rather than life-defining occupation. Having defeated planters' attempts to drive them into gang labor, former slaves and their children viewed industrial wages as key resources in the struggle to preserve family farming as the primary labor arrangement in the rural South.[16]

When men of Brumfield and Holmes's generation fell on hard times, they turned to sawmill work as a permanent livelihood. Dewitt's brother Robert rode a bus fifty miles from his Mississippi birthplace to find work

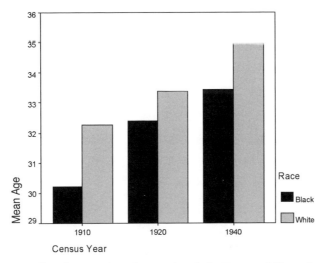

Figure 3. Sawmill and Logging Workers in South, by Race and Mean Age, 1910, 1920, 1940

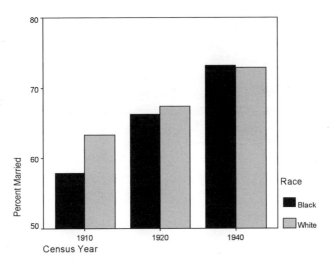

Figure 4. Sawmill and Logging Workers in South, by Race and Percent Married, 1910, 1920, 1940

Source for Figures 3 and 4: 1910 general sample (1-in-250 national random sample of the population), 1920 general sample (1-in-100 national random sample of the population), and 1940 general sample (1-in-100 national random sample of the population), Steven Ruggles, Matthew Sobek, Trent Alexander, Catherine A. Fitch, Ronald Goeken, Patricia Kelly Hall, Miriam King, and Chad Ronnander, *Integrated Public Use Microdata Series: Version 3.0* [Machine-readable database]. (Minneapolis: Minnesota Population Center, 2004), <http://www.ipums.org>.

in Bogalusa in the 1920s. He met his wife Ethel there—she had also recently moved to Bogalusa from Mississippi—and the couple rented a house in Great Southern's "colored quarters." Dewitt followed Robert to Bogalusa in 1937, and he was impressed that his brother's seventeen-cent hourly wage allowed the couple to live comfortably without Ethel working outside their home. "That was good money back in those days," he recalled, noting that his brother's semiskilled position paid "a little bit more than the others." DeWitt, unlike his brother, had no industrial experience—he had done "nothing but pick cotton" in Mississippi—and therefore he had a harder time finding work when he moved to Bogalusa in the depths of the Depression. He nevertheless enjoyed living with Ethel and Robert in Bogalusa, spending his days at the company YMCA, and carrying lunch to Robert before he also secured a mill job during World War II.[17]

Garland Abrams was another member of the generation that came of age in the 1920s and 1930s whose father was proud of the fact that he owned enough land to live an independent life without having to rely on wage work. However, when Garland began his own family in the 1920s, he moved to Chapman, Alabama, and found a job fueling the burners that powered the W. T. Smith Lumber Company's sawmill. His wife, who also came from an agricultural family, found wage work in Chapman as a maid for a white family. Between the two of them, the couple earned enough to rent a home in the company town and to keep their son Ire out of the labor market while he finished school. Ire contributed to the family budget by mowing the lawn at W. T. Smith during his summers, but he completed eleven years at the Chapman school and finished an additional year at a boarding school in northern Alabama. By the late 1940s, the family had saved enough to purchase their own house in nearby Georgiana, a move that reflected workers' conception of independence in an industrial environment. The company provided a "nice house," Ire recalled, but his parents "wanted a place of their own."[18]

A sawmill job allowed George Cheatham to escape the deterioration his and other sharecropping families suffered on one Alabama plantation. "Back then you could count the people on your fingers that [sic] did have land," he recalled, and those who did not were forced to "stay on the white man's place and . . . do what he said." Sharecroppers depended upon landowners for credit, which the sharecroppers used to buy seeds, fertilizer, food, and clothing during the planting season. "All that had to come out of your half of whatever you would make in the run of a year," Cheatham recalled. An honest landlord would deduct debts from the croppers' earnings and pay back the rest, "but [the landlord] had the advantage of it cause it was his land—and every thing." By the time Cheatham reached sixteen years old, "things were so desperate in those days you couldn't get hold of nothing." He found work in a nearby "peckerwood" mill—"the first damn thing I could do"—and held industrial jobs for the rest of his working life.[19]

Industrial wages allowed Cheatham to start a family of his own and gave him some control over his family's living conditions, but also required him to exercise some occupational mobility. After working in the peckerwood sawmill for a time, he left for a better-paying job with the L&N Railroad, which allowed him to get married but forced him to travel frequently between Alabama and New Orleans. Despite this separation from his wife, Cheatham was determined to maintain a stable family life. While many of his coworkers traveled with their families, living in boxcars erected in train yards, he and his wife preferred to keep house in Greenville. After three years of railroad work, his wife made it clear that "she wasn't satisfied" with the situation, and he settled down as a laborer at the W. T. Smith Lumber Company in Chapman. The work was harder than he was accustomed to, and he "dreaded" going to the mill every morning, but the job with W. T. Smith allowed him to maintain the more important ideal of black manhood. In direct contradiction to the prediction that industrial work would undermine black family life, Cheatham admitted, "I didn't like" lumber work, "but I had a family and I had to work."[20]

When black men talked about sawmill work providing them with an escape, it was not from family or responsibility but rather from an agricultural life that they considered oppressive and no longer economically viable. Lonnie Carter left his parents' South Carolina tenant farm when his father disciplined him after Lonnie used a broken bottle to attack a white boy who threatened to assault his aunt. Had Lonnie's older brother not intervened, "I would have ripped his arm open," he recalled. Lonnie's father, who slapped him when he learned of the incident, explained, "Lonnie, I done that to save your life. They would have beat you to death if you had done that." African American parents frequently used such defensive discipline to protect their children from a possible lynching, but Lonnie resented what he perceived as his father's concession to white supremacy and resolved to strike out on his own. A few days later he hitchhiked to Elizabethtown, North Carolina, where he found a job with the Greene Brothers Lumber Company. Ironically, Carter noted later that his father was pleased by his choice to leave farming. He "never did want none of his children to grow up like he was," Lonnie recalled, describing how his illiterate parents saved their pennies to send each of their eleven children to a six-month school.[21]

After a year as a participant-observer in southern Alabama in 1947, sociologist Morton Rubin concluded that sawmill employment actually reflected few of the social problems that previous generations of social scientists had attributed to industrialization. Because lumber workers started work and took breaks according to a set routine, and because they lost pay when they did not show up for work on time, Rubin argued that they lost the "old ways of timelessness and laxidazicalness [*sic*]" that he associated with farming. He also observed that "fairly steady" employment and "good" pay allowed mill workers to send their children to school on a more regular basis and made them "more independent as a consumer" than agricultural workers. Because black mill workers earned "as much as an entire family used to," their wives and children did not necessarily have to enter the labor market. Rubin did express some reservations. He observed that black industrial workers were less interested in education and religion than "older members of the Negro community," and he conceded that occupational changes may have disoriented some who left agricultural communities, "where there are generations of tradition to go by." These losses notwithstanding, he concluded that black men's "best bet for economic and psychological security lies with industry."[22]

Black Women in a Male Industry

Black women did not necessarily share men's enthusiasm for industrial employment. Mabry Shaw's wife opposed her husband's acceptance of a full-time sawmill job because it prevented him from working on their farm alongside her and their children. Shaw's description of farming as "sissy" work and "children's play" also indicated that his employment in an all-male industry reinforced gender inequalities within their household. "A big man needs a big job and that's all there is to it," he said in reference to his motivations for seeking sawmill work. Other male sawmill workers took pride in claiming that mill wages allowed men to remove their wives from wage work. "None of our women worked," Roy Gandy stated with the patriarchal intonation that often accompanied men's descriptions of breadwinning. Such statements support historian Jacquelyn Jones's contention that sawmill town life required that women "acquiesce" to more rigid gender segregation in both work and social life, and accept a less "direct hand in providing for the family's economic welfare."[23]

Despite their reservations about the gendered division of labor, many women seem to have found economic and social benefits in sawmill town life that—despite their exclusion from most mill work—were not available to them in agricultural settings. Hullie Spears, for example, accompanied her husband to Bogalusa and remained in town long after he died. Rather than returning to her agricultural home, Spears paid rent to Great Southern Lumber Company for a company-owned house by renting a room to two young men for $1.50 a week and cooking them meals in exchange for grocery money. Indicating that this arrangement was not controversial, Great Southern management continued to provide water, lights, and cooking wood for her as it did to all its tenants. Another single woman ran a store out of her company-owned cottage located next door to Spears' boarding house. Frances Ginn was another woman who made a living as a single woman in a sawmill town. In the 1920s, she moved to Bogalusa from southern Mississippi with her husband and three sons, but when her husband quit his sawmill job and returned to the family's farm, she remained behind and found work cooking in a boarding house that catered to single white men. Although separated from her husband, Ginn lived and worked in Bogalusa for the rest of her life.[24]

Current scholarship shows that southern women often benefited by moving from agricultural to industrial settings but notes that those gains were dependent upon their abilities to find independent sources of income. In cities such as Atlanta and Durham where textile, tobacco, and domestic employers often favored women over men, women outnumbered men among recent migrants from the countryside. Dolores Janiewski, in her study of the large tobacco town of Durham, North Carolina, argues that black women had less power to negotiate the decline of family farming than whites or black men and therefore were the most likely of these groups to migrate to urban areas in the 1920s and 1930s. Race and gender divisions widened over that period, as black-owned farms failed at a higher rate than those of whites. As in smaller industrial towns, the high levels of marital stability in southern cities contradicted reformers' fears that black families would disintegrate in the face of industrialization.[25]

Sawmill towns differed from cities in the respect that women were almost entirely excluded from industrial employment. Many black women welcomed the opportunity that male industrial wages provided for them to care for their own families while husbands, fathers, and adult children sought wage jobs. Other women, because they were single or wanted to increase their family income, managed to find employment in sawmill towns. By selling goods and services to male workers and managers, black women gained access to male wages without necessarily maintaining a domestic relationship with a male mill worker. In large mill towns such as Bogalusa, black women worked in boarding houses, dining halls, and recreational facilities operated by lumber firms. In Chapman, Alabama, women worked in the company store and in the company-run health clinic. More typically, women operated independently outside the formal economy by taking in boarders or laundry and running small stores, cafes, and beauty salons out of their homes. Some women worked as maids and cooks in the homes of skilled workers and managers. Such full-time domestic employment was limited by the small number of middle-class families in most sawmill towns, but young women could still earn cash by cleaning, cooking, or taking care of children in both black and white workers' homes.[26]

Anthropologist Zora Neale Hurston described the variety of women's employment opportunities in Loughman, a Florida sawmill town that she visited in the late 1920s. She was first attracted to the town by "strong stories of Ella Wall, East Coast Mary, Planchita and lesser jook lights," the single women who frequented the dance halls and house parties that gave the town its boisterous reputation. Upon her arrival, however, Hurston also met housewives such as Clardia Thornton from Alabama and Mrs. Allen, who "ran the boarding-house under patronage of the company." In addition to these conventional female occupations, Hurston also reveals another possible way women could earn money in the sawmill towns of the South. Arriving in Loughman wearing a new dress and driving a late-model Chevrolet, Hurston worried that mill workers would suspect her of being a tax collector or a detective. So she won the community's acceptance by claiming to be a bootlegger—another apparently plausible occupation for a young black woman traveling alone through the rural South.[27]

Conclusion

Just as sharecropping provided freed slaves with a compromise solution to the problems concerning land and labor following Reconstruction, industrial employment offered black southerners with a means to negotiate the difficulties created by a changing rural economy following World War I. By moving to sawmill towns, black men conceded defeat in an earlier struggle to control land. In exchange, they gained higher wages and the ability to withdraw their wives and children from employment in the formal economy. Women gained the options of working in their own homes, working in wage jobs, and participating in the informal economy that they built around men's industrial wages. Often freed from economic responsibilities, children were able to attend school.

As with the earlier transition from slavery, negotiations about proper gender roles within black families played an important part in shaping the labor relations that emerged in an urban industrial setting. Since Reconstruction, the family-based farm labor system had narrowed the gendered division of labor in agricultural communities. But in mill towns where men had nearly exclusive access to industrial wages, black men established new identities as the family's primary breadwinners. Even when women provided critical economic income, some men came to see themselves as providers for their families and patriarchs in their homes. Acceptance of the industrial regime did not, however, render black women powerless and isolated in the domestic sphere. Through participation in the informal service economy that catered to male wage earners, some black women established a degree of economic independence from both black men and white employers. When they moved to sawmill towns and logging camps in the 1920s and 1930s, black men and women weighed new income-generating opportunities against the advantages of agricultural life.

3 Race, Class, and Leisure in the Industrial South

I'm a hardworking woman, and I work hard all the time.
But if you hear my baby, he just isn't satisfied.

I have to go to my work baby, between the night and day.
I didn't think my baby would treat me this way.

I'm a hardworking woman, but I'm becoming a rolling stone.
And the way my baby treats me, Lord I ain't gonna be here long.

—"Mississippi" Matilda, "Hardworking Woman Blues"

In 1936, "Mississippi" Matilda recorded two pairs of songs that expressed the transformation of black working-class communities in southern sawmill towns over the previous decade. The first pair—"Peel Your Banana" and "A&V Blues"—were standards of the barrelhouse circuit, a network of working-class saloons that connected the sawmill towns and logging and mining camps of the Gulf Coast during the earlier "cut-out-and-get-out" era. Typical of "barrelhouse blues" songs, Matilda's standards alluded to sex and migration—topics that musicians and their promoters believed would appeal to the young, single men who sought seasonal wage work in southern sawmill towns early in the century. In addition to the standards, Matilda Witherspoon (as she was known offstage) recorded two of her original compositions: "Hardworking Woman Blues" and "Happy Home Blues." The originals were similar in style to the barrelhouse standards. They were simple twelve-bar blues that were shortened to fit on a record side but contained ample space for extended solos when played before a live audience. Their lyrics focused on a topic rarely addressed in standard barrelhouse songs, however—the tensions between men and women within a wage-earning household. In contrast to the standards, which often had male protagonists, Witherspoon's originals took the perspective of a wage-earning woman, presumably herself or another one of the thousands of black women who established homes in southern sawmill towns following World War I.[1]

Scholars Daphne Duvall Harrison and Angela Y. Davis have pointed out that blues songs provide valuable insight into the historical experience of working-class African Americans—particularly women—who left few other artifacts of their social and political consciousness. Witherspoon was in many respects typical of black women who settled in southern sawmill towns in the 1920s and 1930s. She had been born in Hattiesburg, Mississippi, in 1914 and spent her early years moving with her parents as they sought work in the farms and small sawmills that dotted that state's southern piney woods region. After her mother died in 1919, Matilda's father Dallas settled the family in Bogalusa, just over the state line in Louisiana, where he found a job with the Great Southern Lumber Company and set up house with his wife's cousin, Minnie Long. Matilda completed the eighth grade at one of Bogalusa's "colored" schools, and at twelve years old she started singing in the choir at the Mt. Zion Church. She earned money cleaning and caring for children most likely in both black and white working-class homes in town, and also as a seasonal hand on the farms that surrounded the industrial town. She also began to earn money performing in Bogalusa's many saloons and cafes. The songs that she recorded in 1936 testified to the rich cultural world that black men and women created in southern sawmill towns in the 1920s and 1930s, as well as the degree of economic autonomy that black women often found within that world.[2]

It is important to remember, however, that Witherspoon's songs were produced within the context of a rapidly modernizing and industrializing rural South, in which black working-class culture rarely operated independently of the economic, social, and political influence of white workers, employers, and cultural entrepreneurs. The recordings that give us insight into Witherspoon's life also reflect the degree to which her experience was bounded by the race and class hierarchies that were so powerful in the Jim Crow South. The fact that Witherspoon grew up in Bogalusa reflected a concession by her father and other black men who accepted industrial employment as an alternative to family farming following World War I. Her musical skills emerged initially in black-controlled educational and religious institutions, but they were nurtured and documented by a commercial recording industry that emerged out of the often conflicting interests of record companies, industrial employers, and black and white audiences throughout the nation. In addition to illustrating changing relationships between men and women in southern sawmill towns, the songs that Witherspoon recorded also demonstrated the changing relationships between working-class African Americans and white employers who had an interest in shaping black working-class leisure in southern sawmill towns. The fact that Bluebird Record Company released her originals and not the standards reflected the changing marketing strategies of record firms and the evolving social policies of industrial employers as much as the artistic creativity of Matilda Witherspoon.[3]

My point is not to diminish black cultural creativity but rather to emphasize that African Americans retained cultural influence in spite of the racial and economic limits placed on them by the Jim Crow system. Barrelhouses emerged as part of a recruiting strategy for southern mill owners who hoped places for drinking and dancing would attract single young men to work in their mills. According to barrelhouse musicians, however, the establishments provided them with instruments and wage earning audiences that were critical to their ability to become professional musicians. Barrelhouses lost popularity in the 1920s and 1930s as African American communities became more stable and as black men and women began to establish churches, schools, and homes that provided alternative centers of leisure culture in southern mill towns. Even then, mill owners retained significant influence over black working-class leisure by sponsoring baseball games and swing dances that catered to the mixed-gender and multigenerational communities that had appeared in their towns. When barrelhouses persisted alongside those alternatives, mill owners launched ambitious anti-vice campaigns aimed at forcing working-class communities to comply with their new social policies. Sawmill town leisure culture was not a product of one race or class, but of constant negotiation among them.

Barrelhouse Blues

When she fashioned herself as a blues singer in the 1920s and 1930s, "Mississippi" Matilda drew upon an older tradition that emerged in the barrelhouses, or sawmill town saloons, of the "cut-out-and-get-out" era. "Poor" Joe Williams, a singer and guitarist who performed throughout Mississippi and Alabama, remembered that traveling musicians provided young men with a welcome break from the hard work and isolation of seasonal industrial wage work. "Boy, they'd have a wonderful time on Saturday nights in those camps," he recalled. "When somebody like me went through there it was like the President coming there. They'd come from all over [when] they hear of a man coming there with a guitar."[4]

Industrial work sites had a profound impact on African American leisure culture in the rural South. Farm families lived and worked in isolated units, and the largely cashless economy of southern agriculture made it difficult to divert resources toward commercial forms of leisure. Mill workers, on the other hand, lived in cramped boarding houses and "colored quarters," and their cash wages supported a thriving network of saloons and professional entertainers. Barrelhouses became the "social center of every work camp," according to musicologist Mike Rowe, and they attracted audiences from surrounding communities as well. Robert Johnson, famous today as the prototypical rural blues musician, realized as a young man, according to biographer Steven C. LaVere, that "if he ever wanted to be anything other than a sharecropper, he would need to get himself and his music together." To do so, Johnson moved to Hazelhurst, a sawmill town in the piney woods of southern Mississippi, where he married, studied with older musicians, and gained his reputation by playing in nearby sawmill towns and logging camps. Acknowledging his schooling in industrial towns, he sang, "we can still barrelhouse" in his now classic "Traveling Riverside Blues."[5]

For women as well as men, barrelhouses were important training grounds for a class of black professional entertainers that emerged in the rural South early in the century. Designed to appeal to young single men, barrelhouses gained a reputation for selling liquor and sex. Texas pianist Robert Shaw described typical sawmill town saloons as "sheds lined with barrels of chock beer and raw whiskey, an open floor, a piano on a raised platform in the corner, a back door opening on a line of rooms, each with a woman in a bed." Shaw's reference to prostitution supports historian Steven Reich's observation that exclusion from industrial jobs forced the few women who lived in early sawmill towns to support themselves through an "informal economy of gambling, bootlegging, and especially prostitution." Reich's list overlooks the significant number of female musicians and singers who also worked the barrelhouse circuit, however. Historian Daphne Duvall Harrison traces the roots of the 1920s "blues queens" to the "southern working-class women" who "went to work in the cafes, honky-tonks, and dance halls where men from the lumber camps, foundries, and mills spent their money." A collection of songs recorded by blues queen Elzadie Robinson between 1926 and 1929 includes "Barrel House Man," "Sawmill Blues," and "Arkansas Mill Blues."[6]

Early blues musicians were successful, according to Harrison, because they "brought a reality to the stage that struck a responsive chord in the hearts of their listeners." They appealed to a diverse audience, but barrelhouse songs often focused on the ambivalent experience of leaving home in search of industrial wage work. Pleasant Joseph's "Sawmill Man Blues" voiced a young man's fear that his lover would not be faithful while he was away. "And when I'm on my job, mama, I don't want no man hanging around," moaned the song's fictional mill worker. At the same time, the song expressed the narrator's satisfaction with his life as a lumber worker: "Yes, I'm working on the sawmill, sleepin' in a shack six feet wide. I see my gal every pay-day and I'm perfectly satisfied." Another protagonist promised to send for his sweetheart after finding work in Lewis Black's "Gravel Camp Blues." Black's character was confident that he could find work: "Ain't gonna be long," he assured his sweetheart, "hey pretty mama, ain't gonna be long." On the other hand, he anticipated having to accept less than ideal employment—"If I don't find a log camp," he predicted, "I'll find a gravel camp sure." "Log Camp Blues," written by blues legends Gertrude "Ma" Rainey and Thomas Dorsey, took the perspective of a woman planning to visit her man in a Mississippi lumber camp. Capturing both the pain of separation and the romance of a possible reunion, that song's protagonist proclaimed, "If I can't get no ticket, put on my walking shoes. I'm going to Mississippi, singing those logging camp blues."[7]

Because of their references to mill workers' lives, barrelhouse songs attracted the attention of some of the earliest scholarly studies of black working-class life in the South. Howard Odum and Guy Benton Johnson published a collection of *Negro Workaday Songs* in 1926, which they described as "spontaneous products of the Negro's workaday experiences and conflicts." The final chapter focused on the experiences of Leftwing Gordon, a wandering wage earner that became a prototype for Black Ulysses. Historian Benjamin Filene points out that by treating popular music as a direct reflection of black working-class consciousness, Odum and other scholars reified images of isolated black men that pervaded early blues songs. While many barrelhouse songs expressed ambivalence about leaving home in search of wage work, others celebrated the freedom that young men gained when they left agricultural homes. "I'm so glad I'm twenty-one years old today," sang Joe Dean, in a song about a young man leaving home. In James Wiggin's "Evil Woman Blues," a young man escapes an abusive relationship by moving to the sawmill town of Bogalusa. "Mr. Conductor man, I wanna talk with you," Wiggins sang, "I wanna ride your train from here to Bogalu." Odum and Johnson interpreted the contradiction between Leftwing Gordon's longing for home

and what they believed was his penchant for migration as a "striking paradox to the realism of his practice."[8]

Ironically, early scholars often documented these reputedly authentic expressions of black working-class consciousness in social settings
that undeniably were shaped by whites. An extreme example of this er-
roneous practice was Library of Congress folklorist John Lomax's recordings of prisoners, whom he described as "the Negro who had the least
contact with jazz, the radio, and the white man." Barrelhouses were certainly not prisons, but neither were they places of refuge from white
authority. Joseph E. McCaffrey, the white manager of a Georgia logging
camp, explained that lumber companies allowed drinking and gambling
among their black employees because they believed that such activities
would attract single men to their work sites. Whereas white workers frequented bars in nearby towns, segregation left black workers with fewer options for leisure activities. To accommodate his black employees,
McCaffrey operated dance halls on Saturday nights and hired armed men
to keep outsiders or "ringers" off company property. Company officials
also maintained "reasonable control over liquid refreshments and dis-
turbances," he recalled. "We always had places for entertainment, commonly know as jukes."[9]

Black musicians also testified to white influence over black leisure
space in southern sawmill towns. New Orleans-based musician Danny
Barker recalled his surprise when he discovered official white support for
a "jook dance" that he played while touring in southern Mississippi.
Barker traveled with Eureal "Little Brother" Montgomery, an older pianist who grew up in a sawmill town near Bogalusa. After playing a couple of dances in a Mississippi juke, Barker was horrified when a white
policeman entered the room, a sign that authorities were preparing to stop
the dance. To his surprise, the white officer was followed by "two colored men who carried gallon jugs of 'smoke'—that's what they called
moonshine whiskey" into the hall. Apparently escorting the delivery, the
officer then "took off his two ugly looking pistols and placed them on
the table," where he sat eating chicken and biscuits for the rest of the
evening. Barker noted that "the place really jumped" after that. Anthropologist Zora Neale Hurston reported a similar event at a juke that she
attended in a Florida sawmill town. After two women engaged in a knife
fight, the "only thing that could have stopped the killing" occurred when
a white supervisor, or "Quarter Boss stepped through the door with a .45
in his hand and another on his hip." His timing led Hurston to suspect
that "he had been eavesdropping as usual."[10]

In addition to attracting workers to mill towns, company-sponsored leisure spaces were also designed to protect workers from the often arbitrary power of local police. McCaffrey recalled, "When we established a camp, we'd go to the sheriff and say, 'We're going to set up a log camp and sawmill here. We've got a quarter boss and we'd like to have him deputized.'" The manager also asked officers to notify him when any employee was charged with a crime—to discourage local lawmen from "raiding our camps and arresting the help." McCaffrey remembered, "They always cooperated with us. We never had any trouble in that respect."[11]

Southern mill owners were so involved in their employees' nonwork lives that black social worker and reformer Forrester B. Washington accused them of "forcing upon the Negro a taste for degraded forms of leisure activities." Washington was particularly critical of "industrial firms and railroads, that house Negro employees in bunk houses on company property," who were "deliberately setting up gambling games as part of a recreational program for these men." Historian Carter G. Woodson had more faith in black workers' ability to resist the "evil influences" of their employers. Nevertheless, he agreed with Washington that long hours, low wages, and segregation prevented rural industrial workers from participating in "organized or directed recreation." In a 1930 study of rural African Americans living under Jim Crow, Woodson wrote that "diversions among people thus circumstanced" would necessarily be "restricted largely to drinking and sexual indulgence." After all, he reasoned, "It does not require very much time for a man to get a drink and be happy with his dulcina."[12]

Both writers interpreted the popularity of blues music as a symptom of the broader disintegration of black rural traditions in the 1920s, inaccurately assuming that black people had no influence over the new cultural forms that replaced those traditions. Washington emphasized coercion, charging northern record companies with "almost forcing on the Negro race records that are distinctly immoral in their title and content." In reference to aggressive marketing to black consumers in the 1920s, he contended, "some of these records are so obscene that the companies have not the courage to advertise them in their regular catalogues, but issue special booklets for Negroes." To leave no black community untouched, "these companies also flaunt the suggesting titles of these records, accompanied by obscene pictures, in the Negro newspapers." Woodson, in contrast, included "race records" among the many impersonal forces of modernization—along with radios, motion pictures, and "improved transportation through good roads"—that he saw spreading through the rural South. Even the most isolated rural people, he contended, were no longer satisfied with what he believed were traditional leisure activities such as barn raisings, harvest festivals, hunting, and "the popular picnic in the nearby woods." He blamed the decline of rural culture not on employers but on black workers themselves, who he implied lacked the ability to choose between traditional and foreign forms of leisure: "'Let us have recreation like that in the city,' they say, 'Let it come from without rather than as formerly from within.'"[13]

Making a Modern South

Hurston's *Mules and Men* illustrates the difficulties that scholars faced when they attempted to distinguish black from white influence over sawmill town leisure culture in the early twentieth century. A participant in Harlem's New Negro movement and a student of anthropologist Franz Boas, Hurston believed that black southerners retained a traditional culture that had been forged in slavery but lost to her and other participants in the Great Migration. She sought this "old stuff" initially in Jacksonville, Florida, but was disappointed to discover that the "Negroness" of urban blacks "had been rubbed off by close contact with white culture." Her next destination was Eatonville, the agricultural village of her childhood and a place that she remembered as the "crib of negroism." She found a few stories that she deemed authentic enough in her hometown but learned from the locals that better sources of folklore were the mill towns and railroad camps of Polk County, "where dey makes up all de songs and things lak dat." Charlie Jones told her "strong stories" of jook dances and "jook lights" as Hurston described the black women "around whom the glory of Polk County surged." After hearing stories of "sawmill town and turpentine bosses," she recalled, "I knew I had to visit Polk County right now."[14]

Hurston discovered upon entering Polk County that this legendary source of black culture was hardly the isolated "folk" setting that she had set out to explore. Her first glimpse of Loughman, the Polk County sawmill town where she gathered much of the material for *Mules and Men*, was overshadowed by "a huge smoke-stack blowing smut against the sky," and a "big sign" reading "Everglades Cypress Lumber Company, Loughman, Florida." She drove directly to the "quarters," where "despite the signs all over that this was private property and that no one could enter without the consent of the company," she found a room at the boarding house that a black woman operated "under the patronage of the company." These markers of industrialization and white influence did not dispel Hurston's enthusiasm upon discovering that unlike her insular agricultural village, Loughman was home to "several hundred Negroes from all over the South." She spent a few weeks in Loughman and then continued on to "a locale of sawmills, lumber camps and fisherman" near Mobile and farther west to Bogalusa, "a huge industrial center, sawmills, paper mills, chicken hatcheries and reforestation nurseries." Her selection of field sites indicates that diversity and change—rather than isolation and tradition—were critical components of the southern industrial culture that she documented in *Mules and Men*.[15]

Hurston revealed the dynamic nature of sawmill town culture in the variety of leisure activities that she observed in Loughman. Her introduction to mill town nightlife came not at the juke, as could have been expected, but at dances that several families organized in the houses that they rented in the company quarters. These events were coordinated with payday at the mill and advertised by bonfires lit outside the homes where dances were held. The sponsoring family sold roasted peanuts and fried fish or chicken, and they paid a musician—often with alcohol—to provide entertainment. Whereas jooks supplied musicians with pianos, house parties employed only those who could bring their instruments with them. As a result, Hurston observed, "the only music is guitar music" and the "only dance is the ole square dance." With amateur musicians and country dancing, these events may have represented the retention of agricultural styles as black people moved into industrial settings. That they occurred in working-class households in company towns points to the degree to which rural African Americans had claimed those settings as their own. Rather than attempting to distinguish between black traditions and white impositions—as Washington and Woodson did—we might ask how black lumber workers and their families adapted leisure activities to suit the industrial world in which they now lived.[16]

House parties were particularly important leisure activities in towns where mill owners did not sponsor leisure activities for black workers. The McGowins, who owned W. T. Smith Lumber Company, were devout Unitarians who did not allow alcohol in their company town of Chapman, Alabama. Instead, company managers allowed residents to operate cafes and small juke joints in a section of black rental houses located on company property but separated from the rest of the mill town by the Rocky Creek Swamp. Make Montgomery, a black worker who lived closer to the center of town, recalled that company officials generally condoned such activities and suppressed parties "across the creek" only when the music got too loud. A few families were so successful in the entertainment business that they purchased pianos and hired musicians from nearby Greenville and Montgomery, Alabama. Rufus "Tee Tot" Payne, a native of nearby Georgiana, was a regular performer at house parties in

Chapman. The black blues musician is credited with giving white county music star Hank Williams his first guitar lesson.[17]

Another indication that black men and women were making permanent rather than seasonal homes in the industrial South was the appearance of black working-class churches in sawmill towns. As with black music, scholars have often treated religious forms as if they were the property of a particular race or class. Historian Evelyn Brooks Higginbotham observes that "the most imaginative and analytically sophisticated studies" of black working-class culture have been limited by "the belief that African American Christianity is white-derived, middle-class in orientation, and thus less authentically black." Hurston for one demonstrated this limitation in her own work. *Mules and Men* includes an entire section devoted to the practice of Hoodoo religion in New Orleans but makes no reference to mill town churches. Her one account of Christianity in Loughman involves an unflattering description of a "stump-knocker," or itinerant preacher, and his two female assistants who "detached themselves from the railroad track and came walking into the quarters" one Saturday evening. "Everybody thought he was a bootlegger and yelled orders to him to that effect," Hurston reported. When they discovered his true identity "some fell silent to listen" while "others sucked their teeth and either went back to their houses or went on to the jook." After a dramatic sermon, the trio collected a "sparse contribution" and "drifted back into the darkness of the railroad."[18]

Despite Hurston's contention that black sawmill workers were not interested in organized religion, a mill town of the size of Loughman would almost certainly have been home to a permanent African American congregation by the late 1920s. In Chapman, Alabama, mill workers paid Baptist and Methodist ministers to visit them from Montgomery, and they convinced the company to lend them a dilapidated shack for weekly services. In Bogalusa, the Great Southern Lumber Company boasted that its black employees attended "churches of every denomination" in the 1920s—failing to mention that such institutions had been built by workers with no help from the firm. In Elizabethtown, Greene Brothers Lumber Company provided no space for church services, but black workers attended weekly services in the nearby village of Newtown. White employers often misjudged their workers' commitment to Christianity, for example, when the owner of a North Carolina mill discouraged Reverend Cary Miles Cartwright from building a church in the 1920s. "You have come to preach to the triflingest [sic] set of damn niggers I have ever seen," the employer stated when the minister entered his sawmill town. As evidence, he recalled that workers used for firewood the timber that he had given them to build a church a few years earlier. It is likely that these workers had supported churches in the agricultural communities from which they came, and therefore saw no reason to build a new one in their seasonal home. That Cartwright succeeded in building a church with no aid from the employer later in the 1920s indicated that his congregation had decided to settle more permanently in the sawmill town.[19]

Employers made half-hearted attempts to support black working-class churches even as they supported other leisure activities that they deemed more appealing to their workers. One mill owner acknowledged the diversification of leisure activities among his black employees when he provided two "clubhouses" for their use: "One for the pious folks, whose chief amusement is the lodge and revival meetings, and another at the other side of the 'quarters' for those Negroes who wish to dance, shoot craps, and carry on in a lighter vein than that offered by the brethren of the cloth." When sociologist Abraham Berglund surveyed southern mill owners in the late 1920s, he found that employers exerted only minimal influence over workers' religious lives. This influence typically took the form of a monthly or annual donation, or the provision of a church building. In "but a very few cases," employers also paid the salaries of ministers, a practice that Berglund found "dangerous" but atypical. He reported that one manager insisted he did not attempt to influence white preachers, and that he asked black preachers only "to impress upon their flocks the fact that the company expected six days of work from each employee." Despite lack of support from mill owners, the sociologist found that "as in most communities, the churches and the schools play a very important part in the lives of the people of the sawmill villages."[20]

"The New Welfare Emphasis in the Southern Lumber Industry"

While most southern lumber mill owners took little interest in their workers' personal lives, a small but influential minority of them began to adopt welfare capitalist strategies that aimed to attract loyal workers through the provision of healthy living conditions for them and their families. In his 1914 presidential address to the Yellow Pine Manufacturing Association (which would soon merge into the Southern Pine Association), Alabama mill owner John Kaul called attention to what he hoped would become "the new welfare emphasis in the southern lumber industry." Kaul acknowledged that southern industrialists had grown accustomed to employing seasonal labor, but he argued that even "shifting" workers spent "a large number of their days" in company towns and that they adjusted their "lives of work, play, and love and worship, according to the facilities offered." The following year, the trade journal *American Lumberman* printed a detailed description of Kaulton, which they endorsed as a model of "a proprietary village scientifically planned to attain definite objectives." By making comfortable housing and clean living conditions a central part of his labor relations program, the journal contended, Kaul had disproved the "old fallacy" that southern workers do "not appreciate desirable conditions."[21]

Early welfare efforts embraced the theory that employers could shape working-class behavior, typically in an effort to encourage loyalty and efficiency among their employers. The *American Lumberman*, for example, explained that Kaulton's planners appealed to "the home and community spirit" of workers by separating their housing from the noise and pollution of the sawmill. Even "Progressive Lumbermen," as Kaul and other welfare advocates called themselves, retained the belief, however, that African Americans could not respond to such initiatives. Implying that African Americans were part of the nuisance that white workers associated with lumber production, the journal explained that a "separate passage" ran from the mill "to the negro quarters." Managers of the Great Southern Lumber Company also assumed that segregation contributed to welfare strategies designed to attract white workers. Great Southern erected homes for white workers on Bogalusa's aptly named Pleasant Hill, which was separated from the sawmill by an administrative complex and the company hotel. The firm situated the "Negro quarters" on the opposite side of town, on a triangle wedged between the commercial district and the sawmill.[22]

The combination of the "new welfare emphasis" and strict segregation built on the "peculiar paternalism" that historian Steven Reich identified in early southern sawmill towns. In 1912, a white school principle complained that Great Southern failed to support schools in the company town and as a result a "general feeling prevailed" among workers "that Bogalusa was just a mill camp." In an effort to counteract that sentiment, the firm secured a state charter in 1914, incorporating what they claimed had been the nation's largest privately owned town. The terms of incorporation included race, gender, and property restrictions that restricted voting rights to a small group of white men, nearly all of them Great Southern managers and executives. Those voters preserved direct company control over the town by electing general manager William Sullivan as mayor and filling the city council with managers from Great Southern. By extending the town's limits to encompass previously independent communities such as Richardson Town and Poplas Quarters, the new charter granted company officials legal authority over neighborhoods that workers originally established as semi-independent enclaves. While city officials did not challenge workers' claims to land ownership in these communities, their first act of civic legislation barred African Americans from renting houses or businesses outside of the "Negro quarters." Demonstrating that segregation laws were intended to improve the lives of white workers, the city council made an exception for "bonafide servant or servants" who were housed in white neighborhoods, granted they were provided with sanitary facilities and prevented from loitering.[23]

Efforts to legislate residential segregation pointed to an emerging contradiction between the ideological basis of Great Southern's early welfare strategies and the reality that African Americans were beginning to establish permanent homes in Bogalusa. That contradiction was highlighted in 1919 when union activists demanded a "family wage" for both black and white common laborers. It also appeared in company accounts of a massive celebration that William Sullivan threw the following November in an effort to restore "cooperation" between workers and management after he drove union leaders out of town. "It was a night when directors and men got together, shook hands with one another, and joined democratically in an evening of fun and entertainment," declared the *Mill Whistle,* Great Southern's company newsletter. The *Mill Whistle* noted that managers staged the event not only for company employees— "everybody in town was invited to come and take part"—but it also emphasized the strictly segregated nature of the celebration, with whites congregating at the Employees' Building and blacks at the "colored Y.M.C.A." Rather than simply excluding black workers from activities planned for whites, as they had in the past, company officials also addressed "over a thousand men and women" gathered at the "colored Y." Mill owner A. C. Goodyear "made them the same promise of a square deal" that he had made to the whites. Indicating that managers were not convinced that black workers would be motivated solely by improved living conditions, Mayor Sullivan followed Goodyear's offer to African Americans by "telling them that they had all done good work, and urging them to speed up a little more." The *Mill Whistle* reported that the speeches were followed by a company-sponsored dance, another indication that Great Southern officials still believed that black workers were motivated by individual pleasure rather than responsibility to their families or communities. "A well known jazz band from New Orleans had been secured and all enjoyed themselves thoroughly."[24]

Managers at Great Southern found that in order to promote Bogalusa as a "healthy place" for "a [white] man of family," they had to counteract images of mill towns as places of black male pleasure that they and other southern lumber firms had propagated during the "cut-out-and-get-out" era. That effort was illustrated in a pamphlet entitled "Bogalusa: City of Families and Factories," produced by Great Southern's department of publicity in the early 1920s. Clarifying the racial distinctions that separated Pleasant Hill from the dirt and danger that many associated with mill town life, the firm promised, "Every house occupied by a white person has all the conveniences of any modern city home." Upwardly mobile white workers were ensured that Bogalusa's schools would prepare their children to attend "any college or university in the nation." The pamphlet also made it clear that such advantages would not be overshadowed by the large African American population that also lived in Bogalusa. "Everything is done to keep our negro citizens healthy, happy and productive," managers assured potential white employees. The firm boasted its support for black churches, "the colored Y," and schools, and described African American housing as "neat" and "comfortable." Lest white workers suspect that company support for black institutions might compete with welfare programs for whites, Great Southern pointed out that black schools taught "domestic science and useful occupations" designed to cater to white needs and that black recreational facilities were reserved "exclusively for the use of the colored people." While Great Southern encouraged white workers to rely on company welfare strategies, the firm encouraged black workers "to develop pride of race and in every other way to promote their individual welfare."[25]

Over time, large mill owners came to support community-building efforts that black employees and their families initiated in the late 1910s and early 1920s. "The colored race has awakened to the advantages of education," proclaimed Great Southern's company newsletter in 1923. Company officials claimed that "by sending their children to the public schools," parents were demonstrating their commitment not only to reading and writing but also to raising "clean, honest, respectful and better citizens for the communities in which they live." The firm also claimed responsibility for black marriages in town. Director D. L. Smith offered lectures on family life to young men at the colored Y, and he invited older men "to stop by the 'Y' and hear him talk to the young men—he had good advice for you," claimed the *Mill Whistle*. "It has been rumored that Dan Cupid will tie a number of love knots in June and July," read the "Colored Section" of the newsletter. Proclaiming their newfound appreciation for black family life, managers declared, "The houses are ready for you girls; the G.S.L. Company is waiting for you, young men—don't put it off for fear of work."[26]

Although smaller firms devoted fewer resources to welfare capitalism, they also adopted the segregated social strategies pioneered by Kaul and Great Southern. In 1919, W. T. Smith sponsored a Fourth of July celebration for 4,000 employees and guests "from every section of the county." Held on a Saturday so as to not interrupt operation of the mill, the festival served as a lavish demonstration of the McGowins' devotion to their employees, their region, and their nation. After a baseball game and dance, workers assembled for segregated barbeque dinners for black and white families. Montgomery judge Perry Thomas addressed the white workers, among whom he honored the "goodly number" of Confederate veterans, and asked both black and white workers to donate to a memorial being constructed for the heroes of World War I. According to one local newspaper, the event sent the intended message as "the big hearted owners of the vast industry did all in their power to make their workmen and all visitors have a time that will long be remembered by all who were there."[27]

W. T. Smith faced no strikes during World War I, but the mass exodus of workers from southern Alabama convinced the firm to pay more attention to living conditions in Chapman. Having resided in Brewton, Alabama, during the firm's first decade of operation, owner J. Greeley McGowin bought a farm outside Chapman in 1918 and used it for hunting and family picnics until he built a mansion there in 1926. The firm donated space and equipment to open a medical clinic in town and deducted fees from workers' paychecks to pay two full-time doctors. The McGowin women organized a Chapman Welfare Association in 1924 for feeding needy families and "taking care of charity" in surrounding communities. In 1932, the company donated nearly $3,000 to the school for white children in Chapman. They also gave $700 to the "Negro School," which enrolled more children than the white school. Convinced that paternalism increased their father's control over employees, McGowin's children later described the mill town as a "benevolent dictatorship."[28]

Having made black leisure activities central to their labor recruitment strategies in previous decades, welfare-minded mill owners devoted a great deal of energy in the 1930s to counteracting their towns' reputations as places of black male leisure. Kaul reminded his constituents that recreation was "one of the greatest factors in modern city life for making morality" and urged southern mill owners to follow Chicago reformer Jane Addams's model for using organized recreation as a "safety valve for the surplus energy which otherwise would lead many to the saloon, dance hall, or the streets for their amusement." Kaul and other welfare advocates recommended athletics in particular as a method for teaching discipline and teamwork to industrial workers. When Great

Southern officials sponsored a Sunday baseball league for white workers in 1922, local churches blocked what they saw as a violation of the Sabbath. Managers seem to have co-opted that opposition by the following year when they applauded the creation of an all-white Church League, which included several Protestant congregations, a Catholic team, the Bogalusa Shrine Club, the Blue Lodge Masons, city officials, and two groups of Great Southern office staff. By sponsoring an official "G.S.L. Plant Team," the firm contributed to an effort that it hoped would "bring individuals, families, churches and other organizations and communities into closer friendly relationships and truer sportsman-like methods" in their personal, work, and social lives.[29]

"The spirit of baseball and good sportsmanship" proved equally "contagious" among black Bogalusans. "One of the best baseball games ever played in Bogalusa," according to the *Mill Whistle*, was the July

Photo 10. Bogalusa "Y Tigers," 1936. Seated, left to right: Leonard Barnes (No uniform; mascot, Bogalusa, La.); Fred "Maggie" Magee (2nd base, Mt. Ollie, Miss.); Walter Bibbins (outfield, New Orleans, La.); E. Hamilton (center field, Mobile, Ala.); Clyde "Stumpy" Brown (3rd base, Mt. Ollie, Miss.); Ishmael Jordan (catcher, Stonewall, Miss.); Willie Moore (pitcher, Baton Rouge, La.). Standing, left to right: Tillie "Lefty" James (pitcher, n.p.); Lynn Powe (pitcher, Waynesboro, Miss.); John Henry Prince (catcher/outfield, Hattiesburg, Miss.); Jesse Green (shortstop, Baton Rouge, La.); ——— Bates (umpire, Bogalusa, La.); Percy Gill (1st base, Bassfield, Miss.); Bobby Robertson (3rd base, Mobile, Ala.); Columbus "Dazzy" Vance (pitcher, Slidell, La.); Claude "Baby Face" Green (pitcher, Mobile, Ala.) Courtesy of Mark Douglas, Elyria, Ohio.

17, 1923, showdown between the "Y" Tigers and the Giants of nearby Bissant, Louisiana. After tying the Giants in three consecutive games, the Tigers had a "good chance" of entering the state championship that fall. Particularly if they could recruit another strong pitcher, the newsletter predicted, the Bogalusa team was on its way to becoming the "strongest club in the South." Great Southern devoted considerable resources toward fulfilling that prediction. They erected a ballpark next to the colored YMCA and purchased uniforms for the team. Managers recruited star players from nearby communities by hiring them as brakemen or "some other easy job." Management also allowed team members to practice on company time. By 1936, the Tigers were composed of skilled players from as far away as Baton Rouge, Mobile, and Hattiesburg. The Colored Athletic Park hosted double headers on Sundays and single games on Monday evenings. The evening games continued until it was too dark to play. "Ball games were one of your basic activities" in Bogalusa, recalled Larry Powe, whose father Lynn pitched for the Tigers in the 1930s.[30]

Whereas baseball was strictly segregated in Bogalusa, smaller firms were not willing to spend the resources necessary to maintain separate facilities. W. T. Smith bought uniforms and equipment for its black and white ball teams in Chapman, and they granted team members a two-week vacation to participate in summer tournaments. As in Bogalusa, local residents matched mill managers' enthusiasm for the sport. According to a member of the black team, the "whole town" flocked to the ballpark on Sunday afternoons. They sat in segregated grandstands and their respective teams never competed with each other, but black and white fans watched the same games and cheered on both black and white teams as they competed with visiting rivals. The T. R. Miller Lumber Company also sponsored black and white teams in Brewton, about fifty miles south of Chapman along the L&N Railroad. Marvin Mantel, the superintendent of education in Butler County in the 1940s, recalled that company-sponsored baseball games were important cultural bases of a regional "geographical, social and business contact area" in southern Alabama.[31]

Working-class communities seem to have had their own reasons for embracing baseball in those towns. Just as white businessmen established social and cultural contacts through baseball, African Americans also forged regional and even national connections at company athletic parks. The Tigers regularly hosted black teams from Mobile, New Orleans, Baton Rouge, and various towns in Mississippi; and professional Negro League clubs such as the Baltimore Elite Giants, the Chicago

Photo 11. Bogalusa "Y Tigers," 1938. Seated, left to right: Leonard Barnes (2d base, Bogalusa, La.); Clyde "Stumpy" Brown (Mt. Ollie, Miss.); Jake Sheihan (n.p.); Fred "Maggie" Magee (2nd base, Mt. Ollie, Miss.); Leroy Aker (catcher/outfield, n.p.); Rachel Simmons (2nd and 3rd base, n.p.); Percy Gill (1st base, Bassfield, Miss.); Ishmael Jordan, (catcher, Stonewall, Miss.). Standing, left to right: Ike Mealy (manager); George Patterson (catcher); A. D. Brown (3rd base); Pete Fields (pitcher); Claude "Baby Face" Green (pitcher, Mobile, Ala.); Cliff "Jelly" Nelson (3rd base/outfield, n.p.); Columbus "Dazzy" Vance (pitcher, Slidell, La.); Lynn Powe (pitcher, Waynesboro, Miss.); Charles Hutchinson (scorer). Courtesy of Mark Douglas, Elyria, Ohio.

Brown Bombers, and the New York Cubans occasionally barnstormed through Bogalusa. Black fans flocked from Bogalusa and surrounding agricultural communities to catch a glimpse of Negro League heroes Satchel Paige and Roy Campanella when they played in the Colored Athletic Park. Claude "Baby Face" Green, who moved from Mobile to Bogalusa to play with the Tigers, later played with the Negro League's Chicago Brown Bombers. Before he moved to Bogalusa from Jackson, Mississippi, in 1945, John Oatis heard it described as a "sawmill and baseball town."[32]

Alongside baseball, swing music replaced barrelhouse as the most popular musical form in many southern mill towns. In fact, sports and music seem to have developed in tandem. The Colored Athletic Park became "the center of cultural activity" in Bogalusa, according to Larry

Powe, after Great Southern began sponsoring swing dances at a pavilion near the grandstand. The impetus for swing music came from black residents themselves, with company support. A. M. "Appie" Wadell, an older black man who had worked as a chauffeur for manager and mayor William Sullivan, started a jazz band for young men at the colored Y. Great Southern executives A. C. Long and Harry Hoppen bought instruments and provided financial support in the band's early years. Young men who joined their families in the migration from farm to industrial town provided a pool for musical talent. Henry Sims joined the band soon after his family moved from Franklinton, Mississippi, in 1923. He and Willie "Hump" Manning took formal music lessons at the local high school, but they adopted musical styles from older musicians in town and from sheet music that they bought at Wurliner's music store. Eventually, they learned to transpose songs directly off popular swing and blues records. "When we get through with it," Sims boasted, "you couldn't tell it was, you know, just off the record." By the late 1930s, this band, the Rhythm Aces, traveled regularly between Jackson, Mobile, New Orleans, and Baton Rouge, the same communities frequented by the baseball Tigers. The band also maintained a regular gig at the Washington Parish Fair, which allowed them to attract fans from throughout the surrounding communities. The Aces recorded a single with the Decca label in 1940 although it was released under the name of Lorenzer "Good" Lewis, a drummer who joined them at the New Orleans studio. Sims maintained a day job during this period at the Great Southern commissary, but indicating the extent to which they had become financially independent from the company, John "Duke" Oatis lived off his share of the band's earnings after he joined the Rhythm Aces in 1945.[33]

W. T. Smith Lumber Company also supported the introduction of swing music to Chapman, where it rivaled older blues styles in the 1930s. The management sponsored dances at the Chapman colored school in the mid-1920s and hired Claude Shannon and other bandleaders who traveled from Montgomery and other cities. In the early 1930s, the Civilian Conservation Corps (CCC) erected a dance hall for young black men who were housed at a federal work camp on land that W. T. Smith donated to the New Deal work program. Marie Cobb remembers lying on the front porch of her family's company cottage as a young girl, listening to the swing music that floated through Chapman from the CCC camp and the schoolhouse.

Similar to baseball, swing music brought black working-class southerners into dialogue with the black commercial culture that emerged across the South and the United States in the 1920s and 1930s. "Race"

Photo 12. Willie Manning, Oliver Austin, and Sherman "Einstein" Thompson. Horn Section for the Rhythm Aces, Bogalusa, La., 1940s. Star Studio, Bogalusa, La., courtesy of Henry E. Sims, Bogalusa, La.

labels such as Decca, Okeh, and Bluebird broke into the record industry by selling blues and jazz records to an African American audience that major labels assumed were too poor or too backward to support their own market. After black consumers bought out two Mamie Smith records in 1920 and then packed theaters to see her and other blues acts in New York, Chicago, and St. Louis, these pioneering labels searched for ways to sell their products in the South, where the vast majority of African Americans still lived. "We want live agents everywhere," declared a manager of Black Swan, the only black-owned label of the era. This and other independent labels advertised for sales representatives in southern drug stores, furniture shops, hair salons, and cafes. Salesmen peddled records in black neighborhoods, bars, and workplaces as well as through the mail. Record companies also combed the South for new artists, paying musicians to travel from small southern towns to studios located as far away as Grafton, Wisconsin, and Richmond, Indiana. Before the Depression curtailed their operations, several "race" labels also operated studios in Atlanta, New Orleans, and Dallas. The lumber towns where black southerners developed new musical forms in an industrial setting provided some of the first music released by the race labels. The earliest of these recordings popularized barrelhouse musicians. Later sessions introduced a national audience to artists such as "Mississippi" Matilda and the Rhythm Aces who had moved onto newer forms such as swing.[34]

The emergence of new musical forms from within rural industrial towns presented a challenge to contemporary observers who viewed industrialization as a foreign imposition on black southerners. Perhaps because they disrupted her vision of an isolated folk world, Hurston omitted any reference to baseball or jazz from *Mules and Men.* An unreleased film that she made in Loughman in the early 1930s shows black men and women wearing suits and fancy dresses and gathering for an event at a baseball stadium. The film does not reveal what its subjects were gathering for, but it does show a man entertaining them with a saxophone. In later works, the anthropologist analyzed the increasing significance of commercial popular culture that she had observed in southern sawmill towns. Race records were "greatly affecting the originality of the Negro songs," she wrote in 1936, even in the "farthest-removed places" such as "remote turpentine, logging, phosphate, and other camps." She observed that nationally known recorded music such as "Pinetop's Boogie Woogie" and "Mistreating Blues" had become more popular than songs that "had formerly been more or less peculiar to the particular section in which they were sung." These observations led Hurston to reject Boas's relativistic approach to culture in favor of a functionalist approach that saw black people as participants in modern American culture. "Negro folklore is not a thing of the past," she wrote shortly after *Mules and Men* was published. "It is still in the making. Its great variety shows the adaptability of the black man: nothing is too old or too new, domestic or foreign, high or low for his use."[35]

As Hurston began to acknowledge the modern character of black culture in the South, she also recognized that commercial recording provided a venue through which local musicians could preserve and extend the reach of traditional styles. "Pinetop's Boogie Woogie" was a recorded version of a barrelhouse piano classic developed by sawmill town musicians in the 1910s. "For some time," she wrote from Florida, "one of the best known phonograph singers has been a man known as Tampa Red; Tampa Slim is another favorite." Historian Lawrence Levine argues that race record producers "understood the music they were recording imperfectly enough so that they extended a great deal of freedom to the singers they were recording." As a result, according to scholar

John Fahey, "by 1931, the companies had been performing for three or four years the function of passively allowing hundreds of Southern Negroes to sit in their studios and record the songs which they had been singing for decades." Rather than replacing live performers, recorded music often inspired them to improvise. Solo pianists often pounded their foot pedals "to give the effect of a drum," Hurston noted, and they played "loudly and insistently" to replicate the sound of amplified juke-boxes. "There is little need for other instruments if he knows his 'jook' music well."[36]

Recording technology also limited the extent to which records could compete with live performances. Producers eliminated the "strongest part" of the barrelhouse tradition, according to musicologist Mac McCormick, when they discouraged extended instrumental solos that would not fit on one side of a record. Because they recorded "theater style," with the artist standing in front of a microphone, studios also prevented musicians from playing their own accompaniment as they did in live performances. Early blues women such as Victoria Spivey, Hociel Thomas, and "Sippie" Wallace "developed their own versions" of barrelhouse piano standards, according to McCormick, but there is little evidence of that in their recordings. Race records obviously could not capture the "frequent cheerful volunteer vocal assistance" offered by live audiences. Due to such limitations, Hurston observed in Florida, "the nickel phonograph" had "not yet entirely displaced the traditional piano player always found where groups of Negroes live in the State, and the often-improvised jazz band."[37]

In contrast to the fears expressed by Washington and Woodson, rural African Americans seem to have greeted industrialization and commercialization as opportunities to expand the scope of their leisure activity. Ire Abrams, a black man who lived in Chapman in the 1930s, recalled that juke joints "across the creek" were "more fun" than dances in town. "The school dances were run by the company," he pointed out, "and they didn't want people dancing all night before work." Managers restricted such events to Saturday and prohibited alcohol. Marie Cobb preferred the dances, however, which were more elegant than juke joints and where she could dress up in "crazy hats" and dance popular steps such as the Charleston and the jitterbug. As black working-class communities found alternatives to barrelhouses, some within them rejected older institutions as tainted by the male-dominated and often rowdy environment of early sawmill towns. Gospel composer Thomas Dorsey recalled that association with such places led some African Americans to avoid blues music entirely. "But it wasn't nothing wrong with the blues," he insisted, "it was just the places where they was playing 'em in! Up there some guy'd get killed every Saturday night, or get cut up, or something like that." John Oatis agreed that Bogalusa's saloons gained a bad reputation in the 1930s, but this did not prevent him and his wife from meeting to dance and listen to the blues at them after performing at swing dances with the Rhythm Aces.[38]

Redrawing the Color Line

The transformation of sawmill town culture in the 1920s and 1930s held contradictory implications for mill owners. Having sponsored barrelhouses with the intention of recruiting single black men early in the century, employers now funded activities that they believed would encourage marriage and permanent residence among their African American employees. In so doing, they assumed that black men were capable of such a response and not inherently transient, as employers had described older generations who had refused to abandon family farming. Lumbermen complained about "shiftless" labor well into the 1950s, usually as justification for the low wages and poor living conditions that they continued to provide for their employees. Starting in the 1920s, however, their social policies were shaped by the recognition that black workers were no longer resistant to making permanent homes in their towns. By sponsoring alternatives to barrelhouse culture, southern mill owners challenged—implicitly at least—the myth of Black Ulysses.

Because new social policies assumed that black and white workers responded to similar incentives, these policies also challenged the social basis of segregation in mill towns. According to Evelyn Boyette, a white woman whose husband and father worked at Great Southern, swing music provided her with a space to enjoy black music without compromising respectability in the eyes of other working-class whites. "A girl wasn't caught in a barroom," she recalled, "It was strictly a man's place." That black women did not always share such prohibitions reinforced white people's criticism of saloons. Black mill worker William Bailey does not "remember prostitution being widespread" in the 1930s, but he speculated that whites believed it was because "there was a lot of honky ponky going on, men getting' with the women." He insisted that such activities were romantic—"It's just my sweetheart, you know. It wasn't that she was out sellin' it"—but he understood that such behavior may have enticed white men to "hang around in black neighborhoods" in search of prostitutes.[39]

Swing dances were strictly segregated by race, on the other hand, which allowed them to attract enormous mixed-gender crowds in both black and white communities in southern mill towns. "We played for everybody, white, colored, whatever," recalled Rhythm Aces member Henry Sims. Police allowed the Rhythm Aces to entertain whites as long as dancers remained segregated. They even permitted white musicians to join black bands on stage. Whites could also observe black dances, although Sims recalled that interracial dancing provoked police to "come in there and close it down, run everybody out of there and bust some heads." These local examples were part of a regional trend toward biracial working-class leisure in the South, one that anticipated the confluence between black and white popular culture that historians Pete Daniel and George Lipsitz have traced to the 1940s and 1950s. In reference to bandleader Duke Ellington's southern tours in 1933 and 1934, one observer claimed that swing "erased the color line" between black and white music.[40]

The convergence of black and white leisure activities compelled southern employers to seek alternative methods for shaping the social lives of both black and white workers. Having operated towns as an extension of factories, southern lumber firms established formal legal institutions in the 1920s that increased their ability to discipline the nonwork activities of employees and their families. Those efforts were intended to enforce the new policy of creating social environments that managers believed would attract both black and white workers to settle in their towns. While W. T. Smith never attempted to incorporate Chapman, the firm did establish a "police court" to maintain legal order in 1914. For the first decade of its existence, Chapman's "court" served to protect the firm's labor supply by assuring local officials that criminals would be punished when turned over to management. Starting in 1928, managers started to use the institution to shape the town's social climate. Of the 409 arrests made over the following ten years, one third were for fighting or in other ways "disturbing the peace." Another third punished drunkenness or possession of alcohol. In 1936, company officials drew up the "Criminal Code of the Town of Chapman," which focused primarily upon such social offenses as "allowing loud, drunken or disorderly people to disturb the neighborhood from your house." Clarifying their intent to create spaces for mixed-gender leisure, town officials specifically outlawed disturbing "females in any public assembly met for the purpose of amusement, instruction, or recreation, by rude or indecent behavior, or by profane or obscene language."[41]

Racial distinctions were difficult to maintain in small mill towns, where black and white communities were separated by only a few hundred feet and where black and white workers interacted at baseball games and on the streets as well as in the mills, logging operations, and, in the case of black women, white homes. In towns such as Chapman and neighboring Georgiana, whites and blacks often mingled over common interests in music and dance. Historian George Lipsitz attributes white musician Hank Williams's appreciation for black music to his friendship with black musicians Rufus Payne and Connie "Big Day" McKee. Marie Cobb recalls that Thigpen's Log Cabin, an officially white roadhouse where Hank Williams performed occasionally, was in practice an interracial establishment. Other whites-only roadhouses permitted African Americans to purchase liquor at a back window and a few allowed them to stand inside and listen to the music. Williams also studied guitar with white merchant Jim Warren, who had been attacked by the Ku Klux Klan for renting a house to a black man. W. T. Smith Lumber Company maintained strict residential segregation in Chapman but, like other southern firms, viewed the KKK as a threat to their influence in local politics. As in the case of Warren, who "struck it out in Georgiana, even though the town was ashamed of him," company suppression of white supremacists may have had the unintended consequence of allowing interracial contact.[42]

The Green Brothers Lumber Company, which operated two mills in eastern North Carolina, also attempted to exclude certain leisure activities from its company town in the mid-1930s. Having operated mills in Alabama earlier in the century, the brothers retained traditional social policies in the "shanty houses" that they erected at their Beach Island mill in 1931. They hired mostly single young men and, benefiting from the Great Depression, provided no incentive for them to bring their families with them. "So many people were up there trying to get jobs," one manager recalled, that the company had to turn workers away. Company housing "was so crowded," that fights broke out frequently. Only after two workers shot each other did Greene Brothers begin to rethink their social policies, and they created a much different environment when they opened a much larger mill at Elizabethtown in 1938. Having grown frustrated with the workers they recruited in Beach Island, managers built better housing to attract experienced workers to their new "Negro quarters." They provided space for entire families and prohibited drinking and parties to ensure what they believed was a more suitable environment in which to live. As in Chapman, such restrictions simply pushed working-class drinking and dancing outside of company control. Unlike W. T. Smith, however, Greene Brothers' mill was located within a town that was even more rigidly segregated than "the quarters." African Americans were barred from most businesses in Elizabethtown, and therefore patronized stores and cafes in Newtown, a black village just outside the town limits. With few options for recreation within their own community, mill workers walked to Newtown most evenings, where they danced to the jukebox at Old Man Hatches' or to bands at the Dew Drop Inn. "Folks weren't used to them bands coming in a little place like this," black worker Waymond Tyson recalled, but musicians "made plenty of money" after mill workers started patronizing Newtown.[43]

The most dramatic shift in leisure policy came in Bogalusa, where Great Southern launched an outright attack on drinking and other activities that managers had once viewed as essential to their ability to recruit young black men to the company town. E. R. Cassiday, who replaced Sullivan as both general manager and mayor of Bogalusa, called an emergency meeting of the city council on May 2, 1931, to discuss the "matter of law enforcement in this city." Commissioner of public health and safety J. B. Lindsley set the tone for the meeting, stating that it was "a well known fact that for many years in the past the Commission Council of this City has, for economic reasons surrounding the operations of our great industrial plants, followed a policy of regulation rather than suppression of gambling and of illegal sales of intoxicating liquors." Explaining that access to liquor and prostitutes had served to attract workers to the town, Lindsley pointed out that such policies had convinced many in the surrounding communities that "certain members of the police force [were] in league with bootleggers, houses of prostitution, etc." Other members of the council agreed with Cassiday that "the time has come to the city of Bogalusa for the rigid suppression of vices that have been permitted to flourish too long." Upon his recommendation, they granted "unlimited authority" to police chief T. A. McGee "to wage a continuous war of annihilation upon the violator of the prohibition law, upon the professional gambler and upon the keeper of the houses of prostitution."[44]

Bogalusa's "dragnet," as local newspapers called the town council's 1931 crackdown, completed Great Southern's effort to bring its social policies in line with a new labor regime based on the establishment of black and white working-class communities in Bogalusa. Earlier that year, city officials had instructed McGee to "suppress the gambling houses that catered to white people, and to more strictly enforce the prohibition acts relating to the sale of intoxicating liquors." They launched a more "general clean-up of the city" only after police recognized that both black and white people frequented many such institutions. A newspaper reporter commented on the "strange mixture of the human race" that assembled before the criminal court following the initial wave of arrests. "There were men and women, young and old, white and colored, one man on crutches, and another bent and crippled. Some looked prosperous, while others appeared to be on the brink of poverty." Meanwhile, according to the *Bogalusa Enterprise,* townspeople "congregated on street corners to discuss the queer quirk of fate that had transformed portions of Bogalusa from oases to veritable Saharas."[45]

The convergence of policies directed at black and white workers required Bogalusa officials to invest unprecedented resources in maintaining what a 1945 law described as "accommodations equal in quality but divided for the white and colored races." Starting in 1933, the city council passed a series of laws that legislated—for the first time—racial divisions that the company had previously maintained through distinct social policies for black and white workers. The first of these laws emerged out of the council's concern that interracial "boxing and other similar exhibitions" were being "operated in such a way that the peace was frequently disturbed." Indicating that city officials still considered racial separation central to the peaceful order, city councilmen passed a law requiring match organizers to provide segregated seating for "colored and white patrons." In 1939, the city prohibited the sale of liquor "for consumption on the same premises to persons of the white or Caucasian race and persons the Negro or black race." Two years later, the council made it a crime for blacks and whites to use the same athletic facilities, and in 1945 city officials required transportation companies to segregate riders on local buses.[46]

Conclusion

By creating communities in southern sawmill towns, African Americans had a significant impact on the cultural history of the rural South. Black workers and entertainers had shaped sawmill town leisure since the birth of the industry in the 1880s, but seasonal employment patterns led them to focus their community-building and recreational energies primarily upon agricultural communities to which most of them intended to return. When they settled in mill towns in the 1920s, black working people helped mill owners make the transition toward sustainable development. They also sacrificed a level of cultural autonomy that may have existed in agricultural communities. Rather than rejecting their traditions to embrace a foreign culture, however, African Americans used the financial and spatial opportunities of industrial life to create a new culture. As Zora Neale Hurston discovered, this new culture was informed by the commercial popular culture that was forming across the nation in the 1920s, but it was also rooted in social and political dynamics that were specific to the rural South.

By endorsing community-based leisure as an alternative to older, male-dominated barrelhouses, southern employers acknowledged black workers' connections to families and communities. An implicit rejection of racist assumptions about black transience, biracial welfare strategies created a cultural basis for interracial exchange and even interaction. Depending upon their scale and capitalization, lumber firms were able to counteract that dynamic by shifting from informal to legal methods of enacting social policy. In the smaller town of Chapman, mill owners may have reinforced interracial exchanges by excluding most nightlife from the company town, where they had the power to enforce segregation. Greene Brothers officials also relinquished control over working-class leisure, although they pushed it into the rigidly segregated context of Elizabethtown. Much larger than most lumber firms, Great Southern expended the resources necessary to legally segregate working-class leisure within Bogalusa.

The history of working-class leisure in southern sawmill towns demonstrates the futility of distinguishing between rural African American culture and some white, northern, or commercial "mainstream." Even before they settled in mill towns, black mill workers helped to shape some of the earliest commercial recordings of black music. It may be that this music was descended from a more autonomous black culture that existed in agricultural communities, but most of what we know of that legacy was gathered in the context of industrial settings. Rather than evidence of a counterculture that black working people created outside the influence of whites, sawmill town leisure was the product of constant dialogue and negotiation within an interracial and increasingly national popular culture. Barrelhouse music, for example, spoke to the hardships and opportunities that black men found in seasonal wage work, but it also articulated the trope of disconnected wanderers that justified employers' disregard for black families and communities. Likewise, baseball games and swing dances served employers' efforts to stabilize their workforces during the period of conservation, but they also provided avenues for rural participation in regional and national black popular cultures of the 1920s and 1930s. Finally, these activities created opportunities for cultural exchange between black and white workers. Black lumber workers were largely excluded from formal political activity. As we have seen, however, they used leisure culture as a vehicle for participation in a very public dialogue. This participation challenged fears of cultural destruction advanced by Washington and Woodson. Nevertheless, the complexity of white involvement in black working-class culture cannot be explained through models that isolate black culture from

some white or middle-class "mainstream." In fact, it was black southerners' refusal to accept cultural isolation that gave sawmill town culture its particular dynamism—a dynamism that forced black people and
cultural styles into the popular mainstream of the 1930s.[47]

Two events allowed black southerners to expand their reach into
national political discourse in the 1930s. In 1933, the federal government
extended to all industrial workers—including black southerners—the
right to protection under federal wage and hour laws. It also granted the
legal right to join unions and bargain collectively, although black southerners were effectively robbed of those privileges until much later in the
decade. As they did with the cultural transformation of the 1920s and
1930s, black lumber workers used these political changes to support their
responsibilities to wage-earning families and communities. As the following chapters make clear, their success in asserting these new roles
depended upon cultural identities and social relationships forged during
the transformations of the 1920s and 1930s.

4 The New Deal
and the New Tradition

Movement into sawmill towns provided black southerners with increased opportunities to participate in the interracial popular culture of the 1920s and 1930s, but it also highlighted the sharp distinctions that persisted between black and white working-class income in the South. Lonnie Carter left his parents' tenant farm after hearing that the Greene Brothers Lumber Company paid three times what he earned as a farm hand. His uncle had died in a mill accident, and his mother insisted that "none of my boys ain't gonna work in no sawmill." She stopped protesting after he visited her for Christmas, however, with two new suits and matching shoes. After seeing his dapper attire, he recalled, "She knew I was doing good." Carter stayed with the Greenes, and after a few years worked his way up to a "top rate" position, loading the re-saw for twenty cents an hour. He followed the firm to Elizabethtown in 1938, where he rented a small cottage in the company quarters with his new wife, Pauline. Despite the obvious pride with which he described his work experience, Carter noted that his job was only "top rate" in comparison to other black workers. Another Greene employee stated, "No black man sawed," for example, in reference to band and circular saw operators who earned as much as three times Carter's wages. Even after he gained more experience than most whites in the mill, Carter found himself barred from the best-paid positions. "Along then it didn't make any difference about what you could do," he stated. "You had to show the white man how to work and he got paid more."[1]

Carter's story illustrates the "new tradition" of racial wage discrimination that according to historian Gavin Wright emerged with the stabilization of industrial employment in the South during and after World War I. Black workers had been excluded from the highest-paid craft positions in southern sawmills since the 1880s, and white-controlled unions maintained this color bar in the 1920s and 1930s by preventing even experienced black workers from entering apprenticeships. Unlike the nearly all-white textile industry, however, lumber firms hired laborers indiscriminately from agricultural labor markets, and they paid black and white workers relatively equal wages for those positions. This horizontal system of segregation gave way to a vertical pattern as black men advanced into positions that were not claimed by craft unions. Migration and strikes forced employers to raise laborers' wages significantly during World War I, and the movement toward mechanization and conservation created a new segment of "semiskilled" machine-operating positions that fell outside jurisdictions claimed by craft unions. As Carter and others gained experience that enabled some black men to move into operative positions, they observed that similarly experienced white men often advanced directly into craft jobs. As a result, white men's wages increased steadily during the 1920s and 1930s while black wages stagnated. By 1934, sociologist Charles S. Johnson observed that gaps between black and white wages were "now so well established in custom that they are frequently maintained where work is identical." Discrimination had become so deeply entrenched in southern employment policies, he asserted, that "Separate wage rates for Negroes are thus in a sense a fixed tradition."[2]

Having committed themselves to earning a "family wage" through industrial employment, black lumber workers became increasingly critical of wage differentials during the Great Depression. They found allies in this criticism from small groups of labor and civil rights activists who blamed the Depression on the extremely low wages paid to African Americans and to women of all races. These activists used the National Recovery Administration (NRA), a federal program designed to stabilize the industrial economy, as a vehicle for pushing for higher wages. As they had anticipated, their efforts also gained support from white common laborers in the South, forming the basis for a small interracial labor movement that emerged in southern industrial towns. Southern employers generally supported the NRA, in large part because they retained the power to ensure that federal regulation typically served their own interests. Through the Southern Pine Association, for example, southern sawmill owners convinced federal officials to set southern minimum wage levels well below those of the rest of the nation. Unlike employers in agriculture and domestic service, however, southern industrialists conceded to federal officials their right to determine wages and hours of work in their operations. For African American lumber workers, this was the first time since Reconstruction that the federal government played any positive role in their lives. The ensuing struggle between southern employers, black and white workers, federal officials, and labor and civil rights activists illustrated the "revolutionary" nature of black workers' struggle for higher wages in the 1930s.[3]

"Black Wages for Black Men"

Wages for U.S. sawmill and logging workers stagnated in the 1920s after doubling between 1915 and 1919. One year before the stock market crash that ushered in the Great Depression, average hourly wages stood at thirty-seven cents—one cent more than they had been in 1919. Wages fell back to thirty-six cents in 1930 and then plummeted to twenty-six in 1932. What these averages do not reveal are the dramatic wage differentials among various classes of lumber workers. Wages for sawyers peaked at seventy-five cents in 1919 and fell to a 1932 low of fifty-four cents. Doggers—men who attached cables to logs before they were dragged into mills—earned on average thirty-five cents in 1919 and twenty-one cents in 1932. These occupational distinctions were compounded by regional differences. Northwestern sawmills paid an average of fifty-five cents per hour in 1930. Midwestern mills paid an average of thirty-eight cents that year, while southern mills paid twenty-eight. Sawyers averaged $1.06 in the Northwest, and eighty cents in the South and the Midwest. Northwestern doggers averaged fifty cents per hour, more than twice the earnings of their southern counterparts (tables 7 and 8).

Black men were concentrated in the lowest-paid positions in the South and therefore suffered the most from both regional and occupational differentials. After surveying seventy-five member firms in 1933, the Southern Pine Association was happy to report that every one of those mills paid black and white workers according to "the same wage scale for [the] same work." While that may have been true, the same report revealed a racial division of labor that resulted in black men earning far less than their white counterparts. Ten of the surveyed companies hired no African Americans in skilled positions, and five admitted that they paid lower wages to skilled black workers than they did to skilled whites. More generally, according to the SPA, "Negro skilled labor is classified by some as 'semi-skilled' and usually need closer supervision than white skilled labor."[4]

Table 7. Average Hourly Sawmill Earnings, 1910 to 1932, by Occupation and Year

Year	Industry Selected Occupations	All Occupations	Sawyers[a]	Doggers
1910	.180		.543	——
1911	.176		.550	.179
1912	.178		.546	.181
1913	.185		.557	.184
1915	.169		.539	.178
1919	.360		.768	.358
1921	.308	.334	.797	.306
1923		.362	.883	.343
1925		.357	.877	.332
1928		.371	.887	.335
1930		.359	.886	.306
1932		.256	.652	.212

a. These figures are for head sawyers on band saws. Head sawyers on circular saws earned slightly lower wages.

Source: "Wages and Hours of Labor in the Lumber Industry in the United States, 1932," *Bulletin of the U.S. Bureau of Labor Statistics,* 586 (August 1933): 3–4.

Table 8. Average Hourly Sawmill Earnings, by Occupation and Region, 1930

Region	Industry	Sawyers	Doggers
South[a]	0.28	0.81	0.22
Midwest[b]	0.38	0.80	0.43
Northwest[c]	0.55	1.06	0.50

a. Includes Ala., Ark., Fla., Ga., La., Miss., N.C., S.C., Tex., Va., W.V., Ky., Tenn.

b. Includes Mich., Minn., Wis.

c. Includes Calif., Ore., Wash., Idaho, Mont.

Source: "Wages and Hours of Labor in the Lumber Industry in the United States, 1932," *Bulletin of the U.S. Bureau of Labor Statistics,* 586 (August 1933): 7, 24–25.

Racial segregation of southern lumber work was not a holdover from slavery, as some assumed in the 1930s, but rather it emerged in the context of technological and economic changes at the turn of the twentieth century. The earliest southern logging operations employed "lumberjacks," mostly white craftsmen recruited from New England and Midwestern operations in the 1880s. Lumberjacks used axes to fell large trees, and they commanded relatively high wages by carrying their own equipment and by imposing a craft apprenticeship system. The development of crosscut saws allowed firms to replace lumberjacks with "unskilled" "fellers" after 1900, and they reduced wages by training and equipping local men for these positions. By the 1920s, southern pine was felled almost exclusively by African American men, known as "flatheads" for the wide-brimmed hats that they wore for protection from the stifling heat of the southern lowlands. Black men also predominated as "graders"—or "road monkeys"—who erected rail lines to carry steam skidders and log trains that replaced mules and wagons in the 1890s. Illustrating the extent to which southern employers attached racial classifications to lumber jobs, the Bureau of Labor Statistics reported in 1946 that a steam-powered arm that replaced common laborers in many sawmills was commonly referred to as a "steam nigger."[5]

As such terminology suggested, employers came to associate certain skills with qualities that they believed were innately African American. "The really skilled guys in the mill were black," recalled Ben Greene, who managed his father's Elizabethtown mill in the 1940s. The elder Greene recruited experienced black men from South Carolina and Alabama in the 1930s, because "there weren't many people in North Carolina with experience in a large mill and who know how to work in the woods without getting hurt." The firm reserved craft positions for whites but relied on African Americans to fill the vast majority of their labor needs. Lumber work "was something [black men] grew up with and knew how to do well," according to Ben Greene, and his firm paid "premium wages for it." Ben Greene's cousin Alvin claimed that the most qualified workers were "geachies," members of an African American linguistic group that lived on the heavily lumbered coasts of South Carolina and Georgia. That assumption also informed an article on the Greene Brothers' logging operations written by white journalist Staley Cook, who stumbled across "a crew of approximately 30 men; some 'geachy' Negro men, some not of the 'geachy' strain," while hunting in 1938. Using language that evoked romantic adventure novels of the era, Cook described the black workers as natural features of a "water-logged marsh of a remote, almost inaccessible swampland." He marveled at the ease with which two black men felled a massive tree—"muscular, breathing as lightly as one at ease in a porch chair"—suggesting that they were at home in their "jungle" workplace. Alvin Greene agreed that African Americans seemed biologically predisposed to certain tasks, recalling that "riggers," who strung skidder cables between standing trees, were able to climb "like a monkey."[6]

While they preferred black men for physically demanding "nigger work," employers favored white men for supervisory positions that required judgment and initiative. As a result, black men who remained in lumber jobs over long periods of time often found themselves under the supervision of less experienced whites. These included "cruisers," who walked through forests selecting and grading trees that the flatheads would later fell. White men were also preferred as "fitters," who removed branches from fallen trees and assessed the grade and number of boards that could be produced from each log. In addition to following the orders of such men, black men were victimized by their mistakes. Black men were often hired as "setters," for example, who walked behind fitters cutting logs into smaller sections and attaching cables that would drag the logs to waiting trains. When they had completed their tasks, setters signaled to the "drum man," the typically white workers who operated the skidders. In what was perhaps the most deadly moment of lumber production, the drum man engaged a steam engine that pulled the log toward the skidder at breakneck speed. With several setters working at various points in the forest, and with other teams of men, animals, and machinery working nearby, drum men often confused signals, sending enormous logs crashing through the woods without warning. Logs sometimes snagged on standing trees, knocking them over or snapping steel cables that recoiled with enough force to cut a man in half. Unfortunate setters were often caught between the logs and the skidders, or dragged along with a log that they had not finished setting.[7]

By adding speed and power to lumber production, mechanization exacerbated the dangers faced by low-wage workers. In a study of work injuries in the United States, the Department of Labor reported in 1945 that "as in past years, the logging industry led all other manufacturing industries" in numbers of injuries, with a rate of ninety-two disabling injuries per million employee hours worked. "Second, but still far ahead of other manufacturing industries, were sawmills," with a rate of fifty-six injuries per million hours. Iron foundries ranked third at forty-four injuries per million hours; the average for all manufacturing industries was only eighteen. Investigators noted that explosives manufacturing, which was "usually regarded as extremely hazardous," injured workers at a rate of only 3.6 injuries per million hours. In general, manufacturing was far more dangerous than other employment sectors such as agriculture, service, and even mining and railroads. The majority of logging injuries involved hand tools such as saws, but "accidents involving falling trees, limbs, and branches, or moving logs," according to a 1941 report, "tended to be much more serious." Machinery also caused the most common accidents in sawmills—"striking against or being struck by logs or lumber"—and the most severe injuries resulted from misuse or failure of power equipment. Federal investigators noted that most such injuries could have been "reduced by strict and simple measures" such as training, supervision, and installation of safety equipment.[8]

Mechanization heightened the danger associated with historically "black jobs," but it also created space for a few black men to work their way into higher-paying positions. Even after they drove industrial unions out of the industry in 1919, southern mill owners allowed craft unions to control access to "skilled" positions such as carpenter, machinist, and metal filer. Although they typically espoused racial egalitarianism, craft associations used both formal and informal measures to restrict African Americans from these trades. The United Brotherhood of Carpenters and Joiners, which claimed to represent sawmill and logging workers as well as carpenters, drove nearly all black carpenters out of business in the 1920s. Whereas such policies led to a decline in black craft employment between 1910 and 1940, African Americans made slight headway into midlevel operative positions such as sawyer, fireman, and truck and tractor driver that lay outside of craft jurisdictions. These positions proliferated with the mechanization of sawmills and logging operations in the 1920s. They paid far less than craft positions, but they provided significant raises for black men previously employed as laborers, teamsters, and lumbermen (table 9, figure 5).[9]

Particularly for Lonnie Carter and others who worked their way into semiskilled machine operating positions, black men's hopes for job advancement clashed increasingly with their exclusion from even better-paid craft positions in the 1920s. Men of Carter's generation remained in lumber jobs even as they grew older and took on the additional responsibilities associated with marriage and fatherhood. That decision increased the significance that they attached to wage earning, and led some of them to turn to unionization or migration as a means to securing a "family wage." Employers succeeded in destroying early union movements and most African Americans did not leave the South, but these threats led employers to acknowledge some responsibility toward their black workers' families and communities. By supporting institutions such as schools, churches, and recreational facilities, and by endorsing black participation in commercial leisure, lumber firms further raised the expectations that black men invested in industrial wages. By the end of the decade, racial wage discrimination was the most glaring—and perhaps seemingly arbitrary—barrier to black lumber workers' personal and social aspirations. Carter and thousands of other black men would spend the following two decades attempting to destroy that discrimination.

Table 9. Selected Occupations of Sawmill and Logging Workers in South, Percent Black, 1910, 1920, 1940; with Median Annual Wage and Salary Income for All Workers in Occupation, 1940

| Occupational Class | Percent Black (Total Cases) | | | Median Income |
Occupation	1910	1920	1940	1940
Laborers				
Lumbermen[a]	47.4 (213)	40.1 (583)	38.7 (599)	$250.00
Teamsters	n/a	40.8 (125)	29.5 (61)	300.00
Laborers (nec)	57.5 (764)	56.1 (1,751)	56.2 (1,542)	350.00
Operatives				
Stationary				
firemen	34.3 (35)	46.2 (52)	44.7 (47)	368.00
Sawyers	14.5 (55)	19.2 (130)	20.8 (149)	400.00
Operatives (nec)	29.2 (113)	32.7 (113)	33.8 (228)	445.00
Craftsmen				
Carpenters	14.3 (7)	13.6 (22)	9.4 (32)	620.00
Machinists	0.0 (10)	20.0 (20)	9.1 (11)	728.00
Stationary engineers	4.0 (24)	4.0 (25)	0.0 (10)	980.00

(nec = not elsewhere classified)
a. Also includes raftsmen and woodchoppers.
Source: 1910 general sample (1-in-250 national random sample of the population), Steven Ruggles, Matthew Sobek, Trent Alexander, Catherine A. Fitch, Ronald Goeken, Patricia Kelly Hall, Miriam King, and Chad Ronnander, *Integrated Public Use Microdata Series: Version 3.0* [Machine-readable database] (Minneapolis: Minnesota Population Center, 2004) <http://www.ipums.org>.

A New Deal for Southern Lumbermen

The "new tradition" of racial wage differentials came under scrutiny in the 1930s as federal policy makers attempted to standardize industrial production in order to end the Great Depression. Between 1933 and 1935, the Roosevelt administration attempted to establish uniform minimum wages in each of the nation's industries. Authorized by the National Industrial Recovery Act (NIRA), these standards had the dual purpose of stimulating working-class "purchasing power" and also standardizing the price that employers paid for labor. These strategies reflected two competing theories concerning the causes of the Great Depression. The former was proposed by those who blamed "underconsumption," or the inability of workers to support the economy by purchasing the products that they made. The latter aimed to stabilize industrial markets by reducing competition between firms. The NIRA created the National Recovery Administration, which in addition to setting minimum wages, set uniform standards for working hours and the prices of manufactured goods. The administration also protected workers' rights to unionize, although it made no provision

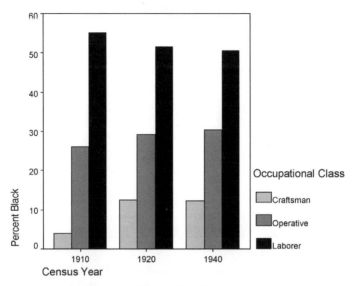

Figure 5. Occupational Class of Sawmill and Logging Workers in South,
Percent Black, 1910, 1920, 1940
[Laborers include lumbermen, raftsmen, woodcutters, teamsters, and laborers not elsewhere classified. Operatives include stationary firemen, sawyers,
and operatives not elsewhere classified. Craftsmen include carpenters; log and
lumber inspectors; scalers and graders; machinists, mechanics, and repairmen;
and stationary engineers.]
Source: 1910 general sample (1-in-250 national random sample of the population), 1920 general sample (1-in-100 national random sample of the population),
and 1940 general sample (1-in-100 national random sample of the population),
Steven Ruggles, Matthew Sobek, Trent Alexander, Catherine A. Fitch, Ronald
Goeken, Patricia Kelly Hall, Miriam King, and Chad Ronnander, *Integrated
Public Use Microdata Series: Version 3.0* [Machine-readable database]. Minneapolis: Minnesota Population Center, 2004, <http://www.ipums.org>.

for enforcement. The NIRA typically allowed employers to draft a "Code
of Fair Competition" for each industry and then held hearings to gain in-
put from interested parties such as organized labor, consumers, retailers,
and state and local government. It then designated regional code authorities to administer each code throughout the nation.

Southern lumbermen generally supported the NRA's effort to standardize production. Composed of hundreds of family-owned firms, the southern lumber industry had struggled since early in the century to escape what
historian George Tindall described as a "remarkably dense thicket of competition." The region's largest firms attempted to merge in 1909, but southern states refused to allow one corporation to control what would have

amounted to 20 percent of the nation's pine production. Leading firms then created the Southern Pine Association in 1914 in an attempt to control competition as well as fight unionization. Following the 1929 stock market crash, the SPA became one of the first trade associations to propose relaxation of federal antitrust laws to allow standardization of prices and production. SPA president C. C. Sheppard urged his constituents to "oppose Government regulation" in 1931, but as the Depression wore on, SPA secretary H. C. Berkes lamented that "the infectious germ of government cooperation" had begun to infect the association. "The industry . . . was seeing attitudes of free enterprise giving way to the necessity of firm controls," Berkes wrote later. "Everyone was being conditioned by circumstances to the acceptance of regulation of prices and production." On June 7, 1933, Alabama senator Hugo Black introduced a union-backed bill designed to limit industrial work weeks to thirty hours. That same day, three hundred SPA members gathered in New Orleans to "commit the industry and to work with the government and other branches of the lumber industry" to ensure the success of Roosevelt's more moderate legislation.[10]

A photograph printed in the August 1933 issue of the Brooks-Scanlon Lumber Company newsletter illustrated the relief with which many firms greeted the enactment of the lumber code. Under the picture, which showed a man and two children driving an ox cart, a caption explained that the "Hoover-Cart" had been "very popular" under the previous administration. Following the "reshuffling of cards that brought the New Deal," the newsletter asserted, such vehicles were "almost extinct." The owner of the cart offered to trade it for a cash register—"now badly needed. Seriously though," the caption continued, "we like this picture. It tells a story typical of today's recovery. We ARE at the END of a LONG, HARD ROAD!" Even SPA secretary Berkes eased his skepticism of government regulation, reporting that "for the first time the lumber industry feels that its conditions can be rectified, and that the Code provides the way out of chaos and misunderstanding." The president of the West Coast Lumbermen's Association stated, "The Lumber Code is not an edict handed by us by Congress or the President. We went to Washington and asked for it."[11]

Convinced that federal intervention could save the industry, leaders of the SPA devoted their "efficient administrative machine" toward promoting and enforcing its wage, price, and production standards. Federal officials authorized the SPA to enforce the lumber code in the southern pine region. Taking up that mandate, industry leaders printed 15,000 copies of the code and issued press releases to 355 daily newspapers, 60 trade journals, and all major wire services. They also organized thirteen local meetings throughout the South where they explained the significance of the code and asked members to post wage and hour standards at mills and to publish them in their employee newsletters. The SPA Traffic Committee sent letters to major railroads and shipping companies in the region, requesting their aid in monitoring regional trade. "No lumber manufacturer can cut or ship pine lumber unless he is registered with the Southern Pine Association," the committee wrote to the Atlantic and Western Railway, "and it is in your best interest to see that the names of those pine manufacturers on your line, and/or connecting short lines, are transmitted to us so that we may contact them for this purpose." The *Southern Lumberman* bestowed "well deserved praise" on the SPA's mobilization in support for the NRA. "The ink was hardly dry on the President's signature before the organization had launched its campaign to lay the code before every mill in its territory and start reaping its full benefits at the earliest possible moment." The SPA already had a "great record of achievement," the trade journal gushed, but its administration of the lumber code promised to be the "brightest page in its history."[12]

Wages and the "Character" of Southern Labor

Even as they embraced the NIRA's plan to limit industrial production, southern lumbermen rejected the related proposal for a minimum wage. At the same meeting that endorsed the NRA, SPA members elected Mississippi lumberman L. O. Crosby to succeed Sheppard as their president. Crosby created "quite an upheaval," according to a local journalist, when he returned from that meeting to declare "very emphatically that he will not tolerate under any conditions organization and bartering [sic] of employees." Unions were not strong enough to protect their rights in southern mill towns, but northern industrialists had an interest in preventing southern lumbermen from undercutting their labor costs. For that reason, the SPA took a more conciliatory approach to wage standards, arguing that their mills were less efficient than northern mills and therefore needed to lower their labor costs in order to compete.

Southern mill owners attempted to justify lower wages with the contention that southern workers enjoyed lower costs of living than their northern counterparts. "The unskilled laborer in the southern lumber industry in the South is relieved from many of the necessary expenses of living that must be met by industrial labor generally," Sheppard explained at a hearing on the NRA lumber code. He clarified that he spoke specifically of pine and hardwood production on the coastal plain and the Mississippi River Valley, and not of Appalachian lumber, "which is accustomed to paying a higher rate." To emphasize the significance of his testimony, Sheppard pointed out that within the region that he addressed, "the Southern lumber industry is the most important, aside from agriculture." The South produced 42 percent of all U.S. lumber in 1929, he asserted, and paid 35 percent of U.S. lumber wages. Nevertheless, southern lumber workers generally lived in company housing, and therefore had to pay very little of their wages for housing, utilities, or transportation to and from work.[13]

Central to Sheppard's argument justifying lower wages was the assertion that between 60 and 75 percent of all southern lumber workers were "negroes." In a statement that was delivered before a hearing on the Code of Fair Competition in the Lumber Industry and then published and distributed by the Southern Pine Association, Sheppard testified, "There is no question but that this class of labor lived in comfort and earned a fair living under the conditions existing in the South during the period prior to the present depression." Noting that living costs were even lower than they had been before 1929, Sheppard proposed setting minimum wages for southern lumber workers at 22.5 cents per hour—just over half the proposed minimum for northern lumber workers—and limiting the work week to forty-eight hours. Such a standard would allow greater earnings for many black men at shorter hours than they were accustomed. "They have, through the past, constituted perhaps the most contented element of our industry and the total absence of labor trouble and dissatisfaction with this class of our people would seem to demonstrate that a resumption of rates of pay which will give them as great earning power as they had during the period prior to the depression would accomplish the basic purpose of the National Industrial Recovery Act."[14]

Southern lumbermen argued that in addition to having fewer needs as consumers, their workers were less efficient. Q. T. Hartner, whose father had pioneered the conservation movement in southern lumber, wrote to his congressman to gain support for Sheppard's proposal. Reminding the representative that lumber employed more southerners than any other industry, he claimed that the "types of operation" and "living conditions and classes of labor employed" put southern sawmills at a disadvantage against those in other regions. In order to compete, he had been forced to employ "twice as many men to produce a given quantity of lumber than what was required by northern operations." Regional wage differentials reflected these differences in productivity, he asserted, but employers relieved workers of any hardships by charging "very nominal" fees for housing and medical care, and by providing free lights and water to those who lived in company housing. North Carolina lumberman F. B. Gault wrote directly to the White House, urging Roosevelt to consider "the vast difference between labor conditions in the South and those existing in the thickly populated sections of the North." He claimed that his "labor has been happy and well provided for" with wages "not so high as those proposed" by Sheppard and warned the president against enacting the "radical changes" pushed by the "organized labor dictatorship in Washington." The only people who would benefit from uniform wage scales were a few "bright-eyed industrialists" in the North, who wanted to "make trouble for southern manufacturers."[15]

To alleviate dissent over wage regulations, NRA officials conducted a series of hearings to consider code exemptions for firms particularly hard hit by the Depression. "Well, gentlemen, we have a kind of peculiar situation down there in Hale County," an Alabama manager explained before one such hearing. "It consists practically of Negroes." Employing the same argument that Sheppard had proposed to counter underconsumption theories, the manager of Greensboro Lumber Company stated, "I guess seventy-five percent of our population are Negroes and they look largely to the white man to give them food and shelter. They are paying no house rent, no water. They buy no wood and unless the sawmills continue to operate there will be several hundred of them that will not be fed in that locality this winter. We cannot raise wages under present conditions." NRA officials remained committed to racially neutral standards for industrial workers, but they granted this one exception on the grounds that the firm hired "mostly farm labor." The deputy of the review board assured the manager that he was also a southerner and understood, "certainly to some extent, many of the problems which you mentioned."[16]

The NRA was limited in its ability to grant such requests by the fact that most firms went along with the code and thus viewed exemptions as a form of unfair competition. Georgia mill owner H. C. Allen wrote to NRA director Hugh Johnson in September 1933, to complain about violations of the code in his region. He understood that Roosevelt intended to raise wages and increase employment, and he gave his "full hearted support" to both the "spirit and letter" of the law. He promised to follow code wages and hours "one hundred percent" but complained that "unless others [in] this territory adopt similar scale wages and discontinue unfair competition," he would be forced to close his mill. Allen promised to "furnish names" of code violators and asked administrators not to "allow them to undersell" him anymore. J. G. McGowin, who owned the W. T. Smith Lumber Company in Chapman, urged leaders of the SPA to "do something as quickly as we can to see that the code is being carried out." Future SPA president P. A. Bloomer convened a meeting in September to discuss the organization's strategy for preventing violations.[17]

Northern mills also objected to the southern mill owners' proposal for a regional wage differential. The mayor of Oshkosh, Wisconsin, in the heart of the Midwestern lumbering region, sent a telegram to Hugh Johnson requesting that "the woodworking code of the South be raised to the woodworking code of the North." A mill owner in southern Indiana pointed out that its competitors in Kentucky—just across the Ohio River—would be able to undercut his prices by 20 percent due to the regional differential. Officials sympathized with the complaint but responded that elimination of the differential "would jeopardize the entire minimum wage structure in his Industry." Dillman Industries, which owned a mill in southern Missouri that the NRA classified as northern, requested a reclassification based on the argument that "Our whole life is southern." Demonstrating the intersections between racial and regional arguments, managers at the mill stated that "Cotton predominates" in the region and "about fifty percent of our population is colored labor." Invoking a stereotype that no longer applied to most southern industrial workers, they explained that Dillman was handicapped by a "very heavy labor turnover on account of the character of the labor that we have, which is Southern labor."[18]

NRA officials resisted overtly racist appeals for "black wages," but they were more sympathetic toward employers who argued that southern workers, particularly African Americans, were unable to produce at a rate that justified higher wages. In response to the Dillman manager's contention that half of his potential employees were black, a member of the NRA review board asked why the firm did not simply "raise prices and hire better labor" in order to meet the new standards. "We haven't any high type of labor down there," another manager insisted, to which a southern board member replied, "we all say that from the South." The manager persisted, however, explaining that a "high type of labor" existed, but that it was already employed as "the key operators" in his mill. He even invited the board to "come down and look over the factory if you want to see the high type of labor we have. Any operator in the South can tell you what that is and I will say that what we call the white trash down there—well, I'd just as soon have negro labor as I would white trash labor." Asserting that southern whites had no better claim to higher wages than blacks, he argued that wage increases would lead both groups to work less. "Take the Southern negro and the Southern white trash, if they have a few dollars in their pockets, they don't work." Apparently convinced by that argument, administrators agreed to reclassify Dillman as a "southern" operation. A dissenting board member predicted that such tampering would doom the lumber industry to an even "worse situation than now."[19]

Race and "Efficiency"

So entrenched was the "tradition" of wage inequality that some black and white liberals accepted the argument that black workers deserved lower wages. Shortly after Roosevelt signed the NRA into law, white southern newspapers began reporting that employers had threatened to fire African Americans rather than raising their wages. The *Norfolk Ledger-Dispatch* warned government officials to acknowledge a "condition which peculiarly and particularly affects the South," whereby blacks enjoyed a monopoly on certain jobs because whites would not accept the wages that they paid. Wage standards would destroy that monopoly, the newspaper explained, by giving "white boys or youths or men" an incentive to compete for black jobs. The *Ledger-Dispatch* urged NRA officials to perform a "work of great humanitarianism" by exempting such jobs from the codes. The *Norfolk Virginian-Pilot* warned that the Blue Eagle, which Roosevelt designated as the symbol of the NRA, threatened to become a "bird of prey" rather than a "bird of happiness" for "semi-skilled or unskilled Negro workers." Reporting that some establishments had already replaced black workers with white ones, the newspaper hoped that others would "act humanely" by retaining African Americans in spite of the increased wages. Charles L. Kaufman, a white lawyer who served on the board that administered NRA codes in Washington, D.C., explained that such reports reflected the fact that "differentials in wages and working hours have kept the colored people in many jobs which would otherwise have been filled by whites." Employers believed that African Americans displayed a lower "standard of efficiency as well as living," Kaufman contended, and therefore hired them only when they could pay them a lower wage. He claimed to have "discussed the matter at considerable length with some of the leaders and most intelligent of the colored group and they have expressed grave concern over the anticipated consequences of the recovery program to the colored people."[20]

It is tempting to dismiss such statements from a self-proclaimed white partisan of "the effort to improve social and economic conditions among negroes," but Kaufman's logic resonated with a strain of black political thought that retained considerable influence in the early 1930s. The theory that wage equality would lead to black unemployment rested on a belief that racial discrimination reflected actual differences between black and white proficiency. As historian Daryl Michael Scott has pointed out, such views were promoted not just by racists but also by liberals who called attention to the damage that racial oppression inflicted on African Americans. Prominent intellectuals such as Booker T. Washington and W. E. B. Du Bois differed on how best to overcome such damage in the 1890s, but neither questioned its existence. By the 1920s, hundreds of black training schools, reform organizations, and churches aimed to "uplift" poor African Americans by teaching them skills as well as moral and social guidance. Only later in the 1930s did significant numbers of black radicals begin to shift their attention from personal to structural causes of racial inequality.[21]

In keeping with the prevailing orthodoxy, representatives of Booker T. Washington's Tuskegee Institute actually lobbied against NRA wage standards in 1933. Washington's successor Robert Moton testified on behalf of a southern manufacturer who claimed that "racial characteristics" prevented his black workers from earning a standard wage. At a hearing on the case, Tuskegee secretary G. Lake Imes urged NRA officials to grant the employer an exemption to the minimum wage until he had been able to "bring up the efficiency of the workers." With additional training, he maintained, black workers had the potential to produce "the equivalent of the minimum requirements of the code." Few black journalists articulated such theories as directly as Imes and Kaufman, but many echoed their implicitly racist warning that wage equality would lead automatically to black unemployment.[22]

Criticism of the "efficiency" argument emerged initially not among black activists but from a group of mostly white "industrial feminists" who worked to raise wages for female industrial workers in the 1930s. Building on efforts to unionize northern sweatshops in the 1910s and 1920s, and bolstered by a wave of militant strikes in southern textile mills in 1929, a small cohort of industrial feminists gained significant influence within the Roosevelt administration and a few AFL unions. Industrial feminists focused upon the low wages and poor working conditions of white women in the southern textile industry, but they also attacked racial discrimination. Lucy Randolph Mason, a white Virginian who served on the board of the NAACP, represented the National Consumers' League at a hearing on the NRA textile code. Countering those who argued that African Americans had no use for higher wages, she argued that black consumers were critical to economic recovery. "If the negro is to live in a little better home and smoke a little better tobacco, and perhaps have a little Ford and buy gasoline for it, it is going to be a blessed good thing for purchasing power."[23]

In addition to offering underconsumptionist arguments against wage discrimination, Mason exposed the duplicity of southern industrialists who complained about black inefficiency. "If it did not pay to employ

Negroes they would not be employed at all," she told a hearing on the crushed stone, sand, and gravel industry. Sawmill owners knew as well as anyone the validity of her point. Having relied upon black workers to perform an increasingly specialized set of tasks over the past decade, many southern lumbermen believed that African Americans were even more qualified for low-paid positions than were whites. To counter charges that southern mills discriminated against black workers, the SPA presented a report to the NRA showing that 90 percent of its members believed that "Negro labor [was] as steady and as efficient as white labor" when employed in low-paying jobs such as laborers. The report was intended to rationalize racial discrimination in higher-paying positions, but it also contradicted C. C. Sheppard's claim that African American inefficiency justified lowering the minimum wage.[24]

Working through the National Consumers' League and a loose network that included the Women's Trade Union League and the Young Women's Christian Association, industrial feminists convinced some labor leaders to adopt an underconsumptionist approach to fighting the Depression. Most AFL leaders opposed minimum-wage laws on the principle that wages were best negotiated between unions and employers without interference from government. Mason and others found a receptive audience, however, among leaders of unions that began to organize mass-production workers in the late 1920s and 1930s. Sidney Hillman, who headed the Amalgamated Clothing Workers Union, and United Mine Workers president John L. Lewis were among the earliest union supporters of wage legislation. In April 1934, Lewis used arguments and statistics provided by the National Consumers' League to counter employers who advocated a lower wage for southern coal miners. Echoing Mason's testimony at the textile hearing, the union leader asserted that black workers accepted low wages not because they lacked standards but because they had no choice.[25]

R. B. Parsons, a professor at the University of Tennessee, wrote to NRA director Hugh Johnson in an outrage over statements against wage equality from manufacturers in his state. Responding to a statement by the Tennessee Manufacturers Association that wage equality would "cause trouble" between black and white workers, he countered that thousands of black and white southerners already worked alongside each other at the same wages. Parsons claimed to have discussed the issue with a "Union Labor man who is an official in the State Department of Labor" and reported that organized labor supported wage equalization to stop blacks from undercutting white wages. "No, General Johnson, the truth is simply this," wrote the professor. "It makes no difference what concession you make to southern capitalists, they will cry for more. Remember this; you can never satisfy the demands of the privileged classes of the South."[26]

While civil rights organizations remained neutral and at times on the side of employers, a small group of young black activists and intellectuals acknowledged the radical potential contained in industrial feminist calls for wage equality. Ironically, this counterposition emerged initially among the staff of the National Urban League (NUL), an organization founded by disciples of Booker T. Washington. NUL field secretary Jesse O. Thomas toured the South in 1933, and he dismissed threats of displacement as the cynical pleas of southern employers. The "most important element in the whole recovery set-up to the captains of industry in the South is can the NRA operate in such a manner as to prevent the Negro from sharing equally with other wage earners?" he wrote in the NUL's journal *Opportunity*. Thomas quoted the *Norfolk Ledger-Dispatch* and others who warned that wage equality would lead to displacement of black workers, but he countered such statements with quotes from southern white liberals who supported the NRA. Dr. W. W. Alexander, for example, who headed the largely white Commission on Interracial Cooperation, charged that racial wage differentials would "undermine the President's program of economic recovery in the South, and at the same time cut the economic foundations from under the feet of the white working man." While G. Lake Imes urged black workers to raise their standards, Thomas pointed out that threats of displacement were based on the racist assumption that black workers deserved less. He characterized the cause of wage equality as "little less than revolutionary."[27]

T. Arnold Hill, who headed the Urban League's department of industrial relations, argued in *Opportunity* that racial wage differentials were merely a method of creating competition between black and white workers. "Few employers will pay more for their labor than they have to," he observed. White employers claimed to prefer white workers, Hill observed, but "if they can get Negroes cheaper than they can whites, the latter will often find themselves unwanted and unemployed." Threats of displacement were simply efforts to intimidate black workers into accepting lower wages, and Hill even urged black workers to call their bluff. "If employers are unwilling to pay Negroes wages equal to those paid whites, then let them be discharged," he wrote. "It is unfair, of course, that the race should be forced into mendicancy, but it is better that Negro workers insist upon wages equal to those paid whites, even if it means their ultimate discharge, than to accept smaller wages and thereby perpetuate the class distinctions that now exist." By sanctioning differentials, the federal government would only "perpetuate the age-old strife between the two groups and make for actual warfare at a time when it takes little to foment either racial or industrial discord."[28]

Hill's argument ran counter to the official positions of both the Urban League and the NAACP, which had long maintained, as the NAACP resolved in 1932, that a "thoughtful or advantageous alliance with white American labor" was impossible. The possibility of cooperation between black and white workers was more widely accepted, however, among the thirty-three "Young Turks" that NAACP president Joel Spingarn invited to discuss the "present situation of the Negro race" at his Amenia, New York, estate in the spring of 1933. The Young Turks battled to convince civil rights activists of the potential for building an interracial movement around the needs of low-wage workers. Howard University economist Abram Harris provided the intellectual basis of that position in his 1931 study *The Black Worker*. Not discounting the racist history of organized labor, Harris and his coauthor Sterling Spero devoted the majority of their five-hundred-page text to the AFL's hostility toward black workers and the resulting legitimacy of black antiunionism. They also criticized the Socialist and Communist Parties for failing to appeal to black workers: either by ignoring racial discrimination in the name of class solidarity or by running "from pillar to post, with an eye for any dissatisfaction that can be seized upon for its revolutionary possibilities."[29]

A genuine working-class movement could be built, according to Harris, only by accounting for the subtle social and economic changes that were shaping the lives of both black and white workers in the 1920s and 1930s. "Most important is the machine, which is rapidly changing the meaning of skill and obliterating old craft lines," he argued, asserting that mechanization undermined previously rigid distinctions between black and white job classifications, thus providing space for black workers to advance into industrial positions previously controlled by racist unions. While "the rising Negro middle class" generally supported "uplift" as a solution to discrimination, Harris saw reason to hope that black workers "may in time develop a labor leadership which will help to educate both the Negro workers and the general labor movement to the realization of the need of black and white unity." This argument formed the basis of Harris's "Future Plan and Program for the NAACP," which he drafted as an unofficial summary of the Amenia conference.[30]

Civil rights leaders balked at Harris's recommendations, but both the NAACP and the NUL lent financial support—along with eighteen other organizations—for the creation of the Joint Committee on National Recovery (JCNR). Harris's allies John P. Davis and Robert C. Weaver launched the JCNR in the spring of 1933 out of frustration that neither civil rights organization maintained a Washington office. Alongside Lucy Randolph Mason and the National Consumers' League, Davis and Weaver were often the only speakers at NRA hearings who spoke in favor of wage equality. "The fact that wage slavery exists in the South is no justification for its continuance," Davis declared before a hearing on the lumber code. Southern workers did indeed earn less than northerners, but such differentials resulted from different "standards of living rather than variations in efficiency or living costs." Even when employers granted wage increases, he contended, they attempted to "recapture" them by raising the fees that they charged for services. Furthermore, housing provided "to the Negro sawmill worker" was often "so poor" as to invalidate any argument that they benefited from low rents. Chastising both "Negro leaders" and the AFL for their silence on the issue, Weaver warned that racial wage differentials would "brand black workers as a less efficient and sub-marginal group" and thereby destroy any possibility for the creation of "a real labor movement in this country."[31]

The immediate impact that the JCNR and the NCL had on New Deal wage policies was mixed. On one hand, NRA officials rejected proposals for an overt racial differential—a victory that prompted NAACP president Walter White to quip: "We cannot always measure effectiveness by things gained; we must also measure results by considering evils prevented." At the same time, however, even relatively liberal policy makers accepted Sheppard's request for a regional differential, which as we have seen was justified on racist grounds. As one NRA official indicated in his reply to University of Tennessee professor R. B. Parsons, this decision grew out of at least partial acceptance among policy makers of the logic of black inefficiency. "Complete elimination of the differential may cause extensive displacement of the negro worker," a member of the NRA Labor Advisory Board wrote in December 1933. "We are between the two horns of the usual dilemma." Attempting to accommodate racial neutrality with southern employers' implicitly racist appeal for a wage differential, the NRA set the minimum wage for southern lumber workers at twenty-four cents per hour. This was just over half of the minimum mandated for northern lumber workers, and only slightly above that originally proposed by C. C. Sheppard.[32]

Due to the extremely low wages previously paid to most southern lumber workers, though, the NRA minimum actually mandated a substantial increase over prevailing wages in the region. U.S. lumber wages averaged twenty-six cents per hour in 1932, but southern lumber wages trailed at between thirteen cents in South Carolina and twenty cents in Louisiana. In other words, the average southern lumber worker gained between four and eleven cents an hour from the NRA standard. Over the course of a year, that raise amounted to between $50 and $270. For a sense of how such increases bolstered workers' buying power, the *New York Times* carried advertisements in January 1934 listing prices for new suits between $25 and $30 and shoes under $10. It is unlikely that men like Lonnie Carter shopped at the exclusive clothiers listed in the *Times,* and so they would have paid even less for such goods. To continue these comparisons, prices for new radios averaged between $10 and $40, and a new Ford automobile was listed at $515. As Lucy Randolph Mason had testified, the NRA wage placed such goods in reach of many southern lumber workers.[33]

As Harris and the Young Turks suggested, however, the significance of NRA wage standards went beyond their immediate economic impact. Even before he proposed the NRA, President Roosevelt excluded from its provisions workers in agriculture and domestic service. A concession to southern Democrats in Congress, this action was designed to ensure that federal regulation did not violate white control over the nearly four million African Americans who worked in those sectors. Southern industrialists also succeeded in extending such exemptions to include semi-industrial jobs that were often filled by blacks. For example, the typically "black" job of loading cotton into textile mills was classified as agricultural. Such exclusions were manipulated to preserve gender norms as well, and employers succeeded in codifying explicitly sexist differentials into a quarter of the NRA codes. In such a context, it is notable that federal officials extended NRA protections to over a million black industrial workers in the South. Despite their very real limitations, the 1933 minimum wage standards represented the first federal recognition of black southerners' economic or political rights since Reconstruction.

The Southern Negro and Southern "White Trash"

The NRA worked primarily to address conflicts among employers, but it also encouraged workers to take an active role in the recovery program. Through press releases to local print media, and through Roosevelt's nationally syndicated "fireside chats," federal officials explained the aims of the NIRA and asked workers to help enforce the codes. Workers responded to this criticism by adopting the language of underconsumption, emphasizing their roles as male breadwinners and participants in a consumer society. Some also emphasized their commonality with other low-wage workers, describing themselves as "working men," "poor devils," and in one case "the people, both black and white." As North Carolina sociologist Harriet Herring observed in October 1933, the NRA had the effect of making southern workers "more self-conscious and more class-conscious, more aware of the power of group action."[34]

In their letters to the Roosevelt administration, southern lumber workers used the language of underconsumption to assert their claims to a family wage. "A wealthy man doesn't know what a poor common laboring man with a family has to put up with," declared a letter signed collectively "McCarroll Lber. Co. employees." Workers at that Louisiana company complained that their employer paid them seven cents below the NRA minimum and that managers evaded maximum hour standards by working them "like stock" for two days and then closing the mill for three. In direct contradiction to the argument that low wages were justified by southern inefficiency, they laid the blame for the Depression at the feet of greedy employers. "The trouble this day and time [is that] the world's full of people that are . . . working the laboring man to death for starvation wages and making about eighty-five percent clear proofity [sic]." They pleaded bitterly, "What can us poor devils do about it to make a little bread." F. E. Brogdan wrote that his Georgia employer was "not acting according to the lumber code at all." Immediately after the authorization of the NRA, the company store had raised prices "beyond all reason," and managers began docking workers for "every minute" that they were not actively at work.[35]

As T. Arnold Hill predicted, participation in debates over wage standards proved to be a politicizing experience, wherein poor black and white southerners articulated a shared economic interest. William McKinley Bowman did not identify his race, but his letter addressed to "His Excellency Franklin D. Roosevelt" revealed the tone of someone not completely at ease with political participation. "I know you are busy," he apologized, "but I am forced to write you on this matter." Bowman explained that his South Carolina employer had cut wages below the lumber code and that he raised prices at the company store to the point that men spent two-thirds of their earnings paying for food. "Please do something for the men Mr. President." Indicating that he risked retaliation for seeking federal intervention, Bowman ended his request by adding, "but don't mention my name." Even letter writers who seemed familiar with political participation expressed a sense that the New Deal brought a new attention to the needs of working people. Mrs. Clyde La Fone, for example, complained to Hugh Johnson that her husband's lumber wages were far below those paid in other industries. Taking literal ownership over her political rights, she promised that she and her husband would do all they could to keep Roosevelt in the presidency—"in fact he can have our part of the white house." She signed the letter, "Yours with two Democratic votes until the children are twenty one years old, and then it will be more," she praised Roosevelt and Johnson as "the only men that have ever help [*sic*] the poor people in our time."[36]

La Fone's letter was one of a few by wives of male lumber workers who also saw in the NRA an opportunity to bolster male wage earning. "Why did you and the President sign such a cheap lumber code?" La Fone demanded of Hugh Johnson. She reported that other industries near her North Carolina home were paying thirty cents per hour, and that federal public works programs even paid forty—while "men working under the lumber code" earned only twenty-four. "Is it fair," she asked, that her husband "and the other men who have been there for eleven years cannot feed their families?" Explaining that her letter had been inspired by one of Roosevelt's radio shows, she wrote, "As you wanted the people that has a kick about the NRA to write you, I thought I would tell you our trouble." Such letters provide further evidence against the theory that male wage earning relegated women to a subservient and isolated position in southern lumber town families. Indeed, historian Jeannie Whayne contends that women were typically better educated than men in the rural South, and that literacy in particular increased their power both within their households and in relationships with more powerful employers. "While southern rural women could use their literacy to counterbalance the power differential between themselves and their husbands, they could also use it to assist their husbands in demanding a fair settlement from planters." Those skills seem to have been useful in negotiating for higher wages as well.[37]

In a few cases, letter writing emerged out of broader movements to enforce NRA standards in sawmill towns. L. C. Barefoot, for example, wrote on behalf of an interracial group of "about one hundred people" employed by a sawmill in Dover, North Carolina. He explained that "90 per cent have families," and that the mill was the "only enterprise in this village of about four hundred population." The company had threatened to close the mill, and Barefoot promised Hugh Johnson that if he stopped them he would "have the thanks of many a woman and child who will suffer if something is not done." In addition to asserting their identities as male breadwinners, these workers also demanded reciprocity from a company that had employed some of them for forty years. After making "millions of dollars out of cheap labor in the past," Barefoot wrote, the firm was now unwilling to operate unless they were "allowed to work labor at the old wage scale." He anticipated that managers would "possibly give all kinds of reasons for closing down" but assured Johnson that "the only reason is that they are fighting the lumber code." Once again expressing these men's pride in their ability to support their families, Barefoot clarified that "what we want is work not charity. This can be averted if some one like you would investigate."[38]

Most letters came from low-wage workers and their family members, but workers also found support from other members of sawmill communities. Barefoot's letter was followed, for example, by resolutions from the Dover board of aldermen and the Chamber of Commerce in Kinston, a larger town twelve miles away. It is unlikely that any of the African American lumber workers in Dover had been able to vote for these political representatives, and it may be that North Carolina's literacy tests prevented even white workers from voting. Nevertheless, the aldermen urged federal action in support of "the people both white and colored," and the Chamber of Commerce supported their contention that the company was closing only in order to evade the code. In a similar act, the executive committee of the Democratic Party of Quitman County, Georgia, invited federal intervention against lumber companies that were "making huge profits" while the "labor that makes it possible is naked and on [the verge of] starvation." T. J. Dowdy, a "planning mill foreman" wrote to support NRA efforts to raise wages in his Georgia lumber town. His was a "very dangerous place to learn a trade," he informed Hugh Johnson, and he and "hundreds of other men" had worked at the mill for fifteen years under the threat of being killed at "any minute." Despite their loyalty, "Common labor at saw mills and planer mills" earned only forty to sixty cents an hour "for long days." Wages had not increased, and during the Depression, "the groceries have gone so high that we can't make ends meet."[39]

Whereas debates over wage standards created space for black and white common laborers to unify around their identities as consumers and breadwinners, they often exacerbated social and economic distinctions between "skilled" craft workers and the "unskilled" and "semiskilled" majority of the workforce. Even T. J. Dowdy, who expressed solidarity with common laborers, greatly overestimated the wages that such workers earned. As a foreman, Dowdy may have earned much more than sixty cents per hour in 1933. The average hourly wage for Georgia sawmill workers was thirteen cents in 1932, and it is unlikely that many common laborers earned more than the NRA mandated minimum of twenty-four cents in 1933. Such figures illustrate the vast economic distinctions between low- and high-wage workers in southern sawmills in the 1930s. Craft workers and supervisors such as Dowdy suffered very little from the regional wage differentials that employers claimed reflected basic economic realities of the South. Whereas southern laborers earned 40 to

50 percent less than their northern counterparts, regional differentials for sawyers and millwrights ranged from only 10 to 20 percent. Sawyers in Georgia averaged fifty-six cents per hour in 1932, which was sixteen cents less than they would have earned in California but only five cents less than Michigan and one cent more than Maine. In contrast, "doggers" averaged thirteen cents in Georgia—compared to thirty-seven cents in California, thirty cents in Michigan, and twenty-six cents in Maine. These differences meant that higher-paid workers supported the NRA as an attempt to fight the Depression generally, rather than an opportunity to alleviate previously existing injustices. Dowdy suggested that both workers and employers needed aid in 1933. He even asked Johnson to "please help them first so they will be able to help us." In contrast to laborers' attacks on exploitation, he stated that "we all want them to make a profit (certainly) so. And I know you folks along with President Roosevelt are going to help the poor as well as the rich. We are banking on you all."[40]

So significant were the social and economic distinctions between craft and common labor that "skilled" workers often expended more energy defending those distinctions than they did in pushing for higher wages. During initial debates over regional wage differentials, Louisiana mill worker F. C. Peters rushed a telegram to Hugh Johnson informing him that "southern lumber industry labor demands" thirty cents an hour for "skilled workers." Such a wage, he explained, would represent a legitimate "proportionate increase" over the proposed twenty-four-cent minimum for common labor. It was true that wages for craft and supervisory workers had fallen more rapidly than those of common laborers between 1929 and 1933, but the NRA instructed employers to counteract wage compression by raising wages for higher-paid workers proportionately. As a result, average hourly earnings for craft workers remained at least ten cents above those for common laborers throughout the life of the NRA, and their weekly wages grew faster than those of common laborers during the first half of 1934.

As letters from craftsmen made clear, the gap between high and low wages was often as significant as the wages themselves. As one Florida "skilled Lumber Worker" explained to Hugh Johnson, he was not "kicking the code" and he was not "sore because the common laborer has been helped." R. B. Brown merely resented the fact that his wages had fallen by 50 percent while the common laborer was "making as much or more than he was in pre-depression days, because he is protected by the codes." Men who were expected to "fill a place of responsibility of skill," he insisted, were "entitled" to earn more than those who did not. In contrast to low-wage workers who embraced the democratic implications of undercon-sumption theory, skilled workers defended their ability to consume as a mark of distinction. In a second letter, this time to President Roosevelt, R. B. Brown complained that decreased "purchasing power" was prevent-ing craftsmen from being the "same kind of citizens" that they had been in the 1920s. He came from a family of skilled workers, and both his fa-ther and brother had grown accustomed to earning "not what they should have been paid" but more than previous generations. "The things that we have enjoyed heretofore, such as radios, cars and education for our children, etc," were no longer in reach. He did not believe it was "selfish to long for the old salaries and standard of living again" and urged the president to restore the status "which justly belongs to us."[41]

Benjamin Smith went so far as to accuse the NRA of furthering a communist plot. By allowing employers to lower craft wages while forc-ing them to raise common wages, the government had placed the bur-den of the Depression on "the skilled workman and no other." Smith suspected that the code had not been "promulgated with this idea in view," but stated that "if it was, then it is entirely communistic." He could not understand why he was expected to "live under a communis-tic code" while "the management, and finally everybody, including your-self" were not, and he claimed that similar strategies had created "an absolute flop" in Russia. To support his claim to higher standards of liv-ing, he included a letter from a former employer, stating that "Smith is a high priced man, but he is worth his money to any big mill."[42]

Lending additional support to the significance that Harris and Weav-er attributed to wage equality, craft workers indicated that NRA codes heightened occupational conflicts that had emerged out of mechanization in the 1920s. A. S. Drew, an "expert wood-turner and cabinet maker," objected that he and other "highest paid skilled mechanics" at a Georgia sawmill earned only forty-two cents per hour. This was "certainly not adequate compensation" for such skilled and dangerous work as his. Drew also put in a word for the "colored" machine operators and the "young men"—presumably white—who had worked for several years as mechan-ics' assistants. While he implied that these men should not earn nearly as much as he did, the craftsmen believed that men of their experience and proficiency deserved more than the minimum wage. The United Brotherhood of Carpenters and Joiners, an AFL union that represented craft workers in many southern sawmills, outlined a similar position on that point in an "official protest and objections" to the NRA. Like other craft unions, the Carpenters protected its members not by negotiating with individual employers but by controlling the training of a "certain class of mechanics to perform a certain class of work." In order to join the brotherhood, a worker was required to convince a "committee of qualified mechanics" that he was a "competent mechanic of good moral character, a citizen of the United States, and able to command the standard rate of wages in the particular branch of the industry he had chosen to follow." The brotherhood protested that "by lumping the skilled mechanic in with a group of workmen that are classed and known as semi-skilled," the NRA had undermined "working conditions built up for him in over fifty years of peaceful negotiations." As a result, craftsmen were forced to accept wages "way and far below that which any skilled mechanic should be called upon to consider."[43]

With black men's advancement into semiskilled machine operating positions in the 1920s, the distinctions between craftsmen and other experienced lumber workers became defined increasingly by race. As we have seen, the Southern Pine Association even admitted to NRA administrators, "Negro skilled labor is classified by some as 'semi-skilled.'" While the Carpenters denounced the "drawing of the color line" early in the century and attempted to organize even unskilled African American workers in 1919, the union adopted these racial definitions of skill in the 1920s. A survey of southern labor union practices conducted by the Urban League in 1928 found that a few "colored" locals survived in the South but that "southern prejudice"—white intransigence—prevented cooperation between white and black carpenters "in most southern cities." Investigators found that "colored and white carpenters meet occasionally in joint session to discuss common problems" in the sawmill town of Jacksonville, Florida, but that otherwise, they had "little or no connections with each other." More typically, black workers received "no protection" from union representatives—regardless of skill. De facto racial job classifications became so entrenched in the 1920s that the union abandoned them only under court order following the 1964 Civil Rights Act.[44]

By challenging the "new tradition" of racial job classifications, NRA wage standards threatened social hierarchies that went far beyond the skill distinctions upon which craft workers based their claims to higher wages. Acknowledging the extent to which such hierarchies were defined in racial terms, a Louisiana union activist objected to C. C. Sheppard's claim that in southern lumber operations "seventy-five percent of the laborers were negroes." His objection was not that black workers deserved equal treatment, but that such statements undermined white workers' claims to better pay. "We want to be fair and square," he wrote, "but we also want a living wage." R. C. LeBlanc, who was president of the Memphis local of the Lumber Inspectors and Millwrights Union, explained that many craftsmen considered one of their most important benefits to be the financial ability not to settle in sawmill towns. Craftsmen and their families resided in nearby cities and paid their own travel expenses to the small towns where the mills were located. He insisted that such places "were not fit to bring our families to as they have no schools or water systems and are unhealthy besides." The financial "obligations" accrued by such migration justified higher wages for "the men whom make it possible for lumbermen to produce lumber for the market at a good profit by our loyal and efficient work." While federal officials had rushed to the aid of common laborers, LeBlanc complained, "We have been overlooked entirely."[45]

"Small Mills" and the Destruction of the NRA

The SPA succeeded in generating an impressive rate of compliance in 1933, but the Lumber Code Authority reported "a small but steady stream" of dissent from southern lumbermen in the fall of that year. By December, W. T. Smith Lumber Company owner J. G. McGowin found it "quite discouraging the way things are turning out with the Lumber Codes and markets." He admitted that his firm had operated at a loss through most of the Depression and speculated that the SPA could do more to address complaints and convince mill owners of the significance of the code. "Broadly speaking," he did not "think there is a thing in the world for anybody to fear from these codes if they undertake to live up to them." Worse than those who were openly violating the code, he charged, were those who were "sniping" by claiming compliance and then committing small infractions. These were mostly smaller mills who believed that NRA assistance was not worth the costs of higher wages, and McGowin predicted that they would "be looked upon more or less in the future as deserters would be in a time of war." Nevertheless, without some dramatic change in their attitude toward the lumber code, he expected "the whole thing to break down by the first part of the new year."[46]

As McGowin indicated, dissent within the SPA emerged from a group of firms that identified themselves as "small mills" and claimed that they were more severely affected by wage standardization. "Small mill men" portrayed themselves as family farmers who offered seasonal "employment for regular farm laborers, many of whom would otherwise be idle." They also claimed to provide housing, firewood, and medical attention to their laborers free of charge, rendering differences between labor costs at small and large mills not "so profound as the mere quotation" of statistics would indicate. "Little sawmills" produced "inferior timbers," they complained, which the code forced them to sell at the same price as the lumber produced by "larger and better equipped mills." Finally, small mills objected to wage standards, according to the Lumber Code Authority, on the grounds that "they have been using negro labor which they claim does not merit fixed wages." Some based this claim on the familiar argument that black workers produced less than whites. "You are familiar with the large percentage of negro labor that we have in the industries here in the South," a Mississippi mill owner stated, "which class of labor is far inferior to the class of labor obtained in the larger industrial centers of the North." Others claimed that "negro laborers have become more inefficient because we are paying them more than former-ly." As one small mill man complained, the SPA had conceded to wage standards only because larger firms saw in the legislation "a chance to break the men that owned the little mills . . . and believe me they surely have made a good job of it."[47]

There was little substance to small mills' complaints about unfair treatment. While they likened themselves to the temporary "pecker-wood" mills operated by many southern farmers, most small mills op-erated year round and produced ten times as much lumber at a far high-er grade than seasonal mills. Ironically, small mill operation had been pioneered by the SPA-sponsored research conducted in the 1920s by J. G. McGowin's son Julian. This research was spurred by the conservation movement, and it allowed many large southern firms to take advantage of smaller, more dispersed timber. Contrary to testimony presented be-fore NRA hearings, such mills were actually less likely to provide hous-ing to their workers than were larger operations. One small mill owner even conceded that family members of many of his workers maintained farm jobs so that they could live in plantation housing. Small mill com-plaints also came from mills that hired as many as a hundred workers. McGowin characterized the "small mill" complaint as a cynical way to evade punishment for code violations. A large mill "like ours just can't afford to violate the Code," he stated, "because we would be handled very promptly."[48]

There was also significant evidence that NRA standards actually improved lumber markets in 1934 just as the complaints of small mills began to mount. The NRA conducted an investigation into the effect that the lumber code had on small sawmill operators in the South. A random survey of 250 mills, most of them small, found "sufficient material" to demonstrate that NRA standards produced a "substantial increase" in the number of small mills in operation. All surveyed sawmills agreed that

March 1933 had been "the lowest point in the history of modern lumber manufacture," and that conditions had improved since May, when the "general outline" of the lumber code had been drafted. Markets had improved with the spring building season, and prices had gone up rapidly when lumber dealers purchased in quantity in anticipation of price increases under the code. A smaller survey showed that lumber orders rose by 75 percent in 1934. Price increases were aided by the fact that production grew by only 5 percent while shipments increased by a quarter. Because they had less storage capacity, small mills had indeed been more susceptible to price reductions early in the Depression. The number of mill closings slowed under the code, however, and the NRA found that closings were "more than offset" by the number of new mills that opened or reopened in 1934. The Lumber Code Authority boasted that employment was 30 percent higher in 1934 than it had been in 1931.[49]

Some countered that "the code has nothing to do with the present demand for lumber," but as these critics themselves revealed, the recovery was inseparable from the broader agenda of the New Deal. A Louisiana company newsletter attributed increased demand to federal home building legislation, government purchases for public works programs, and limited West Coast production due to strikes. The firm urged its distributors to join the SPA in lobbing for the Federal Housing Act, a mortgage assistance program that would create a market for millions of dollars of lumber. "Every city, town and farm in the country is a potential market," declared the *Brooks-Scanlon News.* The Lumber Code Authority agreed that government housing programs represented "the lumber industry's largest new market opportunity." Lumber stockpiles decreased by 680 million board feet in the last five months of 1934, and dealers even complained of a "distinct shortage" of many products.[50]

The complaints of the small mill men nevertheless found sympathy among conservative critics of the New Deal. Late in 1933, Tennessee Manufacturers Association president John Edgerton called a meeting in Chattanooga to organize southern businessmen against the NRA and to "enlist Southern Senators and Representatives in the fight." That meeting created the Southern States Industrial Council (SSIC), which according to Edgerton was designed to "protect the South against discrimination." Speaking before a 1935 NRA hearing, Edgerton charged that the NRA had been based "on the theory that these wage differences were arbitrary, and were not the result of natural and economic forces." Such misconceptions led New Dealers to identify the region as "a particular candidate for social reform," he claimed, by those who believed they could "ostensibly 'lift' the South to the same economic level as the rest of the country." Wage standards were doomed to damage southern industry, however, because they overlooked the handicaps produced by higher transportation costs, lower rates of mechanization, and proliferation of small firms in the South. More importantly, he drew policy makers' attention to the "agricultural background of labor" in the region, which meant that workers had less experience and required costly training.[51]

Gathering together a number of arguments articulated over the course of previous debates, Edgerton stated

> Closely allied to the problem of relative inefficiency of white labor in the South is the problem of sub-normal labor, represented by the negro. It is a well-known fact that negroes are being displaced by white workers to an alarming rate, thus creating an acute relief and social problem, the burden of which the South will be compelled to carry alone.[52]

Initially, Edgerton found little support among southern sawmill owners. The SPA conducted a series of hearings on the small mill problem in Atlanta, Jackson, and Shreveport in 1934. President Crosby emerged from those hearings convinced that the "vast majority" of southern mill owners remained "whole-hearted" in their support for the NRA. The Lumber Code Authority conducted more than 20,000 mill inspections between September 1933 and July 1934. They found 9,655 mills in operation, out of 10,977 mills operated by SPA members. 1,766 of those mills were cited for labor violations, and 2,765 were found to be producing above code limits. Authorities reported that they convinced two-thirds of the violators to bring their mills in line with the code and that production at the remaining mills was "so small that the Authority doubts it will ever be able to secure compliance." While this 10 percent remained intransigent, the vast majority of southern mill owners credited the NRA with rescuing the industry from "slow suicide." A Florida firm contended that "if the Code were to be discontinued we think we would drift right back to cut throat prices and to where we could not pay labor a living wage, which, in our opinion would eventually result in Civil War which was so narrowly averted in 1933." Most others agreed that wages were "not too high," that hours and production restrictions were "fine and should be continued," and that prices, "while low, were very fair." One mill owner reported proudly that he had doubled wages since 1933 and even increased his workforce. "These men now are warmly clad, well fed, and face the winter without dread and the future with confidence," the employer boasted.[53]

Emboldened by strong support from southern mill owners, the NRA stepped up efforts to enforce the code. The Lumber Code Authority was convinced that dissent was strongest in regard to wage and hour standards and suspended enforcement of price standards in December 1934. The Timber Conservation Board reported some price "adjustment" following this test of compliance but reported no significant attempts to undersell established standards. Much stronger measures were needed to stop firms from undercutting prevailing wages. Hugh Johnson initiated a well-publicized campaign against labor violations in July 1934, revoking a Florida firm's Blue Eagle credentials and threatening to arrest the owner of a South Carolina mill. He succeeded in convincing the latter firm to pay back wages and to sign a public apology promising to uphold the code in the future. By September, SPA secretary Berkes reported that Alabama courts had issued indictments to two firms charged with violating the lumber code, and he predicted that the state of Georgia would order the arrest of five or six sawmill owners within the next week. He boasted that publicity of such "rapid court action" had convinced additional violators to mend their policies, and that SPA field inspectors were working with NRA attorneys to prepare a number of additional cases.[54]

By the end of 1934, conflict within the southern lumber industry became a focus of a national struggle over the future of the NRA and even the New Deal itself. One of the Alabama firms indicted in July was the Belcher Lumber Company. Typical of small mills, Belcher owned two mills in central Alabama and had refused from the beginning to conform to NRA standards. The company promptly appealed the case to a federal district court in Birmingham, where Judge William Grubb presided. The New York *Journal of Commerce* reported that Grubb was the "legal nemesis of the New Deal" and was not surprised to report his ruling that collaboration between the SPA and the Lumber Code Authority amounted to an unconstitutional "extension of discretionary powers to non-governmental agencies." Republican senators William E. Borah and Gerald P. Nye, both midwesterners, highlighted "small business oppression" in their criticism of the New Deal on Capitol Hill after the decision was announced.[55]

The Roosevelt administration appealed the *Belcher* decision to the U.S. Supreme Court, but with Congressional and business support for the New Deal eroding rapidly, the government withdrew from the case on March 26, 1935. Hoping to defuse opposition before it destroyed the NRA, Roosevelt had appointed the famed pro-labor attorney Clarence Darrow to head a board to investigate charges of "small business oppression." To the president's dismay, the board returned with a report that charged a "bold and aggressive" administration with encouraging "monopolistic practices" and having "cruelly oppressed" small enterprises. Based on what Hugh Johnson derided as "incompetent, misleading, and one-sided testimony," the Darrow report recommended gutting NRA standards and restructuring code administration. Disgusted by Congressional response to the rhetoric of "small business oppression," Secretary of Labor Frances Perkins remarked, "You can always get sympathy by using the word small. With little industries you feel as you do about a little puppy."[56]

The government's concession on the *Belcher* case provided conservatives with a weapon to finally slay the NRA. The *Wall Street Journal* charged the administration with attempting "to enforce a system of industrial control which it dares not defend in court." The *Journal of Commerce* interpreted the withdrawal as a "tacit admission" that wage and hour regulations overstepped government authority. Only "solid proposals" to make the codes "serviceable to industry," the magazine predicted, could restore business confidence in the New Deal. Even the pro-Roosevelt *New York Times* diagnosed the NRA as being on the verge of "disintegrating completely." Although they conceded in *Belcher*, the administration persisted in *Schechter Poultry Co. v. United States*, a case against a small poultry firm that they believed they could win. In May, the Supreme Court ruled on the side of Schechter Brothers, declaring the NIRA unconstitutional. Congressional debates over how best to extend the recovery program ended with this decision.[57]

Remarkably, the SPA maintained support for NRA standards even after the government had abandoned them. New Deal opponent Gus Dwyer spoke at the SPA's annual convention on March 13, 1935. He solicited laughter with jokes about a frightened "negro" and confused "professors," but criticism of the New Deal's "economic quackery" and its "buying power fallacy" does not seem to have resonated. As late as June 3, SPA members voted to enforce wage and hour standards independently. Without government assistance, however, they succumbed quickly to the competitive pressures that had plagued them before 1933. They were saved from pre–New Deal price fluctuations only by continued demands from housing and public works programs, and from western dealers who were starved by a massive strike in Pacific Coast mills. As historian Colin Gordon has written, for "sick" industries such as lumber, coal, and textiles, "the threat of the NRA paled beside the threat of no regulation at all."[58]

Only after the Supreme Court banned federal regulation of industrial competition did southern mill owners join the conservative backlash against the New Deal. Roosevelt was impressed by interracial working-class support for the NRA, and in 1937 he endorsed a more ambitious federal wage and hour law. The Fair Labor Standards Act, which Congress passed in 1938, set minimum wages at twenty-five cents per hour—with no exemption for the South—and then raised them to forty cents over the following seven years. Both black and white working-class southerners demonstrated strong support for the FLSA, but southern employers saw little reason to support wage regulation without other anticompetitive measures imposed by the NRA.

Retracting its once-enthusiastic support for the New Deal, the SPA invited John Edgerton to address their 1937 convention. Edgerton gained only partial support from southern mill owners in 1933, but he won considerable support among both southern and northern industrialists following the collapse of the NRA in 1934. He did so by linking frustration with New Deal economic policies to fears that federal intervention was undermining the social order—particularly in regards to race. "The NRA was devised, to a very large extent, to reform the South," Edgerton told his new followers. "General Johnson practically told me that when he said, 'We don't propose to allow the Negro labor of the South to debase the living standards of the rest of the country.'"

Hugh Johnson was one of the more conservative and pro-business members of the Roosevelt administration, and it is therefore unlikely that he would have had such goals in mind—let alone that he would have articulated them—in 1933. Nevertheless, Edgerton's claim struck a nerve among even pro–New Deal industrialists in late 1930s as it became clear that New Deal labor laws had in fact begun to weaken the Southern racial order. By 1937, the SPA was devoting $200,000 annually toward the defeat of the FLSA. Former SPA president C. C. Sheppard even won election as chairman of the Southern States Industrial Council, where he echoed Edgerton's threat that southern employers would respond to wage equality by firing their "less skilled, less privileged, sub-standard labor." Attributing a racial significance to the FSLA that he had most likely not seen in the NIRA, Hugh Johnson blasted southern industrialists for their about-face. "The South had better wake up . . . pronto or it will find itself sold down the river to a renewal of some of its problems of reconstruction days."[59]

Conclusion

Scholars have attributed far less significance than did Johnson to the NRA's impact on southern race relations, due in large part to their acceptance of the theory of displacement. Gunnar Myrdal, who authored an influential 1945 study of American race relations, interpreted the NRA as an example of the "wages and hours and the dilemma of the marginal worker." Echoing Edgerton's theory of "sub-normal labor," the liberal sociologist concluded, "When government steps in to regulate labor conditions and to enforce minimum standards, it takes away nearly all that is left of the old labor monopoly in the 'Negro jobs.'" In a more recent publication, Harvard Sitkoff quotes the *Norfolk Virginian-Pilot*—which he misidentifies as the black-owned *Journal and Guide*—to support his claim that black journalists unanimously designated the NRA's Blue Eagle symbol as "a predatory bird instead of a feathered messenger of happiness." A recent textbook on African American history states, "To the relief of many African American advocates and workers, the United States Supreme Court declared the NIRA unconstitutional in spring 1935."[60]

It is hard to imagine that Lonnie Carter would have agreed with scholarly assessments of the NRA. He first moved from agricultural to industrial labor in the early 1930s, just as the Roosevelt administration divided jurisdiction over these sectors between the Agricultural Adjustment Administration (AAA) and the NRA. While the AAA granted unlimited power to planters to stop paying and even evict sharecroppers and tenant farmers, NRA wage standards stopped a three-year decline in southern sawmill wages and put them on a steady climb that would continue through the 1950s. These gains were most significant for common laborers, who saw their wages double twice between 1933 and 1945, but wages for semiskilled and even skilled workers increased significantly as well. The NRA also benefited southern workers more than northerners, bringing southern lumber wages to more than half of West Coast lumber wages for the first time since 1925. As active members in the SPA, Carter's employers most likely complied with NRA standards. Even in mills that evaded them, the wage standards had an effect on prevailing wages that was reflected in regional statistics—as well as in Carter's new suit and shoes.[61]

Southern mill owners recognized that Carter and other semiskilled workers were in fact highly skilled, and their reliance upon those skills prevented them from carrying through with the threats of displacement. In a footnote below his confident restating of that threat, Gunnar Myrdal admitted that it was "impossible to give statistical evidence of the effects of social legislation upon marginal labor." Later in the text, he disputed a liberal white southerner's claim that half a million African Americans were thrown out of work by the NRA. That number, he clarified, "seems more definite than the complicated character of the problem would permit, and is in all likelihood much exaggerated." When Sitkoff wrote that *Opportunity* and *The Crisis* "published expose after expose" critical of the NRA, he overlooked an equal number of articles that ranged from guarded optimism to outright enthusiasm for the early New Deal. Urban League researcher Ira De Augustine Reid contended in a 1934 article that few working-class African Americans agreed with "certain Negro leaders [who] advocated publicly and privately" against wage equality. As evidence, he wrote of one such "leader" who "was forced to have his life and home guarded by a white policeman" after advocating what Reid derided as "black wages for black men."[62]

The significance of the NRA went beyond economics, however, a point that historians have only recently acknowledged. "The principle of an equal wage for white and black workers under the NRA codes . . . struck at the very basis of the southern system," according to Patricia Sullivan, who argues that the NRA debates inspired a liberal political movement that laid a basis for the southern civil rights movement. As the Young Turks and industrial feminists predicted, the NRA also created an economic basis for interracial working-class activism in both the South and the North. NRA codes "whet workers' appetite" for government protection, according to historian Lizbeth Cohen, inspiring an interracial and multiethnic ground-swell for Roosevelt's "second" New Deal in 1935. White working-class voters rejected white supremacist candidates in Florida's and Alabama's 1938 congressional primaries, choosing New Dealers Claude Pepper and Lister Hill who campaigned around the FSLA. Even as mill owners began to turn against federal intervention, a Gallup Poll found that general southern support for minimum wage legislation increased from 51 to 56 percent between 1935 and 1938. For the first time since the 1890s, wage equality created a basis for shared interests between black and white southerners.[63]

5 Race, Region, and the Limits of Industrial Unionism

On May 1, 1935, "young white men massed together with colored workers" at the Empire sawmill in Goldsboro, North Carolina, and walked out to protest their employers' violation of the NRA's lumber code. Less than two years earlier, Empire and most other southern pine producers had embraced the NRA in the hope that standardized prices and production would rescue them from the competitive nightmare of the Great Depression. Encouraged by a conservative backlash against the New Deal, increasing numbers of mills began "sniping" and then overtly defying the federal regulations. The Lumber Code Authority indicted Belcher Lumber Company for code violations at its two Alabama mills in 1934, but withdrew the charges after a federal judge ruled that the NRA had granted unconstitutional powers to the Southern Pine Association. By April 1935, a Department of Labor official reported that "the entire lumber industry in this section is shot to pieces due to the *Belcher* case." Firms that supported the code in the past felt "the Government has gone back on them; that they have been cheated for trying to do right." The Atlas Plywood Company, which owned the Empire mill, followed a regional trend when it cut wages from twenty-three to eighteen cents per hour and added sixteen hours to its employees' weekly duties. After leaving their jobs, the Empire workers "marched over to the Atlas Plant and brought enough pressure to bear on the employees of the Atlas Plant to close that unit also."[1]

The Empire workers were not alone in taking direct action in defense

of the lumber code. A union formed at Belcher Lumber Company shortly after that firm abandoned code wages in 1933, and more than 2,500
southern lumber workers participated in strikes that year. Strike activity was much lower in lumber than other southern industries such as
mining and textiles in 1933 and 1934, most likely because the Southern
Pine Association maintained a relatively high level of compliance with
the NRA. As the Roosevelt administration retreated from the *Belcher*
case, however, and particularly after the Supreme Court struck down the
NRA in *Schechter*, southern lumber workers found that strikes were their
only means of protecting the wage increases gained under the New Deal.
The U.S. Department of Labor recorded seven southern lumber strikes
in 1934 and twenty-four in 1935, involving over 3,500 and 3,700 workers respectively. Strikes were concentrated in northern Alabama and
eastern Tennessee, where they gained the support of union members in
other industries, but they also occurred in regions with few other unions.[2]

As Robert Weaver and other Young Turks had predicted in 1933, black
and white workers' defense of the NRA provided a potential basis for
reviving the southern labor movement. By April 1935, one sawmill owner
complained that northern Alabama had become a "strike hatchery." A
federal investigator concurred, noting that one mill was "surrounded by
strong labor organizations, miners, farmers unionists, and carpenters"
who threatened "violence and perhaps property-destruction," in retaliation for the mill owners' abandonment of code wages. A report from Jas-
per, Alabama, warned of a "danger of violence there unless something can
be done immediately" to dispel tensions at local mills. "Considerable
spontaneous organization" led to unionization of Arkansas's three largest sawmills, and workers at smaller mills followed suit. Federal officials
sent to mediate conflicts in Alabama sawmills "feared that considerable
trouble will be had in this state, due very largely to the dropping of the
Belcher case. Other industries have been affected by the case, only a little less than lumber."[3]

Despite these initial bursts of outrage, lumber workers did not establish an interracial labor movement in the South. As Spero and Harris argued in their 1930 study *The Black Worker*, craft unionism presented the greatest obstacle to interracial unionism in the 1930s. "The
craft is a sort of exclusive club consisting of those who now belong,"
they charged, explaining that AFL unions were dominated by men who
saw the black worker as "not merely an outsider trying to get into the
union, but a social and racial inferior trying to force the white man to
associate with him as an equal." But these authors did not anticipate
the formation of the Congress of Industrial Organizations (CIO), which

built upon the strikes of 1934 and 1935 to establish industrial unionism as a viable alternative to the AFL's craft model. That interracial unions were not established in the southern lumber industry even during the "age of the CIO" reveals additional racial and regional limits to liberal and left-wing union activists' enthusiasm for organizing what continued to be one of the South's largest industries. Since the late 1920s, many radical supporters of industrial unionism had believed that racial oppression prevented African Americans from gaining the class consciousness necessary to build viable labor unions. Young Turks succeeded in challenging such beliefs in the mid-1930s, but many of them retained the conviction that union consciousness could develop only as African Americans migrated to the urban North. In so doing, they reinforced the myth of Black Ulysses, in which black working-class men were viewed as victims rather than participants in the industrial transformation of the South.

The Lines of Craftsmanship

The United Brotherhood of Carpenters and Joiners, which claimed to represent all workers who harvested and processed wood, emerged as the most vocal opponent of industrial unionism in the 1930s. This opposition was based not on a historical conservatism among Carpenters—as some authors have suggested—but on the rejection of a relatively liberal tradition that defined the union until the early 1920s. In contrast to the International Association of Machinists, which had excluded black members since its founding in the 1880s, the Carpenters denounced the "drawing of the color line" in 1903, and chartered fourteen segregated African American locals in the South before World War I. The union resisted the wave of industrial unionism initiated by the Industrial Workers of the World in Louisiana, Texas, and in the Pacific Northwest in the early 1910s, but joined the trend by supporting the biracial International Union of Timber Workers at Bogalusa in 1919. Carpenters president William B. Hutcheson led an effort to expel Ku Klux Klan members from the AFL in the 1920s, and he required Carpenters' locals to keep their organizations "free from either religious or racial bigotry."[4]

The Carpenters' conservatism in the 1930s grew out of their endorsement of the "new tradition" of labor market segregation that transformed southern industry in the years following World War I. Louisiana's largest carpenters' local initiated a boycott of local builders that employed black workers in 1921, and by the end of the decade the union had nearly eliminated skilled black carpenters from the South. Carpenter officials insisted that racial exclusion was an unintentional by-product of the economic strategy of limiting the supply of skilled craftsmen. After studying black participation in the labor movement in the late 1920s, however, black economist Ira De Augustine Reid concluded that "organized labor in many instances does not treat the matter as an 'economic question.'" He cited as an example an Alabama union official who justified the boycott on the grounds that black carpenters did "more work in a day, [which] causes jealousy on the part of whites." As a result of white boycotts in other industries as well, the number of black AFL locals plummeted from 169 to 23 between 1919 and 1929.[5]

The belief that it was skill that distinguished white craftsmen from the African American majority of southern lumber workers led some skilled workers to actually oppose the wage and hour standards mandated by the NRA. As early as 1933, a Mississippi "machine man, moulder man, and foreman" informed NRA director Hugh Johnson that the lumber code "sure put the skill labor in bad shape this part of the country." He "and the rest of skill labor here" disapproved of the "strikes and disorder" that common laborers had initiated in defense of wage and hour standards, and he hoped that "the President would throw the NRA in the river and forget about it." A Louisiana carpenter agreed, and in 1934 he complained to AFL president William Green that the lumber code granted a "substantial raise" to common laborers while "we of the skilled labor never received one cent." Assessing the program that had doubled the wages of many of his coworkers, he concluded, "It appears to me that the NRA has very little to offer the skilled labor in the South."[6]

Carpenters president Hutcheson took up his members' concerns and led the charge against industrial unionism within the AFL. "The American Federation of Labor has been brought to the point that it has through following the lines of craftsmanship," he declared at the AFL's 1935 convention, and he urged union leaders to protect the rights of craft workers in their response to common laborers' demands for union membership. The AFL executive council achieved that goal between 1933 and 1935 by organizing noncraft workers into Federal Labor Unions, which were affiliated directly to the AFL and had no formal influence over the craft-based International Unions that controlled the federation. Hutcheson convinced the AFL to group all federal unions at sawmills and logging operations into the Sawmill and Timber Workers Union (STWU), a nonvoting subordinate of the Brotherhood of Carpenters.[7]

Despite opposition from craft unionists, support for industrial unionism did emerge within the ranks of the AFL. Primary among the supporters were Sidney Hillman, who headed the Amalgamated Clothing Work-

ers of America, David Dubinsky of the International Ladies' Garment
Workers Union, and John L. Lewis, the president of the United Mine
Workers of America. Hillman and Dubinsky embraced industrial unionism in the 1920s, lending support to the organization of mostly immigrant women in the sweatshops of northeastern cities. Lewis needed more
convincing, but he was persuaded by a wave of interracial strikes that
swept West Virginia coal mines in 1931 and 1933. All three union leaders were also pushed toward industrial unionism by a cohort of left-wing
activists and intellectuals who believed that mass organization and cooperation with the federal government provided an avenue for restoring
the power of organized labor. A few of those activists, such as Lewis's
advisor Jett Lauck, found employment within AFL unions. Others, such
as Lucy Randolph Mason, Matilda Lindsay, and Tom Tippett, worked for
independent pro-labor organizations such as the National Consumers'
League, the National Women's Trade Union League, and the Brookwood
Labor College.[8]

Bolstered by the NRA strikes and persuaded by radical activists and
intellectuals, Hillman and Lewis mounted a spirited campaign against
the craft orthodoxy of the AFL. While other labor leaders opposed government intervention in labor relations, Hillman helped to formulate the
NRA. At the AFL's 1933 convention, Lewis blasted the "labor barons"
who dominated the AFL and called for an expansion of the federation's
executive council to include representatives of common laborers. Lewis
also joined Lucy Randolph Mason and John P. Davis in testifying against
regional wage differentials in the NRA code for the coal industry. More
importantly, he assisted common laborers who were attempting to unionize in defense of code standards. According to Lewis's biographer, the
UMWA leader risked the entire union treasury to support organization
of Alabama mine workers in 1933. More than half of those miners were
black, and Lewis himself expressed hesitations about their ability to support the labor movement. The gamble paid off, however, and by 1935
Lewis headed the largest union within the AFL. The federation as a whole
grew by 30 percent between 1933 and 1935, nearly recovering the membership lost during the 1920s.[9]

The burst of organization following the NRA complicated William
Hutcheson's effort to protect the interests of craft workers. Southern
sawmill unionism was concentrated in the coalfields of Walker County,
Alabama, where lumber workers cut mine timbers and moved frequently between mining and sawmill jobs. The UMWA forced 95 percent of
Alabama coal companies to sign contracts with workers in 1935, and that
strength facilitated organization in other industries. By 1936, Walker was

"said to be the best organized county in Alabama," according to a federal investigator who reported, "Even a farmer cannot sell his produce [there] unless he carries a union card." Lumber unions grew even more rapidly on the West Coast, where sawmill workers gained the support of the Communist-led International Longshoremen's Association and where Communists concentrated their efforts to radicalize the Carpenters' Timber Workers Union. Communists had isolated themselves from the AFL before 1935, choosing instead to build small but militant independent unions. After changing that policy, they took part in a massive strike that resulted in more than thirty-five thousand lumber workers joining the Timber Workers Union in Washington and Oregon. By the end of 1936, nonvoting sawmill and timber workers represented 43 percent of the Carpenters' entire membership, demonstrating the degree to which common laborers threatened craftsmen's control over the labor movement.[10]

Craft traditions were undermined further in July 1935, when Congress passed the National Labor Relations Act. Designed to preserve New Deal labor protections in the wake of the *Schechter* decision, the act created a National Labor Relations Board (NLRB) to monitor union campaigns and to conduct elections to allow workers to choose their representatives. While the law expanded union rights granted under the NRA, it also extended government authority into the selection of workers' representatives. "The new law in fact contradicted historic premises of American trade unionism," according to historian David Brody. "No longer was the Federation's authority to assign union jurisdictions paramount, nor were its affiliates absolutely free to enter agreements with employers." Judicial challenges and understaffing crippled the NLRB until 1937, but union leaders recognized even before it passed that the new law threatened craft workers' ability to assign common laborers to the margins of the labor movement.[11]

Conflict over industrial unionism erupted at the AFL's 1935 convention, where Hutcheson and Lewis engaged in what has become a legendary brawl. Lewis had convinced AFL leaders to charter industrial unions in Midwestern auto and rubber plants at the 1934 convention, but he complained that they had not followed through with their decision and in fact allowed craft unions to stifle the new organizations. After several days of fruitless calls to "organize the unorganized," Lewis lashed out at Hutcheson, who repeatedly defended the AFL's craft traditions. In frustration, the Miners' leader called a meeting of those who were committed to industrial unionism. The following month Lewis, Dubinsky, and Hillman formed the Committee for Industrial Organization, which was part of the AFL but funded almost entirely by the miners, clothing, and garment workers' unions. In 1937, the committee broke from the AFL and became the Congress of Industrial Organizations (CIO).[12]

The Popular Front in Black and White

The CIO grew out of an alliance between dissident union leaders, common laborers who were radicalized by the NRA, and radical activists and intellectuals who saw industrial unionism as a way to revive the labor movement. Because no one of these groups could have challenged craft unionism on their own, the implications of their social movement extended far beyond the institutional battles of the labor movement. Indeed, historians have identified the decade that followed the NRA strikes as "the age of the CIO" due to the extent to which proponents of industrial unionism transformed the culture and politics of the United States. Historian Michael Denning argues that this transformation was created not by any one organization or party but by a broad "historical bloc" known as the Popular Front. He proposes such a model to understand how the Popular Front articulated a new vision of American society and realized that vision by influencing a broad array of political and cultural institutions. "'Industrial unionism' was not simply a kind of unionism," according to Denning, "but a vision of social reconstruction."[13]

Denning and other historians have not fully recognized the racial and regional limits of that reconstruction, however. Looking back on the Popular Front in the 1940s, black sociologists St. Clair Drake and Horace Cayton described the CIO as a "crusading movement" that made "racial equality . . . a component part of its ideology." Historian Robert Zieger contends that black workers' exclusion from craft positions "made obvious the need" to include them in efforts to extend unionization to semi- and unskilled laborers. African Americans, women, and second-generation immigrants formed "the natural constituency of industrial democracy," according to Sidney Hillman's biographer Steven Frazer. Even in the South, writes historian Michael Honey, industrial unionists "could not ignore" African Americans who dominated that region's unskilled workforce.[14]

Each of these authors overlook the fact that interracial unionism did not follow immediately from the move toward industrial unionism but in fact gained prevalence nearly ten years later during World War II. This was not an oversight but a result of many industrial unionists' belief that black workers were *not* a natural constituency of industrial unionism. Observing that most African Americans lived and worked in the Jim

Crow South, some industrial unionists assumed—incorrectly—that black workers lacked the social and political freedom necessary to join and support industrial unions. Furthermore, as industrial unionists rejected the craft ideology that associated union consciousness with attainment of skill and prestige, they often reaffirmed the related belief that white workers were more class conscious than African Americans. Finally, even when black activists and intellectuals sought to convince both AFL and CIO leaders of the need to organize African Americans, they often framed that argument in the context of the Great Migration, which some believed was a necessary prerequisite to black participation in the labor movement. As a result, industrial unionists did in fact ignore the organizing opportunities provided by the interracial strike waves that followed the rise and fall of the NRA.

Roots of the Popular Front's racial and regional ideology can be traced to a southern component of the social movement that emerged during the first years of the Great Depression. In 1930, the University of Virginia's Institute for Research in the Social Sciences (IRSS) published a detailed study of wages and working conditions in the lumber, cotton, and furniture industries, which they determined to be "fairly typical of southern industrial development." The Virginia IRSS was modeled on the University of North Carolina's IRSS, which Howard Odum established in 1924 to bring social scientific analysis to bear on what he believed were the social and cultural conflicts created by industrialization. The Virginia publication declared that "A new South is in a process of development which in several respects is not only characterized by new industrial activities and interests, but activities and interests which run counter to culture which is the result of some centuries of growth." The sociologists traced these cultural developments to migration from agricultural to industrial employment, and pointed out that such movement had been "much faster and more revolutionary than in the North." Rather than resisting this process—as the conservative "Agrarian" intellectuals did in their own 1930 manifesto—the Virginia IRSS urged southerners to embrace the economic and political possibilities offered by "what may be called an industrial civilization."[15]

Liberal and left-wing interest in the industrial South was sparked by a series of strike waves that began in 1929 and culminated in 1934 and 1935. The strikes started in textile towns on the Piedmont border of Virginia, Tennessee, and the Carolinas, but many assumed that they reflected a broader sharpening of class conflict in a region many associated with social conformity and political consensus. The Virginia sociologists attributed the violence that followed the 1929 strikes to conflict between the "spirit of paternalism" that employers had inherited from the agricultural South and the emergence of "free labor with its assertion of the right to be self-determining." Matilda Lindsay, a union activist who helped organize the 1929 strikes, likened the actions to a "Declaration of Industrial Independence" for southern workers who had previously "been held up to the country as lacking in initiative, docile, willing to work long hours for low wages and altogether have been painted in a very unattractive picture—except, of course, to the type of employer who regards labor as nothing but a source of profits."[16]

Liberal and left-wing activists hoped that in addition to challenging paternalistic employers, the 1929 strikes would set an important precedent in the emergence of an industrial union movement. Lindsay and other industrial feminists had challenged craft orthodoxy since World War I by encouraging women to take leading roles in organizing the textile and garment shops of the northeastern United States. They expanded those efforts to the South in the mid-1920s as textile firms began to migrate to the nonunion Appalachian Piedmont. Lindsay directed a southern educational campaign for the National Women's Trade Union League during which she emphasized southern white women's leadership in her reports about the textile strikes. "In North and South Carolina and Georgia as well as in Tennessee the workers, especially the women, are beginning to understand the message of the Labor Movement," she wrote, pointing out that "in fact, the first department to 'walk out' was composed entirely of women and girls." Writing in the journal of the AFL machinists' union, Lindsay declared, "Women Hold Key to Unionization of Dixie."[17]

Contemporary journalists and subsequent historians have emphasized the local sources of textile workers' militancy in the late 1920s and early 1930s—in order to counter employers' charges that unions were imposed by northern radicals—but such an emphasis obscures the degree to which textile unionism depended upon outside support. Lindsay's southern campaign was assisted after 1927 by the Southern Summer School for Women Workers in Industry, which was founded by the Young Women's Christian Association and the Brookwood Labor College. These institutions provided critical logistical support to the strikers, and they succeeded in diverting at least some union funds toward what one organizer described as "homegrown unions." Perhaps more important than the support that textile workers wrested from the AFL was the attention they gained from liberal and left-wing authors and activists. The Communist-affiliated National Textile Workers Union lent its support to strikers in Gastonia, North Carolina, and left-wing journalists and novelists rushed to document what Brookwood instructor Tom Tippett called the "second phase of the industrial revolution."[18]

Radicals charged the AFL with "criminal sluggishness" in responding to the 1929 strikes, but they eventually convinced significant sectors of the federation to support organization of southern textile workers. Delegates to the AFL's 1929 annual convention voted to fund a southern organizing campaign, and the AFL's textile union boasted that southern locals grew "in leaps and bounds" during the following year. Between 1929 and 1932, southern textile workers and their allies were able to build a small network of union locals that would prove critical to the burst of organization that would accompany the disintegration of the NRA. "Although victories were local and scattered," writes historian Janet Irons, "successful protests occurred frequently enough to convince at least some observers that a loose federation of local unions was possible in the South."[19]

In addition to winning over sections of the AFL, southern textile strikes also became a "watershed" in turning southern intellectual opinion toward support for the labor movement. This convergence between workers, intellectuals, and industrial unionists created a distinctly Southern Front, according to historian Jacquelyn Dowd Hall, that focused Popular Front activism and analysis on issues such as voting rights, lynching, and interracial unionism that had particular relevance in the region. Lindsay and many other activists were southerners, but most entered mill towns for the first time in the late 1920s. The experience of living in those towns led them to reject prevalent images of white working-class southerners as "crippled by poverty and paternalism" and therefore powerless to effect change. The Southern Front replaced such images with the assertion that textile workers would become the primary agents in a complete transformation of southern society. "In Gastonia they lifted a local strike into a national and even international conflict," writes Hall, "and remade the South into a flash point of political possibility in the minds of people around the world."[20]

Even as they succeeded in calling attention to the southern textile strikes, radical activists drew clear racial boundaries around the "political possibility" they saw in southern working-class activism. Lindsay described the 1929 militants as "100 percent native white workers who come from the mountains and the rural sections of the Southern States." This generalization was not true for textiles—small numbers of black workers participated in the 1929 strikes—but other writers applied it to all southern industry, even when they acknowledged black involvement in union activism. Tippett referred to "the Negroes who are beginning to come into industry even if they are not already there in sufficient numbers to constitute an immediate question now." In 1931, the Communist-affiliated International Labor Defense conducted an investigation of violence directed at striking coal miners in Harlan County, Kentucky. A report from that investigation referred repeatedly to "Negro and white miners" and included an account of brutal murders of two black union activists. In spite of the fact that roughly a quarter of Appalachian coal miners were African Americans, however, the report attributed mine workers' militancy to the "English, English-Irish, Scotch Highlanders and Scotch-Irish" ancestors of white miners. "These were the peoples who contributed bold opinion and great brawn to the Anglo-Saxon tradition," one investigator waxed poetically. "These were the peoples who fought for the Great Charter, fought the English in Scotland, fought the English in Ireland, fought the Catholics, fought the nobles and parliaments and kings, fought the French, the Dutch and the Spaniards."[21]

The Southern Front inverted the cultural determinism of older writing about Appalachian whites, but retained the racial premise that contrasted fiercely independent white "mountain folk" to inhabitants of the paternalistic plantation South. In her study of Popular Front fiction, Barbara Foley found that black workers appear in textile novels and plays only as problems to be confronted as white workers develop their political consciousness. The result was that authors reinforced images of helpless and docile southern blacks even as they rejected similar images of southern whites. In a chapter titled "The Southern Worker's Background," the IRSS characterized "the present-day situation" as one in which both black and white southern workers were making a transition from nonwage family farming to industrial wage work. In contrast to their view that Appalachian whites had begun to reject the cultural heritage of that past, the sociologists argued that African Americans still suffered from a culture of dependency created by slavery. "Little need be said concerning the Negroes," they wrote. "As long as the slave system lasted their living conditions depended upon the capacity and generosity of their masters. While the physical needs of this class of workers were generally looked after there was nothing in the experiences of the Negro which would impel him on the attainment of freedom to maintain a decent standard of living,—still less to strive for a better standard."[22]

Here again was the "damage imagery" popular among liberals intent on exposing the oppressive nature of Jim Crow in the 1920s and early 1930s, according to historian Daryl Michael Scott. One of the most effective spokesmen for that imagery was Howard Odum, whose North Carolina-based IRSS played a central roll in emphasizing the political opportunities created by textile unionism. Odum's most popular publications were not his numerous sociological studies of southern industrialization but his trilogy of poetic biographies of Black Ulysses, the fictional black man who worked in sawmills, mines, and prison camps throughout the South. Whereas Odum portrayed white textile workers as active participants in southern industrialization, he described Black Ulysses as alienated by the process of social change: a "primitive man in the modern world."[23]

The Young Turks and the Southern Front

While the Southern Front emerged out of a rethinking of white working-class culture in the South, a small group of black activists saw the potential to expand that rethinking to include African Americans as well. Abram Harris organized a "Symposium on Negro Labor" at Brookwood Labor College in 1927, which he hoped would initiate a program for black workers' education modeled on the Southern Summer School for Women Workers in Industry. The school never materialized, but Harris gained the support of the black radicals who congregated at the National Urban League in the late 1920s and early 1930s. "Any attempt to organize the workers which ignores the presence of the two million black workers will be fraught with disaster," the National Urban League's journal *Opportunity* editorialized as the AFL began to back organization of southern textile workers in 1929. Pointing out that African Americans constituted a significant portion of the southern workforce, editor Elmer Carter attributed labor leaders' disinterest in black workers to their mistaken belief that "the Negro worker was unorganizable, and was as yet incapable of appreciating the necessity of identifying himself with the American Labor Movement." He contended that those assumptions had cost the AFL black support for the past year's campaign, "which was to see a great deal in the South, [and] even as reported, was a scanty 35,000."[24]

Repeating excuses they had used to rebuff the Southern Front, AFL leaders contended that African Americans were ideologically unprepared for union membership. "Joining a trade union requires something more than merely telling the worker that the union is there and that it can render him a service," AFL president William Green wrote in a letter to *Opportunity*. Overlooking the fact that several major international unions excluded African Americans from membership, the craft unionist complained that "The Federation cannot effectively carry the gospel of unionism until workers are ready to hear and act." Green invited the Urban League to join the AFL in planning "more intensive work in the South" but cautioned against hoping for any rapid change: "these are not purposes that can be accomplished in all industries in a year or a decade."[25]

Ironically, the Southern Front's success in drawing attention to white textile workers may have reinforced AFL leaders' perception that African Americans could not be organized. After complaining that black workers had been slow to appreciate the value of unions, Green noted, "On the other hand, sometimes the change comes unexpectedly and suddenly as it did among the southern textile workers this spring." Such a comment overlooked the extent to which both craft and industrial unionists had in fact carried "the gospel of unionism" to southern textile workers. Radical activists like Lindsay and Tippett did not cause the strikes, as conservatives charged, but they did bring resources and attention that sustained the strikes and allowed them to contribute to a national resurgence of working-class activism. The AFL mocked these efforts in 1929, but in 1930 the federation and its affiliated textile union sent several full-time organizers to help strengthen the new union locals.[26]

Efforts to bring black workers into the new labor movement were also hindered by a history of sectarianism between civil rights activists and the labor-oriented left. At the peak of the 1929 strikes, NAACP leader W. E. B. Du Bois joined a group of prominent activists and intellectuals who gathered to discuss the formation of a left-wing political party. To Du Bois's dismay, the group developed an elaborate program that said nothing about African American voting rights in the South. Brookwood Labor College director A. J. Muste shared Du Bois's concern, and he promised to convene a group to discuss "the problem of worker's education among Negro workers" later in the year. As he had with Harris's similar proposal two years earlier, Muste never carried out his promise to Du Bois. Left-wing and liberal ambivalence toward organizing black workers made it "painfully obvious," according to Du Bois's biographer David Lewis, "that the task of making race an integral part of reform was close to being impossible in America."[27]

The Communist Party, which made interracial unionism central to its platform in the 1920s and 1930s, also failed to unite with civil rights activists who shared that goal. The National Urban League created a Trade Union Committee for Organizing Negro Workers in 1924, but Communists viewed it as a competitor to its own American Negro Labor Congress. Both groups failed to win support from even left-wing unions and dissolved by the end of the decade. Communists launched the Trade Union Unity League to build a "revolutionary" alternatives to AFL craft unions in 1929. Small numbers of black workers joined Communist mining and needle trade unions in northern states, and a few joined Communist textile and dockworkers unions in Gastonia and New Orleans. Civil rights activists were impressed by Communist rhetoric, according to Mark Solomon, but the TUUL remained "a mongrel force on the labor front" between 1929 and 1934 due to its isolation from the AFL and potential allies among civil rights activists and the rest of the left.[28]

Communists devoted tremendous energy toward fighting racism between 1928 and 1934, but these efforts were directed primarily toward exposing government abuse of black workers rather than organizing them into unions. A "second cultural offensive" of the Popular Front emerged in 1931 around campaigns to defend black Communist Angelo Herndon and nine black boys sentenced to death in Scottsboro, Alabama. Whereas the first offensive emphasized white textile workers' agency, however, Scottsboro literature focused on black victims and the white radicals who came to their defense. Langston Hughes's 1931 play *Scottsboro, Limited* ends with a scene of white workers sweeping in to rescue the boys, "helplessly crouching back at the foot of the [electric] chair." John Wexley's 1934 novel *They Shall Not Die* ends with a white lawyer declaring that only protests and court battles "in a thousand cities of the world" would save the Scottsboro Boys. The Communists' most successful southern campaign was the formation of a Share Croppers' Union that claimed 8,000 members in Alabama between 1931 and 1937. Ironically, the party downplayed that success because it failed to attract white members and thus failed to exemplify the ideal of interracial unionism. In contrast to the "political possibility" found in white southerners, Michael Denning observes, radical accounts of the black South ended in "martyrdom and tragic defeat."[29]

While Communists achieved minimal success building alternative unions, a more successful strategy emerged out of the Urban League's efforts to push the AFL toward organizing black workers. T. Arnold Hill, who launched the Urban League's department of industrial relations in 1928, penned a second letter in response to William Green's rebuff of Carter. "The Federation is about to embark on a campaign in the South where Negro wage-earners prevail in large numbers," Hill began. "May we ask you then, whether or not your plans for organizing in the South call for organizing Negroes—not merely permitting them to join—but actively campaigning for their membership?" To counter Green's theory that black workers had not yet attained union consciousness, Hill pointed out that more African Americans had belonged to unions in 1919 than they did in 1929. He acknowledged Green's promise that "the Federation 'stands ready to help' the Negro 'raise his standards,'" but concluded, "judging from past observations and experiences, that the word 'stands' is to be taken literally; for we have seen the Federation stand still, exerting not a single muscle to welcome Negroes into the folds of organized labor, while blaming them for not accepting the restrictions grudgingly offered."[30]

The exchange over the AFL's southern campaign consolidated the cohort of young black activists who older civil rights activists would label Young Turks in the following few years. Abram Harris became director of Howard University's department of economics in 1928, and he was joined shortly thereafter by fellow radicals E. Franklin Frazier and Ralph Bunche. The Young Turks gained a second institutional foothold in the Urban League's department of industrial relations, which T. Arnold Hill created in the late 1920s. Hill hired activist intellectuals Charles S. Johnson and Ira De Augustine Reid and then took over as director of the Urban League in 1933, when the comparatively conservative Eugene Kinkle Jones resigned to accept a position in the Roosevelt administration. That same year, NAACP president Joel Spingarn sponsored the Amenia Conference, where Harris, Bunch, and Frazier drafted their influential "Future Plan and Program of the NAACP."[31]

In addition to pushing civil rights organizations to pay attention to black workers, Young Turks also encouraged black workers to join AFL unions or, when necessary, form unions of their own. In the months after he gained control of the Urban League's national office, T. Arnold Hill organized two hundred Emergency Advisory Councils in thirty-two states to inform black workers of their rights and to fight discrimination under the NRA. He expanded these efforts in 1934 with the creation of Negro Workers' Councils designed to pressure local unions to admit black workers, encourage black workers to demand fair treatment from New Deal programs, and to educate black and white workers "on the history of Negro labor and Negro workers." Lester Granger, who Hill hired to coordinate this campaign of "mass education," boasted that forty-two councils operated in seventeen states in the spring of 1935. Granger emphasized the urgency of black workers' need for organization during the economic crisis. "This is no time for soft words and seeking after industrial amity at the expense of the race's future," he declared in *Opportunity*. Calling upon black workers to fight their way into unions and protest legislation that allowed unions to discriminate, Granger urged them to "organize to demand, with other workers, a new deal for labor."[32]

Between 1934 and 1936, the Young Turks succeeded in building relatively broad support for bringing black workers into the labor movement. Robert Weaver and John P. Davis's success in limiting racial wage differentials in NRA codes convinced even conservative civil rights activists of the need to get more involved in black working-class politics. Black workers also took the forefront in efforts to organize Alabama mining and steel companies, which were supported by the UMW, the CIO Steel Workers' Organizing Committee, and the Communist-led Mine, Mill, and Smelter Workers Union. In 1935, Davis and Weaver cosponsored a conference on "The Position of the Negro in Our National Economic Crisis," which was hosted by Harris, Frazier, and Bunche at Howard University. Communists disbanded their "revolutionary unions" that year and devoted themselves to building a popular front with other left and liberal allies. One of the most successful products of that coalition was the National Negro Congress, which was initiated at the 1935 Howard conference. The congress drew 5,000 activists to Chicago the following year to discuss the needs of the vast majority of African Americans who "win their bread by selling their labor power."[33]

Even as the Young Turks won support for unionizing black workers, however, they failed to retain their initial focus on the South. Alabama miners' strikes convinced NAACP leader Charles Hamilton Houston that interracial working-class cooperation "presented the ultimate solution" to the fight against southern racism, and he emerged from the 1935 Howard conference convinced that working-class African Americans could play an important role in building the NAACP in the South. The southern campaign that emerged out of this realization focused on voting rights and legal challenges to segregation, however, which failed to inspire the enthusiasm with which working-class African Americans had defended the economic goals of the NRA. The National Negro Congress "had initially planned to direct much of its energy and resources to the South," according to historian Robin D. G. Kelley, but national NAACP leaders instructed Alabama branch leaders not to work with the Communist organizer who was selected to lead that campaign.[34]

Popular Front writers also shifted their attention away from the South in the late 1930s, hoping to find an optimistic resolution to the Scottsboro tragedies. Reviving a theme developed by the New Negro movement of the 1920s, black and white radical authors argued that African Americans had been able to create a new political culture as they migrated from the rural South to the urban North. Communist novelist Richard Wright urged black authors to explore the distinctly proletarian nature of that new culture, and, along with writers Langston Hughes and Arna Bontemps, he characterized the Great Migration as a necessary prerequisite to African American progress. In the works of these black radical intellectuals, Denning observes, "the portrayals of Alabama terror became the first act in the grand narratives of African American migration."[35]

While they emphasized the revolutionary nature of black culture in the urban North, Popular Front authors often reinforced traditional images of black southerners. The migration narrative found its clearest in articulation in E. Franklin Frazier's influential 1939 study *The Black Family*. A student of University of Chicago sociologist Robert E. Park, Frazier argued that African Americans were participating in a broad transformation of American society from particular rural cultures to a multicultural urban proletariat. He argued that segregation prevented "the emergence of a black industrial proletariat" in the South but that "as this isolation of the black worker is gradually breaking down, his ideals and patterns of family life approximate those of the great body of industrial workers." Cultural change began with a "steady stream of individuals and families migrating from farms to lumber and turpentine camps and into the towns and cities of the North and the South," but it would not reach fruition until African Americans found acceptance in working-class communities of Chicago and other northern cities. Demonstrating the degree to which new radical visions of northern change emerged in harmony with older views of southern stasis, Frazier cited extensive sociological data to support his characterization of northern African Americans, but simply referred readers interested in reading more about black southerners to Howard Odum's description of Black Ulysses: "In Odum's *Rainbow 'round My Shoulder* one may find a composite picture of the impulsive behavior of this group compressed in a single fictional character."[36]

A few authors focused on black working-class culture in the South, but they also diverted attention from the immediate political context of the region. Zora Neale Hurston presented an extreme version of this strategy in her 1935 *Mules and Men*, which documented songs and stories gathered in sawmill, mining, and fishing towns but made no reference to union campaigns or racial violence that occurred in those same towns within the previous decade. She visited Bogalusa in 1929, exactly ten years after the Great Southern Lumber Company drove an estimated five hundred black union supporters out of the company town. "The Ocoee Riot," an unpublished manuscript that Hurston authored in the late 1930s, recounts the lynching of six black activists who attempted to register black voters during the political ferment of World War I. At least one of those lynchings occurred outside Eatonville, Florida, where she spent six months in 1928. She left Eatonville for Loughman, Lakeland, and other lumber, turpentine, and phosphate towns on Florida's Gulf

Coast. One of those towns was Lacoochee, where Cummer and Sons Lumber Company resettled survivors of the 1923 Rosewood massacre. Not one of these events is mentioned in *Mules and Men,* which as a result, according to biographer Robert Hemenway, has "a disembodied quality about it as if it came from a backwoods so far to the rear that American social history of the twentieth century had not touched its occupants."[37]

Hurston's anti-politics won her scorn from Popular Front writers, but her radical critics did not see any more potential in southern African American culture. Writing in the NAACP's journal *The Crisis,* Marxist literary critic Harold Preece chided Hurston for "devoting her literary abilities to recording the legendary amours of terrapins" while "Angelo Herndon was condemned to break rocks in Georgia." Preece's objection was not that Hurston focused on the wrong aspect of black culture, but that she paid any attention to what he viewed as a hopelessly backward rural society. "When one surveys the development of the Negro culture, he realizes that it has been one of evasion whatever its intrinsic beauty," Preece wrote. "Under the circumstances, one can sympathize with the northern Negroes who attempt so strenuously to escape the traditional culture and who justly avoid the conventional folklorist." Richard Wright derided Hurston for depicting "the psychological movements of the Negro folk-mind in their pure simplicity," and urged her to focus on more "serious" urban topics.

Following the publication of *Mules and Men,* Hurston participated in a Popular Front movement that did call attention to the political nature of black working-class culture. She returned to Florida as director of the New Deal–sponsored Federal Writers Project, and she adopted Writers Project folklore director B. A. Botkin's approach to "proletarian regionalism," which sought to document the regional, ethnic, and racial variety of American culture. The literature of that movement popularized images of class-conscious black southerners that helped generate support for truly interracial industrial unionism during World War II, but it also replicated imagery of alienated black men—such as John Lomax's packaging of Leadbelly—that were little removed from Odum's Black Ulysses.[38]

Even when they were engaged in building interracial movements in the South, some Popular Front activists expressed skepticism about black workers' abilities to support those movements. In 1934, Socialist Party activists Clay East and H. L. Mitchell helped to organize the Southern Tenant Farmers' Union in the plantation region of eastern Arkansas. According to historian Robert Korstad, the organization remained more of a protest movement than a trade union, in part because Mitchell "contended that sharecroppers and tenant farmers were too uneducated to keep records and too poor to pay regular dues." Rather than rely upon union members for financial support, Socialist Party activist Claude Williams conducted a tireless fundraising drive that included speaking and letter writing to northern trade unionists who supported the cause of organizing the South. In 1936, Williams discovered that nearby sawmills had been unionized "on the initiative of the workers themselves when the company lengthened hours and reduced wages following the invalidation of the NIRA by the Supreme Court." He documented collaboration between the owners of these mills and the plantation owners to support a legal case against evictions of tenant farmers, but he made no effort to link the Tenant Farmers' Union to the independent and most likely interracial unions that workers had formed in local sawmills.[39]

Skeptical about black workers' abilities to support the labor movement, Popular Front activists and intellectuals ignored an important opportunity to bring black workers into the AFL. A. Philip Randolph, who headed the nation's largest all-black union, introduced a proposal to the AFL's 1934 annual convention that called for the expulsion of any union that practiced racial discrimination. This was the culmination of a decade-long debate between Randolph and AFL leaders, who insisted somewhat cynically that they could not impose racial egalitarianism upon member unions. Randolph's union grew rapidly in 1933 and 1934, forcing AFL leaders to take his complaints more seriously. Carpenters president William Hutcheson headed off a confrontation by drafting an alternative to Randolph's proposal that created a Committee of Five to "investigate the conditions of the colored workers of the country" and report back to the AFL's 1935 convention. The alternative was adopted, and Randolph's Brotherhood of Sleeping Car Porters and Maids cooperated with the Urban League's Workers Councils to mobilize groups of black workers to attend hearings that the committee sponsored in several cities over the following year. Black activists then staged a mass demonstration at the 1935 convention—meeting with delegates, distributing leaflets calling attention to union discrimination, and plastering the convention hall with signs urging the AFL to "Unite the Labor Movement!" and "Expel Trade Union Politics that Put Personal Prejudice Before the Interests of Labor."[40]

The clash between Lewis and Hutcheson focused national media attention on the AFL's 1935 convention, but radical journalists found little of interest in the closely related conflict over racial exclusion. The Committee of Five, which included several prominent industrial unionists, contradicted Green's position and recommended expelling any union that did not remove racial barriers to membership before the 1936 convention. In addition, it advised AFL leaders to conduct a "continuous campaign of education" aimed at combating racism within the ranks of the AFL. The AFL executive committee attempted to head off this challenge to Green by preparing a "summary" of the report that omitted all references to expulsion, but Randolph took the floor and read the full text of the original report. Blasting the executive summary as "dignified diplomatic camouflage," Randolph charged the AFL with forcing black workers into "dual unions" that had no influence over the Federation. AFL president William Green followed Randolph, defending his previous policies and dismissing his critics as "Negro academic organizations." John Brophy, a radical UMWA activist who would play a central roll in the creation of the CIO, resigned from the Committee of Five in disgust at the "face-saving device" engineered by AFL conservatives.[41]

Recognizing that Lewis's assault had overshadowed their efforts to combat racial exclusion, Young Turks were quick to point out that the creation of the CIO would not lead automatically to interracial unionism. Randolph claimed to be closer to Lewis than any other union leader, but he refused to join the revolt out of fear that the Brotherhood of Sleeping Car Porters and Maids would be dominated by the CIO railway union. The AFL had granted a full charter to the brotherhood only a month earlier, and Randolph preferred to carry on his fight against enemies that he knew rather than unproven friends. "There is no clear-cut pro-Negro or anti-Negro issue involved in the struggle between industrial and craft unionism," Lester Granger wrote a few months after the AFL convention. He applauded Lewis's "direct and savage attack on the time-worn craft machinery of the A.F. of L." and blasted the "traditional Negro leadership" who remained "lukewarm on the matter of Negro membership in unions." Nevertheless, he also cautioned those who displayed "great alacrity in climbing on the Lewis bandwagon in the hope that the new movement spells an end of political maneuvers which have thus far kept Negroes out of many bodies of organized labor." As an example, he cited the case of the United Textile Workers of America, which "made no serious effort" to attack employment discrimination even after 10,000 African Americans joined the union during the 1934 strike. The "central task" facing black workers and activists, Granger insisted, remained organizing black workers—"whether in craft or industrial unions."[42]

The Limits of Industrial Unionism

The slow emergence of interracial unions in the southern lumber industry confirmed Granger's contention that industrial unionism would not lead automatically to organization of African Americans. A few weeks after he led the backlash against the emerging CIO, William Hutcheson headed to the United Brotherhood of Carpenters and Joiners' 1935 annual convention. Union leaders called the convention in Lakeland, Florida, hoping to alienate West Coast sawmill and timber workers who were demanding more power within the union. As a peace gesture, Hutcheson invited the Sawmill and Timber Workers Union to send twenty-seven nonvoting delegates to help the industrial workers "become acquainted" with the Carpenters' "method of doing business." A few of those delegates praised the "yeoman service" they received from Carpenter officials in Washington and Oregon, and stated that they "realize very definitely and appreciate most sincerely the value of being members of this great Brotherhood." When one delegate demanded full voting rights on issues that related to sawmill and timber workers, however, Secretary Frank Duffy flew into a rage, stating that sawmill and timber workers paid lower dues than carpenters but still received financial assistance "when they got into trouble." Charging the sawmill worker with being loyal to the CIO, he declared, "This is a craft organization" and promised "the swellest fight" to any member who sought to change it.[43]

In fact, AFL unions did raise the status of industrial workers in the late 1930s—largely in response to competition from the CIO. In Bogalusa, for example, the Carpenters cooperated with other AFL locals to rebuild the Central Labor Union that had been destroyed during the antiunion violence of 1919. By 1936, the union movement was strong enough to win recognition by the Great Southern Lumber Company. Mayor and general manager E. R. Cassiday declared Labor Day an official holiday that year and even welcomed an AFL-led march into the city park for a celebration. In stark contrast to 1919, Bogalusa hosted the Louisiana Federation of Labor's 1938 annual convention, where six hundred delegates heard an address by populist lieutenant governor Earl Long. The resurgence of Bogalusa's labor movement was facilitated by the organization of semiskilled white men in several industries and even white women who worked in Great Southern's bag and box factories.[44]

Relaxation of skill requirements did not weaken the racial barriers that craft unions had embraced in the 1920s. Great Southern converted gradually in the late 1930s from lumber to paper production, a highly mechanized industry that tolerated unions for white machine operators but relegated black workers to nonunion logging and janitorial positions. As late as 1941, the Negro Firemen and Oilers remained the only union open to African Americans in Bogalusa, despite the fact that several saw-mills continued to employ "a large percentage of negro labor." When AFL officials asked why those workers had not been organized, the Central Labor Union responded that "no one has come to organize them."[45]

West Coast sawmill and timber workers responded to Duffy's out-burst at the 1935 convention by initiating what would become the CIO-affiliated International Woodworkers of America (IWA), but they proved no more enthusiastic than AFL activists toward the prospect of organiz-ing their industry's largely African American southern workforce. The United Mine Workers maintained northern Alabama lumber worker lo-cals after the Carpenters abandoned them in 1935, and the CIO transferred those locals along with a few in Arkansas and West Virginia to the IWA in 1937. Nine thousand southern sawmill workers belonged to these lo-cals, and UWM activists informed the IWA that another 30,000 could be brought into the CIO with assistance from experienced organizers. IWA president Harold Pritchett toured southern sawmill towns in the spring of 1938, and he concluded that the union could double its membership by moving into the South. "Organization of the great southern lumber industry is crucial," he wrote in the union newspaper, "if only for pro-tection of the Northern wage scale and working conditions." Despite his confidence, however, Pritchett failed to convince union members to sup-port a dues increase to fund a southern organizing drive. Between 1938 and 1940, delegates defeated three additional proposals to fund a south-ern organizing drive through increased membership dues.[46]

One factor limiting the Woodworkers' support for the southern cam-paign was a factional dispute among left-wing leaders of the new union. While Communists earned a great deal of respect within the union for their leadership in the 1935 strikes, they faced stiff competition from former members of the Industrial Workers of the World. These "Wob-blies" opposed the southern organizing campaign on the grounds that it diverted resources from strengthening existing locals, an argument that they attributed to their old union's anarcho-syndicalist tradition. Pritchett was not a Communist but many of his close allies were, and the "Wob-blies" succeeded in convincing many Woodworkers that his proposal was only a cynical effort to channel union dues toward Communist political campaigns in the South.[47]

The failure to win northern IWA members' support for a southern organizing drive illustrated a broader limit to Communist influence in the Popular Front. While dissolution of "revolutionary unions" allowed party activists to win unprecedented influence within the CIO, it also forced them to temper political ideals in order to preserve those positions. This tension led the party to shift its attention from the all-black Share Croppers Union to the mostly white Alabama Farmers Union in 1935, and according to Robin Kelley, that shift accompanied a general decline in Communist efforts to organize black workers in the South. Communists played important roles in interracial CIO mining and steel drives in Alabama, but they did little to distinguish themselves politically from the broader trend of the industrial union movement. Southern Communists muted their radicalism even further in 1937, when the party resolved to reach out to white liberals who were beginning to speak out against lynching and antiunion violence. This democratic front proved critical to generating white liberal opposition to the most obvious injustices of Jim Crow, but it also diverted attention from the struggle to bring black southerners into the CIO. By the end of the decade, according to Kelley, Communists were "not so much influencing Alabama liberal opinion as constituting a critical section of it."[48]

Opposition to the IWA's southern organizing drive was also inspired by a vision of southern society that had been popularized by Communists during the most radical phases of the Popular Front. When a Wobbly from Washington State was asked to explain why he and other mill workers had joined the 1935 strikes, he stated that they were radicalized by a superintendent who had been transferred from the South. The new manager had "worked with colored people his whole life," the worker explained, and conflicts erupted when he "started driving us the same way." Another union supporter agreed that strikes were provoked by a manager who "came here from Louisiana where he had nothing but niggers and poor kind of white men to deal with." Implying that African Americans had lower standards of self-respect than white workers, he complained that the new supervisor "cannot, or will not, get used to dealing with a white man."[49]

Even after the CIO severed its remaining ties to the AFL, industrial unionists continued to act on the assumption that white southerners would be more reliable union members than blacks. John L. Lewis announced a major organizing campaign in March 1937, but he focused the southern wing of that campaign almost exclusively on the textile industry. Robert Zieger contends that this decision made sense given the size of the industry and the fact that textile workers had "most recently and relevantly" demonstrated the region's "vigorous traditions of labor protest." Industrial unionists also singled out textiles because "one of the most difficult obstacles to organizing southern workers—the seemingly irreducible barrier of racial antagonism—was not a factor in textiles." As we have seen, such statements were not an objective accounting of historical reality, but rather a subjective assessment shaped by ten years of left-wing and liberal efforts to understand southern working-class consciousness. Textile strikes of 1929 and 1934 were relevant not only for their size and militancy, but also because of the radical potential that radical activists and intellectuals identified in them earlier in the decade. The effort to avoid black workers was not simply an effort to avoid conflict—the textile strikes were hardly uncontroversial—but also to avoid a population that many radicals believed were too oppressed to play a significant role in the labor movement.[50]

On the same day that the *New York Times* announced the CIO's intention to break with the AFL and extend the "right to organize, the privilege of being American" to all workers, the same newspaper ran a third-page story revealing that southern lumber workers would not benefit from that campaign. The paper announced that two hundred men, "mostly Negroes," had launched a strike against the largest hardwood flooring plant in the South. Memphis-based E. L. Bruce Lumber Company had avoided the attention of union activists even as AFL and then CIO garment workers' unions organized the city's white textile and newspaper workers. An "epidemic" of "strikitis" swept through the city in the spring of 1937, according to a local paper, culminating in a march of several thousand union supporters on March 8. That support did not extend to black lumber workers, however, and the day after the garment workers' march, AFL Labor Council president Lev Loring scolded the Bruce workers for striking without first gaining permission from union leaders. "Wildcat strikes hurt the labor movement and the city as a whole," he argued, overlooking the fact that existing unions in the plant had refused to admit the mostly black industrial workers. Local union leaders took a similar position in opposition to one hundred black women who struck a nearby nut processing plant the following week. Testifying to the limits of militant working-class action without at least some support from experienced union activists, a Bruce striker confessed to a reporter that, "We haven't got a union. We don't know how to organize one."[51]

Worse than Jim Crow

Black radical journalist George Schuyler visited Memphis in 1937 during a national tour to assess black participation in the industrial union drives. He reported that thousands of African Americans had joined CIO unions in Pennsylvania, Ohio, and Illinois, and quoted numerous labor organizers who recounted "the loyalty of the Negro workers to the union and their solidarity with the white workers in this struggle. Even in Memphis, AFL leader Lev Loring admitted that "there have been more Negro workers susceptible to labor organization than ever before." Despite evidence that black workers had been eager to join the CIO, however, Schuyler contended that industrial union leaders had failed to nurture their support. He credited the growth in black union membership not to CIO leaders but to black activists—Socialists and Communists, members of the National Negro Congress, and even Garveyites—who viewed unionization as a way to strengthen black working-class communities. He pointed out that leaders of the labor movement had not even taken what had been the first step in bringing southern textile workers into the labor movement—"a training school like Brookwood College . . . , where educated young men and women could be schooled in labor philosophy and tactics." Abram Harris had first proposed such a school of black workers ten years earlier, and Schuyler noted, "Considering this shortcoming the accomplishments of the union in this area is the more surprising."[52]

Southern radicals shared Schuyler's dismay at the CIO's failure to take advantage of the interracial organizing opportunities offered by black working-class militancy, and some feared that this failure would pave the way for a social system even more oppressive than Jim Crow. "The South is Fascist," Lucy Randolph Mason wrote in 1937, "—its domination of the Negro has made it easy to repeat the pattern for organized labor." Reflecting on her work for the National Consumers' League, Mason confided to a friend that she "thought labor was at least getting strong enough to defy the politicians. I was wrong." Popular Front activist and sociologist Katharine DuPre Lumpkin wrote in a 1940 publication that the failure to improve "living standards and civil liberties" in the South had created the danger that "something menacingly akin to fascism" would replace the moment of political possibility created by the New Deal. Members of the Communist-organized Southern Negro Youth Congress agreed, and in 1941 they warned President Roosevelt that antiunion repression in Memphis represented "the beginnings of an American fascist stronghold within our very borders, with its race hatreds, enmity to labor, and suppression of civil liberties."[53]

Those fears inspired a revival of Popular Front activism in the late 1930s. John L. Lewis hired Lucy Randolph Mason to coordinate publicity for the CIO's 1937 southern organizing drive, and she cooperated with other Popular Front activists and intellectuals to promote industrial unionism as a positive force in southern society. The new movement retained some of the racial biases that shaped earlier Popular Front activism in the South, but it also showed more willingness to include African Americans as partners and not simply beneficiaries of radical activism. That willingness was demonstrated at the founding meeting of the Southern Conference on Human Welfare, a coalition of liberal and radical activists that Mason helped form in 1938. Roughly 20 percent of the 1,200 attendees at the meeting were black, and after Birmingham police forced the meeting to segregate itself, a majority of those present voted to hold future events only in places that allowed integrated meetings. The Southern Negro Youth Congress was formed in 1937 by a group of young black Communists who had studied at Howard University earlier in the decade. That group called attention to black working-class militancy by lending their support to a strike of black tobacco workers in Richmond, Virginia. Strikers formed an independent union, but the CIO was impressed enough to fund efforts to extend organization to larger firms over the following few years.[54]

Contrary to the assertion that interracial unionism emerged organically from the industrial union movement of the 1930s, CIO unions devoted significant attention to organizing southern industries with large black workforces only during World War II. Inspired by the Richmond tobacco workers' strike, CIO leaders awarded jurisdiction over southern tobacco workers to the United Cannery, Agricultural, Packing, and Allied Workers of America, a left-wing union that emerged out of interracial farmworkers' movements in the late 1930s. Cannery Workers' organizer Harry Koger organized a two-week leadership training school for Memphis workers in July 1940 with aid from his union's Communist leaders and Socialist activists Claude Williams and Myles Horton. Koger was hired by the International Woodworkers of America a few months later, and CIO unions cooperated to build a vibrant and mostly African American Industrial Union Council in Memphis. "I have not seen anywhere more spontaneous activity on the part of workers," Lucy Randolph Mason reported from Memphis in the fall of 1940, "with the large number of Negroes especially interested and desperately needing organization." Over the next decade, black lumber workers would play a central role in building on the support that industrial unionists began to give to interracial organizing in the South.[55]

6 Black Working-Class Politics in the Postwar South

A labor shortage and increased federal protection provided black and white lumber workers with an opportunity to finally translate their shared economic aspirations into a coherent and sustainable social movement during World War II. The movement also depended upon support that both AFL and CIO leaders began to lend to interracial unionism in the South during the war. Impressed by black workers' enthusiastic support for union movements in several cities in 1941 and inspired by A. Philip Randolph's 1942 March on Washington movement, union as well as civil rights leaders became convinced that working-class African Americans could play an important role in the political transformation of the South. Support for interracial unionism declined in 1943, following a series of violent protests by white workers who opposed racial equality, but even AFL leaders remained committed to organizing black southerners following the war.

Black lumber workers discovered a variety of strategies for building unions in the postwar South. In Alabama, CIO members adopted a race-neutral approach that sought to unite black and white workers around common economic grievances. This approach did not transcend racial politics. In fact, black workers often gained important protections that white workers already enjoyed. Nevertheless, economics did provide enough common ground for unionization in sawmills where black and white workers were employed in equal numbers. That was not the case in eastern North Carolina, where white workers typically refused to join what they saw as a black union movement. In that context, black union members pushed the CIO to take a more overtly racial approach to organizing than in Alabama. By the early 1950s, mostly black lumber unions were beginning to revive a model of "civil rights unionism" that left-wing unions had developed in that state during the war. A third approach developed in Louisiana, where overtly racist AFL unions relegated black union members to essentially powerless subordinate organizations of white-dominated locals. Rather than abandoning those unions to whites, black industrial workers used the emerging civil rights movement to force those union to represent them. Finally gaining institutional support for their economic agendas, black lumber workers demonstrated that they could exert a conscious and influential working-class voice in southern politics.

"The Army Needs Lumber"

Having rejected government cooperation following the collapse of the NRA, southern lumbermen once again reversed their position when wartime mobilization offered a lasting solution to the Great Depression. British military orders began flowing into southern lumber firms in the spring of 1940, and by the fall U.S. military orders topped two billion board feet per month, making the government the nation's largest lumber consumer. Southern Democrats dominated congressional defense committees, and Roosevelt secured their support for the war mobilization by locating 60 of 100 planned bases in southern states. "The need for lumber and lumber products in this war can hardly be over-emphasized," said Undersecretary of War Robert P. Patterson. "Southern lumber is now filling a big share of this need, but the demand is far ahead of the supply and is growing steadily."[1]

The benefits of cooperating with the government were "incidental but very large," according to the Southern Pine Association. In addition to furthering ongoing efforts toward price stabilization in the chronically competitive industry, military contractors demanded far more southern pine than firms could produce between 1941 and 1945. Proclaiming that the war effort required "more than ordinary means of cooperation," the SPA repeated Patterson's challenge proudly: "The production of lumber will play an important part in determining the date of final victory." Metal shortages increased the demand for lumber as builders replaced steel girders with wood beams for heavy construction. Government inspectors relaxed grade specifications, allowing a wider use of less valuable wood and allowing government buyers to pay more for high grades when low grades were not available. Rather than waiting for low-grade lumber to cure, contractors used high-grade lumber (which did not warp as quickly) for everything from airplanes to railroad ties. Ben Greene noted with pride that Greene Brothers Lumber Company's high-grade mark adorned the pine beams in a Texas airplane hanger that he toured during the war.[2]

On September 21, 1940, the *New Orleans Times-Picayune* reported that the SPA had "voted unanimously to forgive and forget its quarrel with President Roosevelt and his New Deal policies, and to rally the whole Southern Pine industry with all its resources to support the emergency of national defense." Resuming a role perfected under the NRA, the SPA organized a Southern Pine War Committee (SPWC) "for the sole purpose of helping the Government in every way possible to secure its requirements in lumber." C. C. Sheppard left his position in the anti–New Deal Southern States Industrial Council to head the SPWC. He promised that in addition to raising government-imposed price ceilings and maintaining access to timber and equipment, the SPWC would work with the government to ensure access to "adequate manpower," which was "by far the gravest problem" faced by southern lumber firms during the war.[3]

Having fought so heartily against increased wages in the 1930s, southern lumber mills found themselves unable to compete with "high wage war industries" such as shipbuilding, base construction, and airfields. Competition forced prevailing wages for common sawmill labor above the minimum in 1943, the first time since NRA established a minimum ten years earlier. Prevailing wages in southern mills reached forty cents per hour, but starting wages for unskilled workers rose to sixty cents in some competing industries. North Carolina sawmills reported a "rather acute labor situation" due to competition from a Marine Corps air base. Lumbermen in several states complained that military contractors were sending busses and trucks into sawmill communities looking to recruit laborers. Others complained "of so many local government projects that are paying higher wages than we can pay." A Louisiana mill reported the loss of several "good men" to the laundry at a nearby Army base. The operator of the mill, along with an SPA field man and a U.S. Employment Service representative, visited the head officer of the base to "explain the critical need for workers in lumber plants." The SPWC "hoped these workers can be released for return to the sawmill," and blamed labor and timber shortages and government price controls for a 30 percent drop in lumber production between 1941 and 1943.[4]

Wages and working conditions in southern lumber mills remained so poor that mills began losing workers even to agriculture. An Alabama lumberman complained that his workers were "leaving for farm work."

North Carolina sawmills faced "considerable difficulty" from nearby shipyards and wartime housing construction, but claimed that they lost even more workers during the agricultural season. Mill owners even complained of a "Back to the Farm" movement in 1943 caused by draft deferments granted to workers who could prove that they were "necessary to and regularly engaged in an agricultural occupation." White workers had organized "Back to the Farm" movements in the 1930s to force black workers out of urban industrial jobs. The war had so thoroughly disrupted southern labor markets that African Americans were now returning to farms voluntarily with the hope of gaining draft exemptions. With farm labor excluded from the draft, lumber firms claimed to be supplying the bulk of draftees from rural areas. The SPWC predicted that 10 million lumber workers would be drafted by the end of 1943.[5]

By the fall of 1942, southern lumbermen were desperate to stabilize their labor supply. A survey of 597 mills, representing 40 percent of total southern pine production, showed that over 19,000 workers left the industry between January and July 1942. Sixty-three percent of them went to military construction jobs and railroads, while 15 percent joined the military. Roughly 17,000 workers replaced them, according to the SPWC, but most were aged or inexperienced. One exasperated Louisiana employer told a War Manpower Commission representative that "if some of these experts can tell us how to get men to swamp and cut down trees during the hot summer months, they will go far in solving our problems." Members of the SPWC traveled to the Pentagon in 1943 where they and the War Department drafted a "comprehensive program of morale-building in the Southern lumber industry." The "main feature" of the program was a 375–man Army Salute to Wood Caravan consisting of army speakers, soldiers, and "a returned hero," who traveled four thousand miles throughout the southern pine belt speaking to a "representative sample" of the industry's workforce. In a scene reminiscent of a military parade, lumber workers armed with axes and saws marched alongside troops and military vehicles to generate an audience for each show.[6]

According to an SPA press release, the purpose of the caravan was "to impress the lumber industry employee with the importance of his job—the material he produces—the seriousness of the production picture in the South." Working with local chambers of commerce and Boy Scout troops, speakers urged southern lumber workers to increase their production, decrease absenteeism, and reduce "the migration of workers to other industries." To persuade employers to stop production so that workers could attend the shows, the SPWC pointed out that the War Department had removed soldiers from the battlefield to support the effort because "the Army needs lumber."[7]

Such accolades to the southern lumber workforce presented a challenge to employers' long-standing argument that rural southerners were shiftless and inefficient. Sawmills had an easier time holding on to experienced workers because they were closer to towns and offered more regular employment, allowing them to hire women and "a family-type man," according to the U.S. War Production Board. Logging camps, on the other hand, were "usually isolated," rarely provided "accommodations for families" or remained in "fixed locations," and "often involve dangerous work." They attracted "a more nomadic type of labor." In March 1943, southern lumbermen reported being short 48,599 loggers, or 29 percent of their required manpower. One firm had so much difficulty employing experienced loggers that it closed its mill sporadically so that experienced workers could supervise both sawmill and logging operations. Hardwood production was particularly affected, as it required "skill due to number of species and complexity of grading system." Backing off previous complaints about "sub-standard labor," C. C. Sheppard explained that the "hardwood logger is in every sense a skilled worker."[8]

Previous efforts to depress wage scales also meant many experienced lumber workers did not qualify for draft exemptions designed to keep skilled "key personnel" in "essential" manufacturing jobs. To help members deal with "draft problems," the SPA distributed lists of "essential" occupations and worked closely with the Selective Service and the War Manpower Commission to secure releases for "key employees." A North Carolina mill complained that few of its skilled workers remained, and that it depended on "Army rejects" who refused to work "half the time." Another mill reported "working the culls" because shipyards and the military "already have our best men." To remedy this problem, War Manpower Commission officials asked lumber firms to reduce weekly operation to forty-eight hours when possible, and advised local Selective Service officers to increase the number of draft exemptions given to low-wage lumber workers.[9]

Southern lumbermen were infuriated by black men's sudden ability to find better-paid work. At an SPA meeting, one mill owner recounted his dismay with one such worker. "A nigger that I raised—I was quite proud of the nigger, I thought he was pretty smart—come by with a check for $92 for a week's work." Indicating how disrupting the experience had been, the employer exclaimed, "That's more than I make." Another mill owner complained about defense projects that sent trucks into his mill town to recruit "Niggers we raised and that have been there to the third generation—before the third generation was born—we have been operating there for forty years." Claiming to have acted as a doctor, lawyer, nurse, banker, "and everything else" for black employees, the lumberman complained that the workers abandoned him "for those people because they are paid 55 cents and 50 cents." Painting an apocalyptic picture of wartime labor markets, he cried, "I've seen niggers eat canned peaches that we don't even have ourselves. They have raised the standard of living down there."[10]

Some southern pine mills simply closed in the face of labor shortages during the war. In a 1943 letter to the *Arkansas Gazette,* sawmill owner Carl White complained that the labor shortage had gotten worse over the past two years "until labor is practically out of control." He had reduced operations from sixty to forty hours per week due to overtime pay standards; "It seemed the more we paid our men, the less they worked." A year earlier, he complained, War Labor Board inspectors had fined him for failing to pay workers for travel time between the mill and the logging operations. He built a camp in the woods, but "the men refused to stay there." Frustrated by the "outsiders" and "government agencies" who traveled around on "the taxpayer's money, creating discord and disrupting the otherwise pleasant relationships existing between employer and employees," White announced that he was closing his sawmill.[11]

As they had during previous labor shortages, other southern lumbermen attempted to counteract black mobility through forced labor. In May 1943, a Florida attorney reported to a U.S. district attorney that one lumber company hired retired men in logging and stacking jobs but ordered their arrests if they "cannot hold up at the work and wish to be relieved." The Federal Bureau of Investigation pursued the complaint but found "no case for prosecution." Under pressure from the NAACP, the Communist Party, the CIO packinghouse union, and other groups, the Department of Justice began investigating a rash of peonage cases at southern sawmills in 1941. That agency proved slightly more effective than the FBI. In April 1943, Luther Carter left O'Neal Bodiford's Lowndes County, Alabama, sawmill without paying his debt at a local store and took another sawmill job in Bay Minette, on the Gulf Coast. Bodiford and the store owner tracked Carter down, and in the absence of his new employer ordered him at gunpoint to return to "be held as a slave" in Lowndes County. The two men forced Carter into a truck and "beat him severely with a large stick." After hearing of the incident, the new employer had the slave catchers arrested in the adjoining county. The U.S. attorney general declared the men's conviction "a great victory and . . . a forward step in the protection of civil rights."[12]

In addition to being illegal, peonage required cooperation from other local employers. E. P. Ahern, who operated a veneer mill in Allen, Alabama, complained to the Secretary of Labor that logging contractors in the area used physical violence and the threat of "arrests on trumped-up charges" to force African Americans to work for wages at or below the minimum wage. Ahern wrote of Eb Horne, who received death threats after quitting his job and was recently arrested on trumped-up charges and held on a $500 bond. He would soon be convicted, Ahern predicted, and paroled into the custody of his former employers. Another black man quit the local logging operation for a job with the U.S. postal service. When the logging contractor and his two two-hundred-pound brothers confronted the man on a "lonely road . . . The negro 'sassed' them, so the white men set upon him and beat him unmercifully." Ahern observed that "it was a mighty feeble minded colored man who would, 'sass' three men of their size in the deep south." Nevertheless, he wanted to "compete freely and equally for the labor" and did not "want to see the cream of the labor leave town because of these conditions." His competitors were "strong politically" and could "literally get away with murder in this county." He hoped to persuade African Americans to testify but believed that even whites, "although they do not condone the actions of these men, would not testify against them."[13]

Southern employers also reverted to prison labor during the war. In the fall of 1942, the U.S. Army agreed to relieve crowded British prison camps of 150,000 German and Italian prisoners. Nearly all of these prisoners were housed in southern prison camps, and starting in 1943 the Army began contracting them out to sawmills. While language and lack of experience limited the value of prison labor, white supervisors' racial ideologies helped them overlook those barriers. Ben Greene recalled that one foreman told him that German prisoners "caught on a lot faster than the average person around here," a comment that Greene interpreted as a "racial slur." Greene remarked that the German prisoners "were just Anglo-Saxon, some of Hitler's elite, apparently. And they were pretty sharp people."[14]

In addition to using forced labor, mill owners supplemented their labor supplies by hiring women. The SPA reported that roughly 400 white women and 350 black women were employed by thirty-four surveyed mills in 1941. The SPWC estimated that "several hundred more" were working in other plants. Reporting that women provided "practically the same satisfactory service" and efficiency as male workers and that women were "enthusiastic and conscientious" and rarely absent, the SPWC compared this female "battalion" to the WACs, WAVEs, and other government programs that encouraged women to work, thus "freeing men to fight."[15]

As did other employers during the war, southern lumbermen promoted female industrial employment as a temporary response to the wartime emergency. "Nearly all the women workers interviewed at the mills, both white and colored, said they are working in the lumber plants to help win the war—back up their men-folks in the armed forces and to make additional money to increase the family budget," claimed an SPWC pamphlet. Women appreciated their jobs as "lumber Jills," but would "be glad" to give them up when the men returned, the pamphlet continued, since most had families and were working "double duty" during the war. To demonstrate that industrial employment had not disrupted women's traditional roles, the pamphlet described a white employee who, in addition to "felling trees" all week, "kept house for her husband and seven children, a step-brother and a boarder, milked two cows night and morning, made butter for the family and attended to other household duties with the help of her older children."[16]

Black women had long since become accustomed to such double duty, but racial employment practices prevented employers from taking advantage of their willingness to engage in wage work. The SPWC reported that black women were less "enthusiastic about working" in sawmills, which they interpreted as evidence that they felt less "of a sense of duty and interest in assisting in the war effort." A more likely explanation is that black women faced the same job restrictions that led black men to seek other forms of employment. The SPWC reported that white women were typically employed as saw filers and craftsmen's helpers—"lighter work and in certain jobs requiring intelligence, skill and dexterity." Black women, on the other hand, were restricted to the heavy jobs traditionally reserved for black men. Neither black nor white women worked in logging, employers reported, "which is considered too strenuous for their physical capacities." The Kirby Lumber Company, which employed 125 women at five Texas sawmills, reported that white women were "not quite so productive as men" in heavy work but excelled in stamping and stenciling jobs and in cleaning up. Filling traditional black male jobs, two black women operated the trimmer and the rip saw while two others loaded lumber into freight cars. Thirty white women operated stitching machines in a box plant in Brewton, Alabama, while twenty-eight black women fired boilers and handled lumber in the same firm's planing mill.

An Arkansas lumber company spotlighted two female employees who achieved the highest status on their racially segregated occupational ladders. Julia Alice Wilcox, a white graduate of the University of Arkansas, worked as a water chemist. "Florence S. Hill, colored, operated the ripsaw, which required knowledge of lumber grades."[17]

As prevailing wage scales rose, neither black nor white women accepted the lowest-paid jobs that southern lumber firms had previously filled with black men. "We cannot solve our labor problem entirely with woman-power, because a large number of sawmill jobs are too heavy for them to handle," complained an Arkansas firm. Women also showed the same tendencies as male workers did, leaving sawmill work when they could find better-paying jobs. A Florida mill owner complained that a local airfield had begun running daily buses to his mill town, taking women to work as maids and laundry attendants for $25 per week. A Louisiana sawmill owner complained that his female employees "went to the laundries because it was easier work." Revealing the economic dynamics involved in such decisions, the SPWC concluded that black women avoided sawmill work because "their husbands are generally making more money than ever before."[18]

Opening a Window of Opportunity

One alternative to leaving lumber employment was to raise wages through unionization, and the labor shortage sparked a resurgence of the interracial militancy that plagued southern lumber firms in the 1930s. The first interracial union to sign a contract with a southern lumber firm in the 1940s affiliated not with the CIO but with the AFL's Sawmill and Timber Workers Union. The location of this development could hardly have been more symbolic than Lacoochee, Florida, the company town where Cummer and Sons Lumber Company had settled its black employees after the Rosewood massacre in 1923. It is unclear whether any members of the new union had actually witnessed the racist attack, but many certainly knew survivors or had heard of the incident. Managers capitalized on the memory of Rosewood when they warned union activists to "stop your members from mass picketing and going about the negro quarters. This can only lead to trouble, which we all desire to avoid." Federal investigators reported that provocations were working to stir up tensions between black and white workers, and warned that the town was on the brink of "bloodshed" and "extreme violence." Nevertheless, black and white workers found enough common ground to organize a union in the fall of 1940, and by March of the following year, 489 of Cummer's 750 employees voted for unionization in an election conducted by the National Labor Relations Board (NLRB). Building on that mandate, local union leaders enlisted nearly five hundred blacks and two hundred whites by July 4, 1941.[19]

Economics provided a basis for cooperation between black and white workers in Lacoochee, but the union could not avoid the racial politics that so deeply marked the social and political lives of its members. Cummer and Sons refused to bargain with the new union initially, but a month-long strike forced the firm to raise wages five cents above the current minimum wage and to pay time and a half for overtime and holiday work. For black union members, the very fact that they had voted in a federally supervised election represented a transformation that only deepened when they sat down to negotiate with their employers. Workers were empowered to elect a committee of their peers that would represent them "in the adjustment of all complaints with the management of the Company in the manner hereinafter set forth." In the context of a political system that granted few legal protections to black workers, the democratic provisions of the new union contract must have seemed revolutionary to all involved.[20]

The first grievances taken up by the new union demonstrated the degree to which unionization undermined social relations that had become the norm during more than a half-century of Jim Crow. A group of black workers charged the company with cheating them out of overtime pay, a dispute that union representatives discovered grew out of mutual confusion over complicated work schedules and weather-related work stoppages. The union persuaded managers to simplify the work schedule and to pay the wages that workers believed were owed to them. The second conflict erupted when managers suspended credit lines that they had previously issued to workers at the company store. Workers had not objected to losing credit—they had just won a significant wage increase—but the union committee persuaded the firm to collect debts in weekly paycheck deductions rather than the full amount immediately as originally planned. Each of these disputes represented daily, even minor, conflicts that would previously have been settled unilaterally by managers. Starting in 1941, they were negotiated between managers and the democratically elected representatives of both black and white workers.[21]

Following the victory in Lacoochee, both AFL and CIO unions became more willing to support efforts to organize sawmill and timber workers in the South. Three years after they denounced the strike at E. L. Bruce Lumber Company, Memphis AFL leaders lent their support to a strike at a neighboring sawmill in 1941. Four Sawmill and Timber worker locals were "doing well" in Memphis and nearby Helena, Arkansas, according to government inspectors who noted that AFL leaders were "tickled pink" by a contract that workers won by the strike at Gates Lumber Company. Mediators also reported that managers had "followed the closed shop agreement 100%." The CIO Woodworkers' union remained embroiled in factional disputes on the West Coast and even allowed a 1941 strike at Belcher Lumber Company in Alabama (where the NRA strikes had begun) to die for lack of support. John L. Lewis grew tired of servicing Alabama sawmill locals that had defected from the AFL in 1935, and he sent anticommunist troubleshooter Adolph Germer to arrange a settlement between factions. Communists lost support as a result of a Soviet alliance with Hitler in 1939, and Germer supported the Wobblies' bid for control in return for their support for a southern organizing drive. By that point, none of Alabama's sawmill locals continued to operate. IWA leaders chose to focus their efforts on Memphis where AFL unions had already demonstrated the possibility of organizing interracial lumber unions.[22]

Building on the momentum started by CIO organizer Harry Koger, two IWA activists began recruiting workers at Nickey Lumber Company and the Mississippi Valley Hardwood Company in Memphis. Both firms produced wood for defense contractors, which ensured that federal mediators would arrive quickly to ensure that labor conflicts did not hinder production. The president of Mississippi Valley also worked for the federal Office of Price Administration, which made union activists hopeful that he would respect the collective bargaining process. As their counterparts had in Lacoochee, CIO activists found that racial politics became inseparable from the task of building a union. The IWA won elections in both plants in September, and by 1942 IWA activists claimed to have recruited more than two thousand woodworkers in Memphis. "Since the vast majority of employees are negroes," a federal mediator reported, "practically all the negroes belong to the CIO with some of the whites also." Workers elected Lee Christian as president of the Mississippi Valley local, making him perhaps the first black president of a southern lumber union since Sol Dacus was driven out of Bogalusa in 1919. Beatrice Moore became the first female IWA officer when she was elected to the executive committee at Nickey.[23]

Employers also noted the racial implications of the union movement. Federal mediators complained that despite his position in the federal government, the president of Mississippi Valley Lumber Company "acted as if he was doing a great favor by meeting with the union" and insisted that "his word is final in everything." Even after his employees launched an eight-week strike that established black workers as "the core of CIO support" in the city, mediators concluded that "conciliation of differences [is] hopeless in this case." Federal officials avoided mention of the racial dynamics involved in this and other conflicts, but a union organizer noted, "The workers in this plant are all colored, which may have something to do with the Company's attitude toward negotiating seriously." At Nickey, white workers maintained an AFL union even after the black majority had voted to designate the CIO their legal representative. Federal mediators reported that "although legally speaking from the standpoint of collective bargaining they do not exist, there is a constant source of friction between the two rival unions." Ironically, AFL members benefited from the wage increase and overtime pay regulations that IWA activists secured through the strike at that mill.[24]

A base in Memphis allowed IWA organizers to expand into the rural South. In February, the union won a WLB election at the Anderson-Tully sawmill, the largest in Memphis. Hearing of this victory, workers at the firm's three Vicksburg, Mississippi, sawmills wrote to the union asking for assistance with their own organizing campaign. Anderson-Tully was stalling in negotiations with the Memphis local, and IWA officials hoped that the Vicksburg workers could help them turn up the pressure. Frank Davis, a black worker who joined the IWA staff in Memphis, and white Louisiana native Claude Welsh drove 250 miles south in March 1943, hoping to organize 1,200 workers in the heart of the piney woods of southern Mississippi. A mob of white men kidnapped Davis and Welsh after the first union meeting and drove them out of town, where they stripped them naked, tied them to a tree, and beat them with lead-filled rubber hoses. Federal officials arrived in town soon after that, providing enough protection that the IWA won an election 572 to 42 at Anderson-Tully's Waltersville sawmill just outside Vicksburg. After establishing a base at the largest mill, the IWA organizers moved on to the firm's smaller mills. The IWA won elections at Anderson-Tully's remaining two mills on July 16 and at six other Vicksburg sawmills before the end of September. On October 21, 1943, Anderson-Tully became the first Mississippi company to sign a contract with the CIO.[25]

Bolstered by their role in the NRA debates, Young Turks took advantage of this second wave of black working-class activism to finally convince civil rights and labor organizations to unite in support of black unionism. In the summer of 1941, the NAACP and the NUL and nearly every black political or intellectual leader fell behind A. Philip Randolph's call for a march on Washington to demand equal employment in defense industries and the armed forces. Impressed by the breadth of black support for the movement, and desperate to maintain smooth operations in preparation for war, Roosevelt conceded to Randolph's central demand even before the march took place. In an unprecedented federal affirmation of racial equality, the president created the Fair Employment Practice Committee (FEPC) to prevent discrimination by government agencies or recipients of defense contracts. In that same year, a series of strikes in defense plants prompted similar attention to workplace rights that had been highlighted by the industrial union movement of the 1930s. Having hesitated to enforce the National Labor Relations Act during a Supreme Court review of the law in the late 1930s, Roosevelt accepted the strike wave as a mandate for tighter government regulation of labor relations. He empowered a body of federal agencies including the National Defense Mediation Board, the National War Labor Board, the War Production Board, and the War Manpower Commission to prevent industrial conflict through recognition of unions and government-imposed mediation. Illustrating the respect that Young Turks had gained in national political circles, Roosevelt appointed Robert Weaver as head of Negro Employment and Training for each of these agencies.[26]

Cooperation between labor and civil rights activists and protection from the federal government lent a critical boost to black working-class militancy in the 1940s. In Detroit, Chicago, and other northern cities, NAACP, NUL, and CIO activists joined forces to raise wages and improve working conditions while also defending and extending the civil rights of African Americans. Interracial solidarity was more difficult in the South, but in industries such as tobacco and cotton processing where black workers formed large majorities, unions could afford to sacrifice white support by pushing on civil rights. The CIO cannery union (renamed the Food, Tobacco, and Allied Workers of America) united with the NAACP and other civil rights organizations to build black-led unions in Memphis and Winston-Salem, North Carolina. Left-wing unions with large black minorities such as the Packinghouse Workers, the Transport Workers, and the Mine, Mill, and Smelter Workers also succeeded in building support among their white members for black job promotion, desegregation and political equality. When the liberal Rosenwald Fund commissioned Charles S. Johnson to study black activism in 1942, the sociologist concluded that "the characteristic movements among Negroes are now for the first time becoming proletarian, as contrasted to upper class or intellectual influence that was typical of previous movements." It was in that context that sociologists St. Clair Drake and Horace Cayton described the CIO as a "crusading movement" in which "Belief in racial equality was a component part of its ideology, and was kept constantly before the membership by a vigorous left-wing minority within the CIO."[27]

The Limits of Civil Rights Unionism

Having convinced labor and civil rights leaders that black workers could benefit from union membership, the Young Turks faced the more formidable task of winning white working-class support for racial equality. The limits of civil rights unionism were made clear on May 24, 1943, when four thousand young white men and women rampaged through the Alabama Dry Dock and Shipbuilding Company in Mobile using pipes, wrenches, and other weapons to drive black workers from the yard. The riot was touched off by an FEPC order promoting twelve black men into skilled welding positions, and subsequent investigations concluded that racial tensions had been provoked by the rapid influx of both African Americans and white women into jobs previously reserved for white men. Federal officials responded to the backlash by creating a segregated shipyard where black workers could advance into skilled positions without challenging white jobs or racial sensibilities. Civil rights leaders interpreted the compromise as a "step backward" and an "emasculation" of the FEPC. Using the antifascist language that had been effective in fighting racism early in the war, one black newspaper decried the retreat as an appeasement of "Nazi racial theory and another defeat for the principle embodied in the Declaration of Independence."[28]

The Mobile riot marked a turning point in the rise of civil rights unionism. White supremacists attacked black communities in Baumont and Brownsville, Texas; and Detroit, Chicago, and Los Angeles in the months following the incident, evoking memories of the "Red Summer" of 1919. White workers also staged "hate strikes" in Detroit, Chicago, Philadelphia, and Baltimore, refusing to work alongside black workers who had been promoted into previously all-white positions by the FEPC. In places where CIO unions had taken a leading role in protecting black civil rights, they became increasingly concerned that such actions would alienate them from whites. For example, union leaders praised black activist Elijah Jackson initially for organizing black workers in the Mobile shipyard and "restoring to this group confidence in the CIO." Following the riot, leaders of the CIO shipbuilders' union accused Jackson of "functioning solely as a fomenter of racial hatred" and transferred him from the city.[29]

As they had in 1919, southern lumber employers greeted the wave of racist violence as an opportunity to crush the small interracial movement that had appeared in their mills. Alarmed by IWA's success in Vicksburg, the Southern Pine Association called a meeting in Jackson, Mississippi, where members pledged $75,000 to counter unionization efforts in the industry. Establishing a model that would be followed by lumber firms throughout the South after the war, Anderson-Tully fired union leaders in Memphis and Vicksburg and informed the IWA that all negotiations would be conducted through a labor relations firm located in Detroit. The Southern Pine Association created a Labor Information Service to keep records on union campaigns and help members stay abreast of labor laws in the postwar period. Ignoring threats of strikes and government sanctions, Anderson-Tully refused to renew the contract signed in 1943. The NWLB found Anderson-Tully guilty of four counts of unfair labor practices on April 27, 1945, but failed to coerce the employer back to the negotiating table. Supported by the SPA, southern lumber companies used similar stall tactics to roll back the modest gains made by the AFL and the CIO between 1941 and 1943. By April 1944, the IWA held only two contracts in the South, with Nickey Brothers in Memphis and the Cleveland Lumber Company in Walker County, Alabama. The Carpenters fared slightly better, with five contracts near Crossett, Arkansas, and single contracts in Alabama, Mississippi, and Texas. The UMW maintained one sawmill local in Walker County and another in Macon, Georgia.[30]

Industrial unionists were divided on how best to respond to white workers' rejection of racial equality in 1943. On one hand, left-wing leaders of CIO Food and Tobacco Workers and Packinghouse Workers unions argued that racial differences could be overcome in the same way that industrial unions had overcome ethnic and national differences in the previous decade. In Chicago, for example, "the CIO took every opportunity to advertise what a multi-ethnic community it had become" in the late 1930s. Union staff were selected "painstakingly" to reflect the ethnic diversity of their constituents, according to historian Liz Cohen, and members "flaunted their internationalism" by wearing ethnic clothing and sharing traditional food and music at union events. The Tobacco and Packinghouse unions adopted similar strategies when they organized largely African American workforces in Memphis, Winston-Salem, North Carolina, and Fort Worth, Texas. Even after 1943, those CIO unions made a point of developing black leadership and highlighting African American history and culture at union events.[31]

On the other hand, leaders of more powerful CIO mining, textile, and shipbuilding unions responded to the 1943 backlash by tempering their support for racial equality. "We are not mentioning the color of people," declared Van Bittner, a UMW organizer who played a central role in shaping CIO southern campaigns in the 1940s. William Smith, who directed unionization at the Mobile shipyard and then headed CIO organizing in North Carolina following the war, denounced the "negro nationalist ap-

proach" employed by Tobacco and Packinghouse unions. He claimed to
support organization of black workers, but argued that civil rights unionism created "material [that] could very easily boomerang on us and be
used" to turn white workers against the CIO. Phillip Murray, who succeeded John L. Lewis as president of the CIO, told the *Saturday Evening
Post* that he hired only "practical" organizers to lead CIO campaigns in
the South and avoided "theorists who want a freshly laundered world next
Monday morning." The conservative *Post* approved of this direction and
reported favorably that "Bittner and his associates are hewing singly to
the job of building unions, and they have no desire at the moment to
undertake a crusading job on race relations. That, they think, is someone
else's wrestling match."[32]

Left-wing unions made impressive gains in the South during the war,
but white backlash against racial equality and a related backlash against
the Communist Party limited their influence within the CIO after 1945.
That year, Murray named Bittner to head Operation Dixie, an ambitious
southern organizing drive endowed with a million-dollar budget and 250
organizers. Returning to a racial strategy adopted by AFL and CIO leaders in the 1930s, Bittner focused the campaign on southern textile mills,
with the intention of expanding into interracial industries after he had
established an initial base in the largely white industry. AFL president
William Green announced that his federation would also launch a southern organizing drive in 1946, and *Fortune* magazine observed that the
CIO's retreat from racial equality meant that similarities now "far out-
weighed the differences" between the two union federations.[33]

What distinguished the postwar campaigns from earlier efforts to
organize the South was black workers' ability to sway both CIO and AFL
unions toward addressing racial inequality. Empowered by labor shortages and federal intervention and emboldened by increased cooperation
between civil rights and labor organizations, black workers emerged from
the war prepared to use labor unions as vehicles in their struggle to establish industrial wage work as a basis for economic and social security.
Operation Dixie's initial textile campaigns faltered due to well-organized
opposition from employers and lack of enthusiasm from white workers.
Bittner fired campaign leader Dean Culver for lack of progress after a few
months, and he dismissed two more leaders before the end of 1946. The
CIO lost more than half of the representation elections that they requested in southern textile mills, and most union leaders agreed that the campaign had been defeated even before it began. Reporting from Alabama,
however, an IWA organizer insisted that "the relative slowness of the
drive in textiles does not reflect the success of the drive as a whole in this

state." Bittner had barred the IWA from North Carolina and Georgia—so as to focus on the "larger potential" that he saw in textiles—but he allowed woodworkers to extend their wartime gains into southern Alabama. After a year, a union representative boasted, "Tremendous victories have been won in this state in wood, steel, and auto."[34]

Race-Neutral Unionism

While IWA activists challenged Bittner's focus on textiles, they did not reject his belief that unions should avoid addressing racial inequality. Building on its success in Memphis, the IWA supported union drives in six southern Alabama sawmills operated by Chapman-based W. T. Smith Lumber Company. W. T. Smith had gained labor leaders' attention during the war when federal mediators listed it as the largest of four "southern lumber mills known to have low wages and poor working conditions." Except for a mill in Montgomery, which employed "all Negroes," mediators also noted that the firm hired relatively equal numbers of black and white workers. Black union member Ire Abrams recalled that black and white workers "got along well" because they were accustomed to working together at the mill and that IWA activists used that commonality to transcend the racial differences among them. The union adopted a race-neutral approach that coincided with Bittner's efforts to distance the CIO from civil rights unionism. This strategy also echoed one developed by the United Mine Workers in Alabama—the union for which Bittner worked before joining the CIO staff. This "UMW Formula" rested on the belief that unions could survive in the Jim Crow South only by remaining neutral on the question of racial inequality. By addressing only economic issues, union activists reasoned, they could transcend the racial differences that divided black and white workers.[35]

But it was impossible to avoid racial politics in the context of Jim Crow. Central to the UMW Formula was an assumption that white workers would control the top offices in union locals and regional federations, even when black workers predominated among the membership. IWA activists adopted this practice in Chapman on the assumption that managers would not deal with a black-led union. They also erected their union hall in East Chapman, an all-white community outside the limits of the company town. The union launched a strike in 1949 after W. T. Smith refused to renew the contract that had been in place since 1945. Even as union leaders applauded the solidarity that black and white workers showed on picket lines, the union maintained segregated seating at union meetings and elected all-white negotiating

teams to deal with W. T. Smith. The union launched a second strike in
1955, the same year that a bus boycott helped launch the modern civil
rights movement in nearby Montgomery. Several black workers at W. T.
Smith also helped to build an NAACP chapter in Greenville, where they
launched a boycott of businesses that did not cater to African Americans. The union "didn't take no specific role" in the fight against segregation, according to black worker Roy Gandy, because that movement
was "not just directed at the company."[36]

Indeed, contrary to the belief that Jim Crow limited black workers'
class consciousness, racial inequality seems to have made African Americans more supportive of unionization than white men. George Cheatham
explained that he and other black men joined the Chapman IWA local in
order to force company managers to "have some respect" for them. "That's
what a union's for, that's the reason more people join them," he recalled,
noting that without a union, "the man just kick you around just like he
want to, mistreat you, do you like a dog." Although white workers certainly benefited from union membership, Cheatham assumed that union
membership was not as important to them as it was for blacks. "The white
man mostly had more rights than blacks did at the time. Part of what we
had to fight for, he probably got anyway." Sociologist Charles Peavey corroborated Cheatham's recollections when he observed a union drive near
Chapman in 1948. He noted that the IWA lost representation elections
only in logging departments, where the majority of workers were white
men, but won in the sawmill and box factory, which employed mostly
black men and both white and black women.[37]

Civil Rights Unionism

The success of lumber unions in Alabama, along with the failure of
textile unions in North Carolina, convinced CIO leaders to invest more
resources toward organizing the southern lumber industry. In a July 1946
article, the *Saturday Evening Post* announced that lumber was "No. 2 on
the CIO agenda." Pointing out that the industry employed "a heavy percentage of Negro labor," the magazine surmised, "A quick look at traditional prejudice easily satisfies the neutral observer that lumber will be a
tough ear to shuck." Skepticism about organizing black southerners also
arose at the IWA's national convention that year, but Alabama organizers
seemed convinced that they could overcome racial barriers to organization.
One white activist recalled a conversation he had with a "colored lady"
that he met at a meeting of CIO local officials in North Carolina. He told
of her local's lack of resources—they did not even have a meeting hall—

but insisted that her "devotion and diligence" surpassed those exhibited by white organizers. "I decided that we don't have too many impossible problems after all." Another organizer reported that in addition to the IWA's gains in Alabama locals, CIO activist Rosella Sessoms had been "working quietly" to initiate an organizing drive in North Carolina. He claimed that "chances are very favorable" for organizing "several hundred woodworkers" in the mill towns on that state's Atlantic coast.[38]

North Carolina CIO director William Smith was impressed by these examples, and he directed black organizer Elijah Jackson and white organizer Dean Culver to coordinate a North Carolina lumber campaign in the summer of 1946. In contrast to their experience in textiles, CIO organizers found the mostly African American lumber workforce eager to join the union. "Organization at the beginning was slow," the team reported to Operation Dixie headquarters, "but it picked up momentum as the campaign progressed." Jackson and his coworkers established an office in the fishing village of Elizabeth City, but they focused their organizational work on Elizabethtown, a county seat fifty miles inland where the Greene Brothers Lumber Company operated the largest sawmill in North Carolina. The team identified Greene Brothers as a potential "toughest customer," which meant, according to Operation Dixie strategy, they would target it for a well-publicized campaign designed to inspire organization at other mills. By October 1946, the CIO had established shop committees in each division of the Elizabethtown plant.[39]

In its struggle to avoid racial conflict, the CIO valued diversity and the appearance of racial harmony over racial justice and democratic representation. An IWA representative reported with enthusiasm, for example, that one North Carolina local had elected a white president and treasurer and a black vice president and secretary. In spite of the fact that the local was two-thirds African American, the organizer praised their selection of a white-dominated executive committee as "somewhat democratic."[40] The CIO lumber workers' newspaper encouraged readers to celebrate "Brotherhood Week" during Operation Dixie, a holiday based on vague appeals to "unity" and "tolerance" that according to historian Harvard Sitkoff "supplanted protests against white supremacy" after the racial violence of 1943. Glossing over the difficult organizational work that had built multicultural solidarity in the 1930s, the *International Woodworker* asserted that Catholic, Jewish, Protestant, Greek, Negro, Yankee, and Swedish union members had learned the "simple truths of democracy" simply by working alongside each other in diverse workplaces. "Remember," the union instructed its members, "democracy begins in every day living."[41]

Democracy was not a part of everyday life in North Carolina sawmills, however, and in contrast to Chapman white workers saw little common ground with their black counterparts in Elizabethtown. Workforce segregation was more intense in North Carolina than it was in Alabama, and over 75 percent of all lumber workers in eastern North Carolina were African American. Of 182 black workers in the Greenes' milling and logging operations, 133 joined the union in 1947. Only seven of forty-eight white workers joined, and of those only one paid his dues. In part, union support reflected the concentration of African Americans in more difficult, dangerous, and low-paid jobs where union support was strongest, but better-paid skilled black workers also joined the union. Of twenty-four black workers in the planing mill, fifteen skilled machine operators joined the IWA, as did Solomon Owens, the Greenes' only black foreman. On the other hand, most white workers sided with the company. During a 1948 strike, one white mill worker traveled throughout Bladen Country selling tobacco sticks that the mill produced during the strike, and a white painter drove a log truck. "Everybody diversified," one manager recalled, noting that the painter's inexperience cost him a finger that he caught in a chain while helping to break the strike.[42]

While white workers continued to oppose unionization in eastern North Carolina, black workers' solid support for the Elizabethtown local convinced CIO leaders to invest more heavily in organization of the lumber industry. After 171 out of 230 workers voted in favor of the IWA in a representation election, William Smith increased the staff to six men and promised two more in the following weeks. Nine other elections had been won in North Carolina, and three more were pending. With four new drives underway in Fayetteville, the union moved their headquarters to Kinston, a more central location than Elizabeth City. "Things have progressed so well," the North Carolina director wrote to IWA headquarters, "that we have decided to extend our activities over the entire eastern part of the state and all the way up to the Virginia line." By October 1948, IWA organizers were convinced that they could win a strike at Elizabethtown and force the Greenes and other employers to enter negotiations with black workers. "We were convinced that we had to pick out a key operation there, organize for a strike," and secure a contract that could serve as a model in other mills, one organizer explained.[43]

Even as they prepared for a showdown, white organizers doubted black workers' ability to challenge their employers. "The Greene Brothers are awful big and powerful people in this little town and this strike is the first time anybody has ever stood up to them in any way," read a report in the union newspaper. "A lot of people were so beat down they wouldn't fight in open defiance of the Greene Brothers."[44] Striving to reduce racial tensions, organizers tried in vain to recruit white workers to official positions within the union. They wanted an overrepresentation of whites—four whites to three blacks on the strike committee and three to two on the relief committee—"if possible," which was unlikely since only seven whites had joined the union.[45] A few days after the strike began, IWA organizer Dean Culver requested that fifteen to thirty white workers be sent from other locals to support the pickets. He also asked for assistance from a white organizer whose "soundness on the colored problem and his size and open friendly personality make him fit this situation perfectly."[46] Culver felt confident that he could win "a straight strike" but reported that he feared "a race riot" if the union did not earn "some white support."[47]

Contrary to Culver's fears, black support for the strike proved strong enough to challenge what remained a solid wall of white opposition. At dawn on July 16, when they would normally have headed for work, union members gathered at the union hall and then "fell out in four groups behind the sound truck, carrying the signs, and . . . marched on the plant to the tune of the stars and stripes forever." Culver described the scene with glee: it was "wonderful," he wrote. "It looked like an army."[48] Solidarity extended far beyond the picket lines, as black community members gave money and other support to strikers and their families. Female relatives of many strikers worked in white homes, and some used their position to monitor anti-strike plans. One striker's sister-in-law, for example, overheard her employer discussing plans to dynamite a union organizer's car.[49] Another striker's wife opened her beauty shop as a meeting place for strikers' wives, allowing union officials to leave relief baskets there for women to collect on their way home from work. Reverend Cotton lent his preaching skills, leading songs and coordinating marches at the company gates.[50] William Smith, the North Carolina CIO director, celebrated the "splendid moral situation" maintained by picketers and praised their ability to "get the scabs out as fast as the company gets them in." His hopes raised by support for the strike, Smith declared that "this strike MUST BE WON," and "we can win it."[51]

After a four-month strike, the *Woodworker* reported, the Elizabethtown local "tasted the sweet cup of victory" when their employers "suddenly capitulated and signed a contract" with the union. IWA organizers built on that success and increased the number of southern locals from forty-eight to sixty-four in 1947, and to seventy-four in 1949. By 1950, six of the eleven IWA locals in North Carolina had secured contracts with their respective employers, and the IWA's southern force peaked in 1952

Photo 13. "The Fight Begins." IWA picket line on first day of strike against Greene Brothers Lumber Company, July 16, 1948. The *International Woodworker* did not print the photo until December 1948, when the strike ended. Reproduced from the *International Woodworker*, courtesy of International Association of Machinists and Aerospace Workers, Upper Marlboro, Md.

when eighty-seven southern locals sent voting representatives to the union's annual convention in Portland, Oregon. Thirteen of those representatives traveled from North Carolina.

Black North Carolinians were not satisfied with economic gains, and they pushed the union to address their social and political grievances as well. When the CIO organized classes in labor history and union management for new union members in 1950, it helped black members who were "determined to be qualified voters" to register for upcoming senatorial elections. More than one thousand lumber workers and their family members gathered for "fun" and "serious talk about labor's problems" at a 1951 IWA Labor Day celebration in Washington, North Carolina. Local newspapers noted the "political angle" taken by the "mostly colored" crowd at the event. A few months later, nine black men and a black woman "took a leading role" in forming the North Carolina CIO Political Action Committee, which conducted registration and voter education drives across the state. The Carolinas Council of the IWA elected a black man to its only permanent office in 1952 and passed a resolution denouncing the Ku Klux Klan.[52]

The IWA never embraced the explicitly left-wing "civil rights unionism" of the Food and Tobacco and Packinghouse Workers unions, but the

Photo 14. Labor Day celebration sponsored by International Woodworkers of America in Washington, N.C., 1951. Reproduced from the *International Woodworker*, courtesy of International Association of Machinists and Aerospace Workers, Upper Marlboro, Md.

Woodworkers did attempt to build on the racial politics that attracted black southerners to the CIO in the 1940s. Despite the work of "organized labor and race relations groups," the *International Woodworker* observed in 1951, black workers still faced "brutality, a peonage system, low pay and long hours," and they were often charged higher prices at company commissaries than were white workers. Emphasizing the extent to which unions had already aided "Negroes in the South," the union newspaper admitted that there was "still much to be done." Throughout the 1948 strike, the *International Woodworker* described the town's workers as "beat down" and impoverished, but it never clarified their racial identity. Readers learned of the Greenes' "attempts to create divisions among workers" but never discovered the nature of those divisions. Not until the strike was won did the newspaper print photographs that had been taken at several times throughout the course of the strike. Only then did readers see that the Elizabethtown local was entirely African American.[53]

The newspapers' coverage of the Elizabethtown victory was the first in an increasing number of stories that revealed and even analyzed racial differences among workers. Pictures of the 1951 Labor Day celebration showed mass meetings of African Americans similar to those that would become common in national newspapers during the civil rights movement of the late 1950s. A report from the Canadian Congress of Labor's

Photo 15. Delegates to IWA-CIO school in Hertford, N.C., 1951. *International Woodworker* reported, "Attendence at schools exceeds that of IWA in Northwest at Portland CIO leadership Training school recently." Reproduced from the *International Woodworker,* courtesy of International Association of Machinists and Aerospace Workers, Upper Marlboro, Md.

1951 convention highlighted a picture of Indian, Jewish, Korean, white, and black representatives discussing "mutual problems." Readers learned of a 1952 southern regional IWA meeting "attended by members of different races and creeds who thus gave conclusive proof that the fraternal spirit of democracy and justice is moving into the South along with the coming of the CIO woodworkers."[54]

Even after the IWA disassociated itself from the left-wing unions that pioneered civil rights unionism, it could not escape the conservative backlash that employers and southern politicians directed at all CIO unions in the late 1940s. Taking advantage of divisions within the CIO and the continued disfranchisement of southern African Americans, conservative politicians passed a barrage of antiunion legislation in the late 1940s and early 1950s. The most devastating of these were state "right-to-work" laws and the federal Taft-Hartley Act, which limited union political activity, weakened their bargaining position, and empowered employers to intervene against unionization. Even as the IWA gained southern members during Operation Dixie, antiunion laws prevented them from represent-

Photo 16. Delegates from International Woodworkers of America locals in Louisiana and Texas at regional meeting in Alexandria, La., 1952. Caption in *International Woodworker* read: "The meeting was attended by members of different races and creeds who thus gave conclusive proof that the fraternal spirit of democracy and justice is moving into the South along with the coming of the CIO woodworkers." Reproduced from the *International Woodworker*, courtesy of International Association of Machinists and Aerospace Workers, Upper Marlboro, Md.

ing those members through collective bargaining agreements. "The picture is an ugly one," read a 1950 report from North Carolina. "We have lost over two thirds of the persons we organized. Consequently, over two thousand woodworkers who placed their confidence in the union have slipped away and have lost their faith in the organization through no fault of their own."[55]

Even in Elizabethtown, union supporters found it difficult to maintain their organization in the face of opposition from white employers and coworkers. After signing an initial contract, the Greenes returned to their early evasion by stalling on meetings and refusing to grant basic union demands in subsequent contracts. The local threatened a second strike in 1950, but union members had not yet recovered from the first and could hardly sustain another protracted struggle. The North Carolina legislature passed a right-to-work law during the first strike, which prevented the union from demanding that all workers pay dues to the union that had won pay raises at the mill. Demonstrating the continuing significance of racial loyalty, local president Jonnie D. Lewis complained that most "free riders" were white, and that "It will take a white man to get them into the union." The union maintained itself until Greene Brothers closed in 1958, but the company stopped negotiating years before that. Elijah Jackson left town in frustration, convinced that white organizers had not supported the local. In 1957, the Elizabethtown Chamber of Commerce boasted, "There is no organized labor in Bladen County."[56]

African Americans continued to press for equality in Elizabethtown, but they did so without the support of labor unions. Adel McDowell and Leah Betty Lewis, whose husbands Thomas McDowell and Jonnie Lewis had led the Elizabethtown local, helped form a Bladen County branch of the NAACP in the late 1950s. In the early 1960s, both women led a series of school strikes that made Elizabethtown the focal point of what one scholar labeled "probably the most serious" school desegregation conflict in North Carolina's civil rights movement. McDowell and Lewis traced the origins of this civil rights activism to the "different attitude" that emerged in the wake of the 1948 union drive. By confronting the Greenes and their supporters, explained Orie Tyson, another strike supporter, African Americans learned that they could "do something for themselves." Watching that defiance, whites also "learned that we're not going to take that kind of treatment now." By confronting both the economic and racial foundations of the Jim Crow order, Adel McDowell claimed, the Elizabethtown strikers "started the ball rolling" for the civil rights movement that would emerge in the following decades.[57]

Working-Class Civil Rights

As in Elizabethtown, racial segregation of labor markets made it difficult to build common ground between black and white workers in Bogalusa, Louisiana. In that case, the shift toward paper production allowed white workers to dominate the AFL unions that organized Bogalusa in the 1940s. While national leaders of the AFL made statements in favor of interracial unionism, they did little to prevent local union leaders from excluding African Americans or marginalizing them within segregated unions. Black sawmill and paper workers turned instead to civil rights organizations, which they succeeded in convincing to fight for better working conditions and influence within the labor movement. In contrast to the civil rights unionism that emerged in eastern North Carolina, a working-class-based civil rights movement emerged in Bogalusa.

AFL unions gained strength in Bogalusa from the merger between Great Southern and the St. Louis-based Gaylord Container Corporation. Starting in 1938, Gaylord closed the mammoth Bogalusa sawmill and converted it into a pulp and paper manufacturing complex. Whereas lumber production was labor intensive and subject to frequent shutdowns, paper manufacturing was highly mechanized and very expensive to interrupt. In contrast to lumber firms, therefore, most paper companies welcomed the stability that unions provided to labor relations and signed contracts with conservative AFL unions that agreed to prevent labor stoppages in exchange for relatively high wages. The United Papermakers and Paperworkers (UPP) took advantage of this relationship when they organized an all-white Bogalusa labor council in the late 1930s. Reflecting the town's new productive regime, mayor and general manager Ivan Magnitzky praised the "high type of leadership of Labor" at the 1940 Labor Day celebration. He credited AFL leaders with having "co-operated to bring about and encourage the development of a better city." The firm also connected its support of AFL unions to an antisubversive patriotism that challenged the Popular Front's claim to liberal democratic values. In an implicit reference to Communist influence within the CIO, a full-page Labor Day declaration in the Bogalusa newspaper called upon workers to "defend if need be our land, our homes and our institutions against an aggressor from without or from within."[58]

Conversion to paper bolstered white men's position in Bogalusa's labor market. The firm also expanded into cardboard box and paper bag construction, sectors that adopted the textile industry's preference for white women. In contrast to lumber production, which was labor intensive, paper could be produced by a small number of well-paid workers. Black men held 40 percent of all logging jobs and more than 50 percent of all sawmill jobs in the South in 1940, but held only 20 percent of papermaking positions. Paper also employed far more white women than lumber, but black women secured only 4 percent of those new positions. The paperworkers union established a segregated "colored" local in the late 1940s, but one of its members explained that "the union wasn't going to battle for you, you could forget about that." Illustrating the union's racial politics, the 1940 Labor Day celebration included a "Negro pie-eating contest." When A. Philip Randolph asked the president of the Paperworkers why the union had so few black members, he received the age-old response: "For some reason I could not understand, the colored workers hold aloof from joining our union."[59]

Mechanization of paper production allowed white workers to build a powerful labor movement in Bogalusa without support from African Americans. In contrast to 1919, when Great Southern had "forced the hand of labor" by hiring black replacements, Gaylord cooperated with the Paperworkers to exclude blacks from most jobs and any influence within the labor movement. By the 1960s, one economist concluded that "seg-regation and discrimination" were "part of the industrial relations sys-tem" in paper and "therefore difficult to change." Black Gaylord employee John Oatis agreed. "Let me put it to you point blank," he stated in an interview, "everybody up there with a white face was your boss. What-ever they tell to do, you had to do it. If you didn't you would get fired." Although the union maintained amicable relations with Gaylord, it chal-lenged the monopoly on political power that company officials had held since Bogalusa's founding. In 1942, a pro-union candidate entered the city's first contested mayoral race. "There is one great issue involved in this campaign," read a campaign statement: "Shall we continue in office a man whose interest is solely that of administering the affairs of a cor-poration office, instead of the affairs of the taxpayers of the City of Boga-lusa?" Gaylord president Ivan Magnitzky won the mayoral race, but AFL Central Labor Union president Godfrey Ruddick and one other union candidate secured two of five seats on the City Commission Council. African Americans gained nothing from this dramatic rise in working-class power in Bogalusa. Not until 1950 did even one black Bogalusan succeed in registering to vote.[60]

In 1955, Gaylord sold the Bogalusa mill to Crown Zellerbach, a Cali-fornia firm that was "sympathetic to Negro aspirations for social and eco-nomic improvement," according to historian Timothy Minchin. In the context of an emerging civil rights movement, Crown's promise to take "affirmative action" to promote African Americans into skilled positions touched off a strike aimed at protecting white control over the firm's se-niority system. Crown placated white workers by backing off the commit-ment to black advancement. Isolated from management and excluded from meaningful participation in unions, black workers turned instead to lead-ership in local civil rights organizations. In 1965, A. Z. Young and Robert Hicks, both former presidents of the "colored" UPP Local 189A, became the president and vice president of the Bogalusa Civic and Voters League, an organization formed after Louisiana banned the NAACP in the late 1950s. "Their union experience," a supporter observed, ". . . equipped them well to voice those fundamental economic grievances that do not surface in every civil rights battle but could hardly be suppressed in Bogalusa."[61]

In contrast to Chapman, where black workers gained white working-class support by distinguishing between economic and racial demands, Young and Hicks had little to gain by appealing to economic pragmatism in Bogalusa. Union leaders refused to concede power to black members, and white workers responded to civil rights activism by creating "the largest Ku Klux Klan concentration per capita of any community in the

South." Demonstrating that white workers also linked economic and racial politics, Klansmen claimed the mantle of the 1919 union movement by characterizing the historic antiunion campaign as "a gang of union busters or hired gunmen [who] were brought into this city to kill those who stood up for the common man." Interracial cooperation was clearly out of the question, and Young and Hicks appealed instead to civil rights organizations and the federal government. A group of black mill workers formed a branch of the Deacons for Defense, an armed group that protected civil rights activists from Klan violence while Local 189A sued both Crown and the UPP for employment discrimination. In the face of stalling from the company and violent opposition from white unionists, a 1968 federal court decision forced both to end racial hiring discrimination and to create one interracial union local.[62]

Conclusion

Contrary to the predictions of many black and white radicals in the 1930s, a biracial working-class political movement emerged in the South during World War II. Where they gained support from unions, black and white lumber workers were able to build lasting unions in places that radicals believed to have been on the verge of fascism in the late 1930s. CIO activists succeeded in extending those gains after the war by focusing on a narrow economic agenda that united black and white workers in spite of their racial differences in Alabama, but that approach failed in places where either black or white workers dominated the labor market. White workers refused to join CIO unions in eastern North Carolina, allowing black workers to transform those unions into vehicles for racial equality as well as economic improvement. On the other hand, white workers excluded African Americans from AFL unions in Bogalusa, forcing black workers to seek alternative means of empowerment. While black working-class political movements took different forms in each of these towns, they all expressed distinctly proletarian politics that ran counter to E. Franklin Frazier's prediction that Jim Crow would stifle black working-class consciousness in the South.

By the early 1950s, black lumber workers had placed themselves near the center of what historians Robert Korstad and Nelson Lichtenstein have described as an early "workplace-oriented civil rights" movement that emerged in the 1940s. While previous studies have traced the emergence of this movement to left-wing unions that emphasized racial egalitarianism as key to organizing the South, the history of lumber unions shows that black industrial workers also asserted a class-conscious politics in places where unions downplayed or even expressed outright opposition to civil rights politics. Interest in union policies has also led scholars to overlook the significance of economic and political changes that prepared working-class African Americans to view unionization as a viable avenue toward political empowerment in the postwar South. As we have seen, these changes were evident as early as World War I, during an early attempt to build interracial lumber unions in the South, and they evolved with changes in production strategy and federal labor law during the 1930s. In this respect, the emergence of southern lumber unions represented the culmination of a political struggle that had begun with the Young Turks' calls to include black southerners in the union campaigns of the early 1930s.[63]

As Korstad and Lichtenstein point out, black union members did not sustain the political momentum that they had built through the organizing drives of the 1940s and early 1950s. They and other scholars emphasize the right-wing political backlash of the early 1950s, which isolated left-wing union activists at the forefront in building interracial unions in the South, bolstered support for state and federal laws that made unionization more difficult, and undermined alliances that had solidified between labor and civil rights organizations during World War II. Less attention has been paid to the economic context in which these changes took place. Just as labor shortages and demand for lumber bolstered efforts to build interracial lumber unions during the war, a decline in production weakened unions following the war and in the 1950s. Even unions such as the IWA that succeeded in adjusting their political stance to the conservative environment of the Cold War could not weather the closing of sawmills that devastated African American working-class communities in the rural South in the late 1950s and 1960s. Ironically, southern lumber workers faced those decades with the same sense of uncertainty that their predecessors had faced in the years following World War I. It may be that observation of that uncertainty inspired the reemergence of scholarly writing that emphasized African Americans' inability to adapt to changing economic situations. The fact that southern economic decline coincided with a similar process of deindustrialization in northern cities encouraged scholars to extend a revived myth of Black Ulysses—borrowed directly from Odum and Frazier's writings of the 1920s and 1930s—and to use it once again as a basis for generalization about working-class African Americans as a whole.

Conclusion:
A Dream Deferred

Orie Tyson formed a house-building club in 1953 with his brother Waymond, his friends Lonnie Carter and Reverend Cotton, and two other employees of the Greene Brothers Lumber Company. Pooling their wages, which were bolstered by the successful 1948 strike, the men bought materials and paid a professional carpenter to inspect their work. They worked in the evenings after shifts at the mill, building five new homes over the next ten years in Newtown, the black community just outside Elizabethtown. Tyson recalls that Alvin Moore, a white foreman at the Greene Brothers, "was amazed" by the sight of black lumber workers moving their families out of the "quarters" and into their own homes. In Elizabethtown and other lumber towns throughout the postwar South, thousands of black working-class families used their wages to move out of company-owned housing in the 1950s. Bogalusa's black families bought residential lots in the old independent Poplas Quarters north of town and in new subdivisions such as Mitchell City, named for a minister who led the challenge to the all-white Democratic Party primary in the 1950s. The Gaylord Container Corporation hastened the movement toward black home ownership by closing sections of the sawmill quarters in 1949 and selling company houses to workers, who hauled them to the new communities on flatbed trucks. In Alabama, Ire Abrams' parents moved from the company town of Chapman to the nearby independent incorporated town of Georgiana in the late 1940s. His family had enjoyed their rented house in Chapman but felt that their money was better spent on ownership. Explaining his parents' move from the company town, Abrams said, "they wanted a place of their own."[1]

These examples illustrate a larger trend. By 1960, 37 percent of all black lumber workers in North Carolina, Alabama, and Louisiana owned or held mortgages on their own homes. Home ownership reflected the culmination of a half-century-long historical process for black men who came of age in the decades following World War I. Black workers looked to industrial work when family farming no longer served as a viable source of income. Federal regulations began to raise the wages of common and unskilled workers in the 1930s and unionization and wartime labor shortages increased wages at an even higher rate in the 1940s. Average wages for southern lumber workers doubled between 1933 and 1935, and they doubled again over the next fifteen years. Higher wages allowed increasing numbers of southern workers to buy automobiles, which were necessary for commuting from independent communities to rural work sites. Like other working-class men in the 1950s, black lumber workers also used higher wages to establish themselves as the primary breadwinners in their households. Nationally, 66 percent of all black married couples lived off the earnings of one wage earner in 1950. In stark contrast to E. Franklin Frazier's portrait of family breakdown in sawmill towns, lumber work provided an economic baseline for hundreds of thousands of black working-class families in the 1940s and 1950s.[2]

In addition to reshaping black men's relationships to their families and communities, industrial employment altered their relationships to white coworkers, employers, and the federal government. Through music and sports, African Americans helped to create a modern leisure culture in the South, one that gave them entertainment as well as contact with white and black workers outside of the region. New Deal labor laws extended minimal political rights to black lumber workers in the South, enforcing their access to higher wages and shorter working hours. For the first time since Reconstruction, federal law challenged social and economic hierarchies that formed the foundation of the Jim Crow system. Unions initially resisted organizing African Americans, particularly in the South, but black workers and their allies succeeded in gaining labor's support in the 1940s. As a result, black union membership rose from 200,000 to over 1.5 million between 1930 and 1950, and the National Urban League asserted that, "unquestionably, the Negro worker has gained ground as a result of progressive union policies and practices." Even when unions remained committed to white supremacy, black lumber workers used their institutional resources to gain higher wages, better working conditions, and even political rights. In a report on "The Negro in Industry and Labor," Urban League researcher Julius A. Thomas observed, "from almost any vantage point, the prospects for further improvement in the economic fortunes of the nation's negro population are brighter than they have ever been."[3]

Orie Tyson and his house-building coworkers belonged to a generation of black men that was similar, in some respects, to that of George Williams and Sol Dacus, who led Bogalusa's interracial timber workers' union in 1919. Like men of the post–Civil War generation, men who entered lumber employment in the decades following World War I developed an employment strategy that provided black working-class families and communities with a measure of economic and social security within an otherwise debilitating Jim Crow system. While Williams and Dacus found that security through migration between family farming and "public" wage work, Tyson and his cohort found it through full-time industrial wage work. The former generation's success relied upon expanding agricultural markets, access to cheap land, and the availability of seasonal industrial employment. Success for the later generation meant that young men would continue to find industrial jobs, and that those jobs would pay wages sufficient to fulfill their responsibilities to families and communities. Williams and Dacus turned to unions after their strategy ceased functioning during World War I, but later generations discovered that unions—and federal regulation—were critical to their ability to extract a family wage from southern lumber firms.

Just as black men began to win the political battles that allowed them to survive through industrial work in the South, they lost the economic foothold that put them in a position to fight that battle in the first place. The Greene Brothers closed their Elizabethtown mill in 1958, eliminating black men's largest source of income in Bladen County, North Carolina. Older workers found enough employment in farming and smaller sawmills to hold on to their homes, but younger people saw little hope for establishing a living in the industrial South. Twelve thousand people moved out of Bladen County between 1950 and 1970, most of them under nineteen years old. By 1969, median incomes in the county stood at two-thirds the state median and just over half of the national median. Black families were much worse off than whites, with a median income of only $2,064, or roughly 25 percent of the median income of the United States as a whole. Nearly 60 percent of Elizabethtown's population lived below the official poverty line.[4]

Lumber companies that did not close mechanized rapidly in the 1960s, eliminating entry-level jobs that were most important for young black men. The McGowins sold their Chapman mill to Union Camp Paper Company in 1966. The new owner maintained a sawmill in Chapman, but shifted from lumber production to more mechanized and less labor-intensive ply-wood production in the 1970s and 1980s. Union membership remained solid among the declining number of employees. The new employer also closed the company town, selling the remaining houses to workers who moved them into surrounding communities. By forcing textile mills to hire black women, civil rights organizations and the federal government created lasting job opportunities in nearby Greenville, but Georgiana held few alternatives to the jobs lost in Chapman. Reflecting the persistent racial divisions in the County, East Chapman survives as a small white community and black former W. T. Smith employees have moved to Georgiana and Greenville.[5]

Crown Zellerbach warned of the "prospect of a declining rate of employment" in Bogalusa in 1965, but the firm did little to offset that possibility. Crown invested $40 million to expand a pulp and paper mill on the other side of Louisiana in the 1960s while it continued to shrink operations in Bogalusa. Black workers won a precedent-setting lawsuit in 1968, forcing both the firm and the union to promote them into previously "white jobs." The firm made a point of training a few black men to work in highly mechanized logging operations in the 1970s but then subcontracted most logging to small family-run operations. A few white families dominated these logging operations by monopolizing contracts and providing credit to loggers. Loggers, 80 percent of whom were black, sold wood to contractors at a piece rate, an arrangement that today some liken to sharecropping because it is covered by no labor laws and because contractors are notorious for unfair pricing and lending practices. Few young men, black or white, have access to the well-paid unionized jobs that remained in Bogalusa. In reference to the 1968 antidiscrimination suit, Judith Stein observes, "the court ruling was a victory in principle only."[6]

Historians have emphasized deindustrialization as an important factor in the northern "urban crisis" of the 1960s and 1970s, but that factor was in some ways more destructive in the rural South where job loss was concentrated in low-wage industries that employed large numbers of black workers. That inattention may be attributed to the fact that overall, southern industrial employment grew by 15 percent between 1947 and 1958 while it declined by 7 percent in the rest of the nation. If we look more closely at jobs traditionally reserved for African Americans, however, the rates of decline equaled and at times dramatically surpassed national figures. Textile jobs, which were reserved almost exclusively for whites into the 1960s, declined at a rate of 8 percent in the 1950s, a figure well below the national rate of 18 percent. Historically "black jobs" in tobacco and fertilizer both disappeared at a rate of 16 percent, on the other hand, while logging and sawmilling jobs declined by 30 and 47 percent, respectively. As historian Gavin Wright observes, "The most dramatic effect was on employment in lumber and sawmills which had been the single most important source of nonagricultural jobs for black teenage males in 1950." Indicating the degree to which deindustrialization dev-astated young men's hopes for supporting their families through south-ern industrial work, black teenage employment in lumber declined by 74 percent in the 1960s.[7]

On the surface, patterns of southern deindustrialization in the 1950s and 1960s confirmed the warnings of those who opposed the NRA on the grounds that minimum wage regulation would lead southern employers to lay off black workers. Gavin Wright points out that job loss was closely correlated to increases in the federal minimum wage, for example. Calls for racial wage differentials were premised on the assumption that Afri-can Americans found work only where they were willing to accept pov-erty wages, and that if forced to raise wage scales, southern employers would replace blacks with machines or better-trained white workers. That logic was borne out by the Second Wave of southern industrializa-tion, which offset declines in lumber, textiles, and other First Wave in-dustries with gains in defense, pharmaceutical, and computer industries. The new industries were clustered around urban areas such as Atlanta, Charlotte, and North Carolina's Research Triangle Park, and they paid wages that were high enough to attract highly skilled migrants from cit-ies in the North and even overseas. These industries undermined the tradition of low-wage industrialization that made the South unique in the first half of the twentieth century, and according to Wright, "the first generation of Second Wave industrial jobs were reserved almost exclu-sively for whites."[8]

The argument that black unemployment was caused by the disap-pearance of black jobs forgets, however, that racial divisions of labor evolved in the context of government and industrial policies that grant-ed blacks and whites differing access to particular jobs. As advocates of wage regulation pointed out in the 1930s, southern lumber firms em-ployed black workers not just because they were cheap, but also because they had developed skills over the past fifty years that were critical to lumber production. Furthermore, African Americans' reliance on low-wage manufacturing jobs in the 1930s and 1940s emerged out of their own efforts to find a reliable alternative to the failing agricultural economy.

Starting in the 1940s, however, federal and state policies turned increasingly toward creating jobs that remained out of reach for most black
southerners. Federal defense spending stimulated growth of high-paying
aerospace and electronics jobs at the same time that federal officials refused to attack racist college admissions policies that would have opened
those jobs to black southerners. Northern and southern industries refused
to invest in predominantly black areas in the 1960s–70s because they
feared racial conflict and because affirmative action laws required them
to employ blacks and whites in proportion equal to the local population.
According to historian Bruce Schulman, southern investors also avoided African American communities because they believed black workers
were more likely than whites to join unions. Black workers found easier
access to civil service jobs in public safety and social work, but they were
often restricted to departments that served black communities. Even as
federal defense investments and agriculture subsidies aided a southern
economic revival in the 1970s and 1980s, southern politicians emerged
as leaders of a conservative backlash against federal labor and educational
programs that may have allowed African Americans to benefit from Second Wave investments.[9]

Ironically, some liberals greeted deindustrialization in the 1960s and
1970s with a fatalism that was adopted directly from Howard Odum's
contention that African Americans were hopelessly damaged by industrialization in the 1920s. The University of Chicago Press republished E.
Franklin Frazier's *The Negro Family in the United States* in 1966 with
an introduction by sociologist Nathan Glazer. Glazer noted that the publication coincided with renewed interest in black poverty and urged those
interested in racial equality to read the book, for "its major framework
remains solid and structures all our thinking on the Negro family." As
Glazer wrote, in fact, President Lyndon Johnson was assembling a team
of scholars and policy makers to address the economic inequality that
persisted between blacks and whites in spite of the tremendous legal and
political gains made by African Americans in the late 1950s and early
1960s. That paradox had been illustrated just a few weeks earlier, when
thousands of mostly young black men rioted for five days in Watts, a black
working-class neighborhood in Los Angeles. Glazer's friend and fellow
sociologist Daniel Patrick Moynihan participated in the White House
discussions, and as Glazer had hoped, he relied heavily on Frazier's study
when he wrote a report for the presidential commission entitled "The Negro Family: A Case for National Action."[10]

The Moynihan report has been criticized for "blaming the victim" of black poverty, but it is important to remember that it was designed to legitimate its author's belief that the federal government had a responsibility to create jobs for young black men. Moynihan avoided explicit calls for jobs creation programs in order to avoid conflict with conservatives, and his grotesque portraits of African American families were designed to inspire action to address black poverty. The problem with Moynihan's report lay not in his prescriptions—the need for federal job creation programs in both northern and southern black communities remains desperate—but in the assumption that black men could only take advantage of jobs that had been open to them in the past. He proposed twice-daily mail delivery and increased military recruitment, for example, in order to stimulate job creation in sectors that were heavily monitored by federal antidiscrimination policies. Rather than intensifying education and antidiscrimination policies that would have expanded black employment in "white jobs," or strengthening labor laws that would have allowed unionization of service and retail jobs that *did* hire black men and women, Moynihan proposed that the federal government shore up black men's access to "black jobs." In place of a proactive strategy for expanding black economic opportunities in a postindustrial future, he offered a nostalgic picture of black success in the industrial past. Such a strategy echoed Odum's myth of Black Ulysses—adopted by Frazier—that discrimination rendered black workers incapable of adjusting to a changing economic and political environment.[11]

As in the 1920s and 1930s, there are signs that black southerners have not resigned themselves to the fatalism shared by Odum and Moynihan. Timothy Minchin has chronicled the legal campaign though which black workers and civil rights activists destroyed racist hiring policies in the southern textile industry in the 1960s and 1970s. While textile jobs remained "low-wage," they paid more than other possibilities and, according to Gavin Wright, may have accounted "for a significant upward jump in relative black incomes in the South." Affirmative action and desegregation also increased black access to higher education, which gave small but significant numbers of black southerners access to Second Wave jobs. The vast majority of black southerners remain in unskilled service and manufacturing jobs, however, where wages continue to stagnate and where racial inequality is on the rise. An important difference between the first and second waves of southern industrialization is the increased attention that unions have paid to the struggles of black southerners. Inspired by the success of the civil rights movement, several unions have supported efforts to organize the packing houses, hotels, and cleaning services that replaced lumber, domestic service, and agriculture as the largest employers of black southerners. Those campaigns have been hindered by state laws that make unionization difficult, poor enforcement of federal labor laws, and unions that are weaker today even than the AFL was in the 1920s. It is my hope that this book has provided insight and inspiration to those who refuse to accept those limits on black workers' ability to find economic and social security in the ever-changing industrial South.[12]

NOTES

Introduction: Rethinking the Myth of Black Ulysses

1. Ayers, *The Promise of the New South*, 454–55; Gavin Wright, *Old South, New South*, 179–80; Howard, *The Negro in the Lumber Industry*, 32–35.

2. My interpretation of Ulysses is inspired by Max Horkheimer and Theodore W. Adorno, *Dialectic of Enlightenment*, 43–80. Thanks to Jim Livingston for alerting me to this connection. See also Shapiro, "Politicizing Ulysses," 17–21.

3. Sosna, *In Search of the Silent South*, 50–51; Odum and Johnson, *Negro Workaday Songs*, 1–4, 206; Odum, *Rainbow 'round My Shoulder*, 127.

4. Faulkner, *Light in August*, 6; Carby, *Race Men*, 104.

5. Hurston, *Mules and Men*, 1–4; Hemenway, *Zora Neale Hurston*, 159–87.

6. Frazier, *The Negro Family*, 368. On proletarian literature, see Denning, *The Cultural Front*, particularly 200–282. Quotes from Frazier, *The Negro Family*, 210, 214, 368, 214.

7. Cash, *The Mind of the South*, 317; Woodward, *Origins of the New South*, 221–34.

8. Hall et al., *Like a Family*; Wright, *Old South, New South*, 162.

9. Hunter, *To 'Joy My Freedom*; Korstad, *Civil Rights Unionism*; Arnesen, *Waterfront Workers of New Orleans*; Lewis, *In Their Own Interests*; Rachleff, *Black Labor in the South*; Honey, *Southern Labor and Black Civil Rights*; Trotter, *Coal, Class, and Color*; Kelly, *Hammer and Hoe*; Kelly, *Race, Class, and Power in the Alabama Coalfields*; Letwin, *The Challenge of Interracial Unionism*; Simon, *A Fabric of Defeat*. For overviews of this literature, see Arnesen, "Up from Exclusion"; and Brattain, "The Pursuits of Post-exceptionalism."

10. On white workers in lumber, see Lewis, *Transforming the Appalachian Countryside*; Sitton and Conrad, *Nameless Towns*; Drobney, *Lumbermen and Log Sawyers*; Armstrong, "Georgia Lumber Laborers"; Jensen, *Lumber and Labor*; Allen, *East Texas Lumberworkers*. Studies that give sustained attention to race or black workers in southern lumber focus on the wave of interracial unionism in East Texas and Louisiana in the 1910s. The best of these is Stephen Reich's dissertation, "The Making of a Southern Sawmill World." See also Norwood, "Bogalusa Burning"; Roediger, "Gaining a Hearing for Black-White Unity"; and Green, "The Brotherhood of Timber Workers, 1910–1913." "Transitional" is from Lewis, "From Peasant to Proletarian," 231. Trotter makes a similar statement in *Black Milwaukee*, 238. "Proletarian synthesis" is from Trotter, *Coal, Class, and Color*, 263. Other quotes from Jacqueline Jones, *The Dispossessed*, 155, 161, 148; Gilmore, *Gender and Jim Crow*, 22; Litwack, *Trouble in Mind*, 137, 143.

11. Orie Tyson interview; "interpretive authority . . ." is from *Like a Family*, xx.

12. Rosengarten, *All God's Dangers*, 182.

13. Kelley, *Race Rebels*, 36; Hunter, *To 'Joy My Freedom*, 183. See also Hale, *Making Whiteness*.

14. Lewis, *In Their Own Interests*, 89–109; Scott, *Domination and the Arts of Resistance*, particularly 36–44. For a critique of Scott in a comparable historical situation, see Cooper, *Decolonization and African Society*, 10. Odum, *Rainbow 'round My Shoulder*, 315. On the scholarly tendency to treat African American experience as distinct from broader American history, see Reed, *W. E. B. Du Bois*, 1–11.

15. On the shift from republican to liberal politics, see Stanley, *From Bondage to Contract*. On black views of land ownership, see Hahn, *A Nation Under Our Feet*. On the evolution of republican politics, see Foner, *Reconstruction*; and Edwards, *Gendered Strife*. On white workers and modernization, see Flamming, *Creating the Modern South*.

16. Black men's struggle for a "family wage" intersected with the broader struggle to define the gendered division of labor in the United States. While I pay attention to that struggle as it played out within black families and communities in southern mill towns, this intersection warrants much further study. For a history of the "family wage," see Kessler-Harris, *In Pursuit of Equity*. On the links between consumption and New Deal wage policy, see Cohen, *Making a New Deal*; and Storrs, *Civilizing Capitalism*.

17. My analysis of black southerners' efforts to adapt new models of family and community is inspired by Moodie, *Going for Gold*, and Putnam, *The Company They Kept*.

18. For a discussion of race and working-class standards of living in the 1950s, see Jones, "As Good as It Gets," 183–87.

19. Scott, "Experience," 25.

20. Kluger, *Simple Justice*, 136; Payne, *I've Got the Light of Freedom*. For a critique of scholarship on class dynamics in the Birmingham, Alabama, civil rights movement, see Eskew, *But for Birmingham*, 229–35.

21. Nathan Glazer, forward to the 1966 edition of Frazier, *The Negro Family*, xi. Jacqueline Jones, *The Dispossessed*. Nicholas Lemann also uses rural sociology from the 1930s to explain urban poverty in the 1990s; see *The Promised Land*, particularly 24–32. For a liberal response to deindustrialization, see Wilson, *The Truly Disadvantaged*. On the conservative response, see Davis, "Who Killed LA?" For the history of deindustrialization, see Sugrue, *The Origins of the Urban Crisis*, and Cowie and Heathcott, eds., *Beyond the Ruins*. For a critique of Jacqueline Jones's use of underclass imagery, see Reed, "Parting the Waters." For a history of how images of working-class African Americans shaped efforts to address poverty, see O'Connor, *Poverty Knowledge*.

Chapter 1: Remaking a Southern Lumber Mill World

1. Ovington, "Bogalusa." On black politics following the Civil War, see Hahn, *A Nation under Our Feet*.

2. Ovington, "Bogalusa," 33; Greer, "Report on the Situation in Bogalusa, LA," in Foner and Lewis, *Black Workers*, 357–62.

3. Norwood, "Bogalusa Burning"; "All City Joins in Great Celebration," *Mill Whistle* (Dec. 1920): 1, private collection of Bernella Birdsong, Bogalusa, La., copy in possession of author; "Bogalusa: The City of Families and Factories," Feb. 1924, folder 16, series 3, GSLC.

4. Betts, "The Southern Pines," 1–5.

5. Wright, *Old South, New South*, 28.

6. Ayers, *The Promise of the New South*, 124; Fickle, *The New South and the New Competition*, 241.

7. Thodes, *Labor and Lumber*, 39.

8. Rosengarten, *All God's Dangers*, 182; Wright, *Old South, New South*, 185.

9. Rosengarten, *All God's Dangers*, 182; Brewer, *Marxist Theories of Imperialism*,

225–59; Cooper, *Decolonization and African Society*, 45; Ayers, *The Promise of the New South*, 454–55; Wright, *Old South, New South*, 160–61.

10. U.S. Bureau of the Census, *Negroes in the United States: 1920–32*, 337–59; U.S. Department of Labor, "Minimum Wages in the Lumber and Timber Products Industry," June 1941; Southern Pine Association Statistical Department, "Labor Conditions in Southern Pine Industry"; folder 161, box 469, SPA. On women's domestic work, see Hunter, *To 'Joy My Freedom*. On railroad work, see Arnesen, *Brotherhoods of Color*.

11. Alex Lichtenstein, *Twice the Work of Free Labor*, 4; Collier, *The First Fifty Years*, 10; Massey, "A History of the Lumber Industry," 4; Flynt, *Poor but Proud*, 153.

12. Captain A. D. Hill, letter to the U.S. attorney general, May 15, 1921, frame 0365, reel 9, PFUSDJ; E. P. Ahern, letter to U.S. secretary of labor, Oct. 24, 1945, frame 0309, reel 10, PFUSDJ; Dinwiddie, "The International Woodworkers of America."

13. Flynt, *Poor but Proud*, 152; W. T. Smith Lumber Company, letter to Mr. I. Herz, June 3, 1905, box 42, WTSLC.

14. Alex Lichtenstein, *Twice the Work of Free Labor*.

15. Leavel et al., *Negro Migration in 1917*; Goodlette interview; Fickle, *The New South and the New Competition*, 290.

16. Leavel et al., *Negro Migration in 1916–1917*; Fickle, *The New South and the New Competition*, 289–90.

17. Drobney, *Lumbermen and Log Sawyers*, 111–47; Garlock, *Guide to Local Assemblies*; Fickle, *The New South and the New Competition*, 22; Emerson interview; Reich, "The Making of a Southern Sawmill World," 261–318; Jensen, *Lumber and Labor*, 92–93; Gardner, *Built in Louisiana*; Wright, *Old South, New South*, 178.

18. Fickle, *The New South and the New Competition*, 22; Norwood, "Bogalusa Burning," 609, 619; Thomas V. Kirk, letter to Honorable H. L. Kerwin, Feb. 17, 1922; "Dastardly Outrage," *St. Andrews Bay [Florida] News*, Nov. 1, 1921; and J. W. Perkins, letter to Mr. Ray Canterbury, Feb. 1, 1922, case 170-1578, "Timberworkers, Bay Harbor, FL," MCSDL.

19. Norwood, "Bogalusa Burning," 613.

20. D'Orso, *Like Judgment Day*, 89.

21. D'Orso, *Like Judgment Day*, 191–96.

22. Bond and Bond, *The Star Creek Papers*, 12–13.

23. Fickle, *The New South and the New Competition*, 290, 296; Haynes and Phillips, *The Negro at Work during the World War*.

24. Fickle, *The New South and the New Competition*, 291, 297; Seligman, *The Negro Faces America*, 311–19; Norwood, "Bogalusa Burning," 203.

25. Berglund et al., *Labor in the Industrial South*; Heer, *Income and Wages in the South*.

26. Unidentified mill owner quoted by Hon. Burnet R. Maybank, "Trees, Nature, and Men of the South," speech before the Senate of the United States, July 30, 1953, folder P.L., box 526, SPA; Boyd, "The Forest is the Future?"

27. Maybank, "Trees, Nature, and Men of the South"; Fickle, *The New South and the New Competition*, 241–59; William Greeley, letter to Mr. John L. Kaul, Dec. 20, 1920, Forest Management File, 1919–1939, KLC.

28. Collier, *The First Fifty Years of the Southern Pine Association*, 78; Fickle, *The New South and the New Competition*, 256–62; Sheppard interview.

29. William Greeley, letter to Mr. John Kaul; Alex Lichtenstein, *Twice the Work of Free Labor*, 185; Ben Greene interview; Collier, *The First Fifty Years of the Southern Pine Association*, 75.

30. Merrick, "History of the Great Southern Lumber Company"; Sullivan, "World's Greatest Lumber Plant"; Quick, "The History of Bogalusa."

31. Quick, "The History of Bogalusa"; Great Southern Lumber Company, "Bogalusa: City of Families and Factories," Feb. 1924, folder 16, series 3, GSLC.

32. Bond and Bond, *The Star Creek Papers,* 11, xxvi.

33. Bond and Bond, *The Star Creek Papers,* 5.

34. Myrick, "History of the Great Southern Lumber Company."

35. Goodyear, *The Bogalusa Story;* Myrick, "History of the Great Southern Lumber Company"; Fickle, *The New South and the New Competition,* 253.

36. Great Southern Lumber Company, "Bogalusa: The City of Families and Factories," 3rd ed., Feb. 1924, folder 16, series 3, GSLC; "Great Southern Plants More Tung Oil Trees," *Franklinton Era-Leader,* Mar. 12, 1936, 1; "Long Ago and Far Away: Bogalusa Once Made Redwood Lumber," *Mill Whistle* (Bogalusa), June 26, 1964; *Tri-State Builder* 3, no. 12 (July 1922), private collection of Bernella Birdsong, Bogalusa, La., copy in possession of author.

37. Maunder, *James Greeley McGowin.*

38. On the L&N, see Woodward, *Origins of the New South,* 126–27; Maunder, *James Greeley McGowin; Industrial Survey of Butler County.*

39. J. O. Dunn, interviewed in "Chapman People at Work," *Lumbering Along,* Oct. 9, 1951, 3, WTSLC; Zell Peagler, interviewed in "Chapman People at Work," *Lumbering Along,* Oct. 26, 1951, 6; Jesse Brown, interviewed in "Chapman People at Work," *Lumbering Along,* Mar. 1952, 5, WTSLC. On efforts to rid southern sawmill towns of malaria, see Humphreys, *Malaria,* 83–87.

40. Bond, *Negro Education in Alabama,* 228.

41. J. H. Lehmann, "Report of Examination of Accounts, W. T. Smith Lumber Company, Inc.," box B8, WTSLC.

42. W. T. Smith Lumber Company File, FHS; N. Floyd McGowin interview in Maunder, *James Greeley McGowin.*

43. Earl McGowin interview in Maunder, *James Greeley McGowin.*

44. "Smith Lumber Company Installs Modern Mill," *Southern Lumberman,* Feb. 4, 1931, McGowin file, APCSF; Leonard W. Dobb, "Poor Whites: A Frustrated Class," appendix 1 in Dollard, *Caste and Class,* 447.

45. W. T. Smith Lumber Company File, FHS.

46. Bond, *Negro Education in Alabama,* 228.

47. Ben and Alvin Greene interviews.

48. Cruikshank, *North Carolina Forest Resources and Industries,* 1–2, 10; Sheppard interview.

49. "Greene Gold," *Esso Oilways,* 1940, 14–17; McCormack, *Forest Statistics for Southern Coastal Plain of North Carolina.*

50. Alvin Greene interview.

51. Orie and Waymond Tyson interviews; Ben Greene interview.

Chapter 2: Black Families between Farm and Factory

1. Orie and Louise Tyson interview; Rudolph interview; Johnson, *Growing Up in the Black Belt.*

2. Wolcott, *Remaking Respectability,* 51; Washington, "Recreational Facilities for the Negro"; Woodson, *The Rural Negro,* 135–39.

3. Odum, *Rainbow 'round My Shoulder,* 68.

4. Edwards, *Gendered Strife and Confusion;* Mann, "Slavery, Sharecropping, and Sexual Inequality"; Reidy, *From Slavery to Agrarian Capitalism,* 136–60.

5. Frazier, *The Negro Family,* 210.

6. Faulkner, *Light in August*, 6, 41.

7. Jacqueline Jones, *The Dispossessed*, 156; Jensen, *Lumber and Labor*, 77.

8. Tolnay, *The Bottom Rung*, 49–50, Jensen, *Lumber and Labor*, 77.

9. Berglund, *Labor in the Industrial South*, 54; Wright, *Old South, New South*, 81–123.

10. Rosengarten, *All God's Dangers*, 182; Berglund et al., *Labor in the Industrial South*, 53; Drobney, *Lumbermen and Log Sawyers*, 103; Brown, *Logging Transportation*; Bryant, *Logging*.

11. Wright, *Old South, New South*, 121; Bond, *Negro Eduction in Alabama*, 229; U.S. Bureau of the Census, "Negroes in the United States."

12. SPA Statistical Department, "Labor Conditions in Southern Pine Industry," June 19, 1933, "Consolidated Approved Code Industry Files—Lumber and Timber," box 3378, NRA.

13. Southern Pine Association Statistical Department, "Labor Conditions in Southern Pine Industry," Mar. 3, 1934, "Consolidated Approved Industry Files—Lumber and Timber," box 3378, NRA; "Estimated Number of Employees in Manufacturing Industries in Alabama, by month, 1949," Oct. 1, 1949, ADIR.

14. Jensen, *Lumber and Labor*, 77; Jacqueline Jones, *The Dispossessed*, 133; Southern Pine Association Statistical Department, "Labor Conditions in Southern Pine Industry," June 19, 1933, "Consolidated Approved Industry Files—Lumber and Timber," box 3378, NRA.

15. On black men's attachment to farming, see Alex Lichtenstein, "Was the Emancipated Slave a Proletarian?" and Wright, *Old South, New South*, 99–115.

16. Brumfield and Holmes interview; Alex Lichtenstein, "Was the Emancipated Slave a Proletarian?"

17. Brumfield and Holmes interview.

18. Abrams interview.

19. Cheatham interview.

20. Cheatham interview.

21. Carter interview.

22. Rubin, *Plantation County*, 129; Rubin, "Labor," Camden and Selma, Apr. 18, 1947, FSMCS.

23. Shaw interview; Gandy interview; Jacqueline Jones, *The Dispossessed*, 163.

24. Oatis interview; Ginn interview.

25. Janiewski, *Sisterhood Denied*, 37–38; Jacqueline Jones, *Labor of Love*, 112–14; Hunter, *To 'Joy My Freedom*, 50–52.

26. McDowell and Lewis interview; Orie and Louise Tyson interview; Cobb interview; Abrams interview. On rates for black women's wage employment, see Jacqueline Jones, *Labor of Love*, 112–14.

27. Hurston, *Mules and Men*, 56–58, 61. Jack Temple Kirby argues that most bootleg liquor was made by men in the Jim Crow South, but that women were as likely as men to sell it (*Rural Worlds Lost*, 208).

Chapter 3: Race, Class, and Leisure in the Industrial South

1. Garon, *Four Woman Blues*.

2. Harrison, *Black Pearls*; Davis, *Blues Legacies*; Eagle and LaVere, "Hard Working Woman," 7.

3. On popular music as a source for social history, see Rose, *Black Noise*, 21–61; Lipsitz, *Rainbow at Midnight*, 303–33.

4. Heide, *Deep South Piano*, 12.

5. Rowe, "Piano Blues," 112–38; Davis, *The History of the Blues,* 148–50; LaVere, *Robert Johnson.*

6. Shaw quoted in McCormick, *Robert Shaw;* Reich, "The Making of a Southern Sawmill World," 247; Harrison, *Black Pearls,* 69; Robinson, *Elzadie Robinson, 1926–1929.*

7. Joseph quoted in Oliver, *Blues Fell This Morning;* Rainey quoted in Davis, *Blues Legacies,* 227–28.

8. *Barrelhouse Blues, 1927–1936; Barrelhouse and Boogie Piano, 1927–1930;* Filene, *Romancing the Folk,* 34–51; Odum and Johnson, *Negro Workaday Songs,* 4, 31–32, 206.

9. Lomax quoted in Filene, *Romancing the Folk,* 51; McCaffrey interview.

10. Gert zur Heide, *Deep South Piano,* 37–38. Hurston, *Mules and Men,* 151–52.

11. McCaffrey interview.

12. Washington, "Recreational Facilities," 279; Woodson, *The Rural Negro,* 132.

13. Washington, "Recreational Facilities," 279; Woodson, *The Rural Negro,* 132.

14. Hutchinson, *The Harlem Renaissance,* 78; Hemenway, *Zora Neale Hurston,* 91; Hurston, *Mules and Men,* 57.

15. Hurston, *Mules and Men,* 59–60; for an itinerary of Hurston's fieldwork, see Hurston, *Every Tongue,* 257–58.

16. Hurston, *Mules and Men,* 61.

17. Montgomery, interview; Lipsitz, *Rainbow at Midnight,* 26.

18. Higginbotham, "Rethinking Vernacular Culture," 157–58; Hurston, *Mules and Men,* 139–42.

19. "Chapman People at Work," *Lumbering Along,* Oct. 26, 1951, 6, WTSLC; Ginn interview; Cartwright interview.

20. Higginbotham, "Rethinking Vernacular Culture," 166; Berlgund, *Labor in the Industrial South,* 57, 65.

21. Brody, "The Rise and Decline of Welfare Capitalism," John Kaul, "The New Welfare Emphasis in the Southern Lumber Industry," folder 41, box 3, KLC.

22. Quick, "History of Bogalusa"; Myrick, "The History of the GSLC"; "Photographs of the GSLC," folder 9, series 1, GSLC.

23. Principle quoted in Russell, "A Historical Study"; "City Code of Bogalusa," 16; Reich, "Making a Southern Lumbermill World," 208–60.

24. "All City Joins in Great Celebration," *Mill Whistle,* Dec. 1920, private collection of Bernella Birdsong, Bogalusa, La., copy in possession of author.

25. Department of Publicity, "Bogalusa: The City of Families and Factories," folder 16, series 3, GSLC.

26. "Colored Section," *Mill Whistle,* July 1923, private collection of Bernella Birdsong, Bogalusa, La., copy in possession of author.

27. "Smith Lumber Co. Give Barbeque," July 7, 1919, McGowin file, APCSF.

28. N. Floyd McGowin and Earl McGowin interviews in Maunder, *James Greeley McGowin;* "Form Chapman Welfare Society," Apr. 12, 1924, McGowin file, APCSF; Lehmann, "Report of Examination of Accounts, W. T. Smith Lumber Company, Inc," WTSLC.

29. John Kaul. "Parks and Playgrounds in Relation to the Modern City," folder 41, box 3, KLC; H. E. Hoppen, "The Spirit of Baseball and Good Sportsmanship Is Contagious," *Mill Whistle,* July 1923, private collection of Bernella Birdsong, Bogalusa, La., copy in possession of author. On sports and welfare capitalism, see Ruck, *Sandlot Seasons,* 8–38; and Hall, *Like a Family,* 137.

30. "Colored Section," *Mill Whistle,* July 1923, private collection of Bernella Birdsong, Bogalusa, La., copy in possession of author; Mike Salinero, "Whatever Happened

to Claude Green?" *Daily News* (Bogalusa), June 14, 1981; Mark Douglas, notes on photo of Y Tigers, in possession of author; Reeves and Chapelle interview.

31. Cheatham interview; Charles Peavey, notes, Brewton, Ala., Oct. 29, 1948, FSMCS.

32. Oatis interview; Mike Salinero, "Whatever Happened to Claude Green?" *Daily News* (Bogalusa), June 14, 1981.

33. Cobb interview.

34. Weems, *Desegregating the Dollar*, 38–41; Harrison, "Classic Blues and Women Singers"; Oliver, "An Introduction to the Recording"; Randolph, "A Pioneer Race Recorder."

35. Hurston, "Florida, Negro Folklore," June 30, 1936, Folklore Project, Traditional Folklore, Florida File, Archive of Folk Song, WPA; Hurston, untitled 16 mm black and white film, MMFC; Hurston, "Characteristics of Negro Expression," 27. On the shift from relativism to functionalism, see Filene, *Romancing the Folk*, 136.

36. Hurston, "Florida, Negro Folklore"; Fahey quoted in Levine, *Black Culture*, 225–29.

37. McCormick, *Robert Shaw*.

38. O'Neal, "Living Blues Interview"; Cobb interview; Abrams interview; Oatis interview.

39. Boyette interview; Bailey interview.

40. Bailey interview; Daniel, *Lost Revolutions*, 121–47; Lipsitz, *Rainbow at Midnight*, 19–44; Hasse, *Beyond Category*, 176–80.

41. Earl McGowin interview in Maunder, *James Greeley McGowin*; "Trial Docket for the Town of Chapman," Nov. 8, 1927–Feb. 27, 1965; "Ordinance Book," box B7, WTSLC.

42. Lipsitz, *Rainbow at Midnight*, 24–25; Cobb interview; Mason McGowin interview.

43. Orie and Louise Tyson, and Waymond Tyson, interviews.

44. Bogalusa Commission Council, "Regular Meeting Minutes," Mar. 31, 1931–Sept. 4, 1936, City Hall, Bogalusa, La.

45. "Bootleggers Sent to Jail, Some Fined," *Bogalusa News*, May 15, 1931, 1; "Many Caught in Dragnet Spread by Vice Raiders," *Bogalusa Enterprise*, May 13, 1931; "Bootleggers Alarmed at Vice Crusade," *Bogalusa News*, May 22, 1931, 1.

46. "Time for Cool Heads," *Bogalusa Enterprise*, May 8, 1932, 4; Bogalusa Commission Council, "Regular Meeting Minutes," Feb. 24–Mar. 27, 1933; "City Code of Bogalusa."

47. On black working-class culture as a counter to the "mainstream," see Kelley, *Race Rebels*, 35–53. Kelley cites *Mules and Men* as an inspiration for his analysis, overlooking Hurston's later criticism of models that distinguish between folk and mainstream culture. On Hurston, see Filene, *Romancing the Folk*, 136–39. For a discussion of isolation vs. destruction in studies of working-class culture, see Levine, "The Folklore of Industrial Society," and responses by Lears and Kelley; and Denning, "The End of Mass Culture."

Chapter 4: The New Deal and the New Tradition

1. Carter interview; "Wages and Hours of Labor in the Lumber Industry in the United States, 1930."

2. Johnson quoted in Wright, *Old South, New South*, 197. See also Cell, *The Highest Stage of White Supremacy*, 123–30.

3. Storrs, *Civilizing Capitalism*, 91–123.

4. "Labor Conditions in Southern Pine Industry: Summary of Returns from 73 Companies (75 Mills) in Eleven States," June 19, 1933, folder 274, box 3378, NRA.

5. Betts, *The Southern Pines*, 3–4; Sawaya, "The Employment Effects of Minimum Wage Regulation"; Sitton and Conrad, *Nameless Towns*, 29; Drobney, *Lumbermen and Log Sawyers*, 61–91; Research and Statistics Branch, "Minimum Wages in the Lumber and Timber Products Industry," folder 161, box 469, SPA; Lowther and Murray, "Labor Requirements in Southern Pine."

6. Ben Greene interview; Alvin Greene interview; Staley A. Cook, "Swamps Yield Riches in Timber," *Daily News* (Greensboro, N.C.), Nov. 6, 1938, B10. On geachies, see Turner, *Africanisms in the Gullah Dialect.* On "primitive masculinity" in adventure novels, see Bederman, *Manliness and Civilization*, 217–39.

7. "Wages and Hours of Labor in the Lumber Industry in the United States, 1930"; Ben Greene, interview; Alvin Greene, interview; Sitton and Conrad, *Nameless Towns*, 30.

8. "Work Injuries in the United States during 1945"; Kossoris and McElroy, "Causes and Prevention of Accidents."

9. Herbert Hill, *Black Labor and the American Legal System*, 209–17; Galenson, *The United Brotherhood of Carpenters*; Gardner, *Built in Louisiana.*

10. Tindall, *The Emergence of the New South*, 441; C. C. Sheppard, "Strengthening an Industry during Times of Depression," Mar. 24, 1931, box 739, SPA; Fickle, *The New South*, 120–21; Gordon, *New Deals*, 62–68, 171; Badger, *The New Deal*, 253–55.

11. "For Sale: 1 Hoover Cart," *Brooks-Scanlon News*, Aug. 1, 1933, Brooks-Scanlon File, FHS; Fickle, *The New South*, 125; "Southern Pine Division Code Bulletin," Oct. 5, 1933, box 209, SPA.

12. "Operating Under Code," *Brooks-Scanlon News*, Sept. 1, 1933; A. G. T. Moore, letter to E. T. Ussery, Sept. 26, 1933, Lumber Files, AWRR; "Well Deserved Praise," *Southern Lumberman*, Oct. 1, 1933.

13. C. C. Sheppard, "Wages and Hours of Lumber in the South," July 20, 1933, folder 274, box 3374, NRA.

14. C. C. Sheppard, "Wages and Hours of Lumber in the South," July 20, 1933, folder 274, box 3374, NRA.

15. Q. T. Hartner, letter to Hon. Cleveland Dear, July 15, 1933, Employment, Wages and Hours Complaints File, box 3374, NRA; F. B. Gault, letter to White House, July 17, 1933, folder 274, box 3374, NRA.

16. E. B. May, testimony before the Hearing on the Exemptions to the Lumber Industry Code, Sept. 15, 1933, entry 44, box 82, NRA.

17. H. C. Allen, letter to Hugh S. Johnson, Aug. 28, 1933, Lumber and Timber Products—Employment—Complaints File, box 3370, NRA; J. G. McGowin, letter to A. G. T. Moore, Sept. 14, 1933, reprinted in Maunder, *James Greeley McGowin*, 126.

18. George F. Oaks, telegram to General Johnson, Aug. 29, 1933, Employment—Differentials—District and Regional Complaints File, box 3370, NRA; A. C. Mortland, letter to Mr. Thomas Taylor, Oct. 31, 1933, Employment—Differentials—District and Regional Complaints File, box 3370, NRA; Frederick F. Robinson, letter to Thomas R. Taylor, Nov. 18, 1933, Employment—Differentials—District and Regional Complaints File, box 3370, NRA; "Complaint of the Dillman Industries," Employment—Differentials—District and Regional Complaints File, box 3370, NRA.

19. "Complaint of the Dillman Industries," Employment—Differentials—District and Regional Complaints File, box 3370, NRA.

20. "About the Negro and the NRA," *Norfolk Ledger-Dispatch*, July 10, 1933; "Victims of the Blue Eagle," *Norfolk Virginia-Pilot*, July 11, 1933; Charles L. Kaufman, letter to Dr. Leo Wolman, Aug. 11, 1933, Regional Differential Folder, box 1, NRA.

21. Scott, *Contempt and Pity*, 19–55.

22. Innes quoted in Sullivan, *Days of Hope*, 50; Sitkoff, *A New Deal for Blacks*, 55; On uplift ideology, see Gaines, *Uplifting the Race*.

23. Fraser, *Labor Will Rule*, 259–88; Levine, "Workers' Wives," 45–64; Mason quoted in Storrs, *Civilizing Capitalism*, 106; On industrial feminism, see Orleck, *Common Sense and a Little Fire*, 10.

24. Storrs, *Civilizing Capitalism*, 106; SPA, "Labor Conditions in Southern Pine Industry."

25. Dubofsky and Van Tine, *John L. Lewis*, 199–200.

26. R. B. Parsons, letter to General Hugh S. Johnson, Dec. 12, 1933, Regional Differential Folder, box 1, NRA.

27. *Thomas*, "Will the New Deal Be a Square Deal for the Negro?" *Opportunity* (Oct. 1933): 308–11.

28. T. Arnold Hill, "The Emergency Is On!" *Opportunity* (Sept. 1933): 280–81.

29. Spero and Harris, *The Black Worker*, 429, 469; Wolters, *Negroes and the Great Depression*, 226.

30. Holloway, *Confronting the Veil*, 4–15, 84–122.

31. Holloway, *Confronting the Veil*, 69; John P. Davis, "Concerning the Proposed Changes in the Code of Fair Competition for the Lumber and Timber Products Industry," n.d., "Employment Differentials—District and Regional—Complaint Files," box 3370, NRA; Robert C. Weaver, "A Wage Differential Based on Race," *The Crisis* (Aug. 1934), 236–38.

32. White quoted in Storrs, *Civilizing Capitalism*, 108; A. Howard Myers, letter to R. B. Parsons, Dec. 16, 1933, Regional Differential Folder, box 1, NRA; Griffler, *What Price Alliance?* 134–35.

33. See advertisements in *New York Times*, Jan. 1–7, 1934.

34. Harriet L. Herring, "Industrial Relations in the South," 130. On a similar dynamic in other industries, see Hall et al., *Like a Family*, 291; Cohen, *Making a New Deal*, 267–83.

35. McCarrol Lber. Co. employees, letter to Hon. Donald Richberg, May 27, 1935, Employment—Wages and Hours—Complaints File, box 3374, NRA; F. E. Brodgon, letter to Mr. Hugh S. Johnson, Sept. 18, 1933, Consolidated Approved Code Industry File, box 3374, NRA.

36. William McKinley Bowman, letter to His Excellency Franklin D. Roosevelt, July 26, 1933, Labor—Wages and Hours File, box 3374, NRA.

37. Mrs. Clyde La Fone, letter to Mr. Johnson, Feb. 19, 1934, box 3374, NRA; Whayne, *A New Plantation South*, 194–95. On women and letter writing in the South, see also Hall et al., *Like a Family*, 309–10.

38. L. C. Barefoot, letter to Gen. Hugh Johnson, June 10, 1924 [*sic*], box 3373, NRA.

39. J. P. Booth, letter to Hugh S. Johnson, July 20, 1934, box 3373, NRA; Board of Aldermen, letter to Hugh S. Johnson, Aug. 1934, box 3373; T. J. Dowdy, letter to Hugh S. Johnson, Aug. 5, 1933, Employment—Wages and Hours—Complaints File, box 3374, NRA. On voting in North Carolina, see Key, *Southern Politics*, 565–66.

40. T. J. Dowdy, letter to Hugh S. Johnson, Aug. 5, 1933; "Wages and Hours of Labor in the Lumber Industry in the United States, 1932."

41. National Industrial Conference Board, "Occupational Differentials—Lumber and Millwork Industry," folder 16, box 3373, NRA; R. B. Brown, letter to Hugh S. Johnson, Dec. 9, 1933; R. B. Brown, letter to Franklin D. Roosevelt, Mar. 3, 1934, Employment—Skilled Workers Complaints File 274, box 3371, NRA.

42. Benj. R. Smith, letter to Hugh Johnson, Mar. 23, 1934, Employment—Skilled Workers Complaints File 274, box 3371, NRA.

43. A. S. Drew, letter to Mr. Hugh S. Johnson, May 18, 1934, Employment—Skilled

Workers Complaints File 274, box 3371, NRA; Mr. Dudley Cates, "Report on the 'Official Protest and Objections by the United Brotherhood of Carpenters and Joiners' Presented to the Hearings on the Lumber and Timber Product Industries Code," Sept. 6, 1934, file 274, box 3372, NRA.

44. SPA, "Labor Conditions in Southern Pine Industry: Summary of Returns from 73 Companies (75 Mills) in Eleven States," June 19, 1933, folder 274, box 3378, NRA; Ira De Augustine Reid, *Negro Membership in American Labor Unions,* and "Lily-White Labor," *Opportunity* (June 1930): 169–73; Thomas L. Dabney, "Survey Reports," box 87, part 1, series 6, NUL; Gardner, *Built in Louisiana.*

45. H. L. Weems, letter to Miss Frances Perkins, Feb. 22, 1934, folder 274, box 3374, NRA; R. C. LeBlanc, letter to Mr. Donald R. Richberg, May 9, 1934, Lumber and Timber Products Employment Complaints file, box 3370, NRA.

46. D. B. Gatling, letter to the chief examiner, Apr. 9, 1934, file 5, entry 39, box 38, NRA; James Greeley McGowin, letter to Mrs. McGowin, Dec. 7, 1933, and letter to R. J. McCreary, Dec. 11, 1933, both in Maunder, *James Greeley McGowin.*

47. Federal Trade Commission, "Effect of the Lumber Code on Small Sawmill Operators in the South," May 7, 1934, NRA Binder, box 162, SPA; "South's Small Plants Facing Grave Crisis," *Nashville Banner,* Dec. 11, 1933; "Small mill man" quoted in Gordon, *New Deals,* 188; "Summary of Labor Protests, 1933–1935," Lumber and Timber Products Employment Complaints file, box 3370, NRA; J. W. Bailey, letter to Hugh Johnson, Employment Differentials—District and Region file, box 3370, NRA; D. B. Gatling, letter to the chief examiner, Apr. 9, 1934, file 5, entry 39, box 38, NRA.

48. Berglund et al., *Labor in the Industrial South;* E. B. May, "Testimony Before the Hearing on the Exceptions to the Lumber Industry Code," Sept. 15, 1933, Transcripts of Hearings, 1933–1935, entry 44, box 82, NRA; Fickle, *The New South and the New Competition,* 61–64; McGowin, letter to R. J. McCreary, reprinted in Maunder, *James Greeley McGowin.*

49. "Hearings Arranged for Lumber Mills," *New Orleans Times-Picayune,* Apr. 12, 1934; Federal Trade Commission, "Effect of the Lumber Code"; "Out in Front," *Brooks-Scanlon News,* June 1, 1934, 1, Brooks-Scanlon File, FHS.

50. "Lumber Dealer Vital Factor in Success of Housing Act," *Brooks-Scanlon News,* Oct. 1, 1934, 1, Brooks-Scanlon File, FHS; *Lumber Code Authority Newsletter,* June 1, 1934, and Feb. 16, 1935, box 184, SPA.

51. "South's Small Plants Facing Grave Crisis," *Nashville Banner,* Dec. 11, 1933; Hawley, *The New Deal,* 82; Tindall, *The Emergence of the New South,* 444; Gordon, *New Deals,* 200.

52. John E. Edgerton, "Effects of Labor Provisions of Codes upon Southern Industry," Jan. 30, 1935, Consolidated Reference Materials, Misc. Reports and Documents, 1933–1937, box 37, entry 39, NRA.

53. "Hearings Arranged for Lumber Mills," *New Orleans Times-Picayune,* Apr. 12, 1934; D. B. Gatling, letter to the chief examiner, Apr. 9, 1934, file 5, entry 39, box 38, NRA; Compliance Department, "General Report," July 1934, "Compliance" folder, box 162, SPA; *Lumber Code Authority Newsletter,* Feb. 16, 1935, box 184, SPA; *Southern Pine Division Code Bulletin,* June 16, 1934, box 209, SPA.

54. Compliance Department, "General Report," July 1934, "Compliance" folder, box 162, SPA; H. C. Berkes, letter to L. O. Crosby, Sept. 1, 1934, NRA binder, box 162, SPA.

55. C. W. Whitehead, "Conciliation and Mediation Final Report," May 3, 1941, box SG10081, ADL; W. A. Belcher Lumber Company File, Dispute Case Files, ADL; Jensen, *Lumber and Labor,* 191; "Reselling the NIRA to Industry," *Journal of Commerce* (New York), Mar. 29, 1935."

56. C. W. Whitehead, "Conciliation and Mediation Final Report," May 3, 1941, box

3G10081, ADL; W. A. Belcher Lumber Company File, Dispute Case Files, ADL; Jensen, *Lumber and Labor*, 191; Hawley, *The New Deal*, 96, 82–83.

57. "Reselling the NIRA to Industry," *Journal of Commerce* (New York), Mar. 29, 1935; "Government Asks Dismissal of Belcher Appeal before Supreme Court," press release, Mar. 26, 1935, book LCA 34-48 through 34-519, box 168, SPA; "President Orders NRA Enforcement Despite Retreat," *New York Times*, Mar. 27, 1935; Robbins, *Lumberjacks and Legislators*, 194; Gordon, *New Deals*, 200–201.

58. Dr. Gus W. Dwyer, "Address Delivered Before 20th Annual Convention and Code Conference of the Southern Pine Association," Mar. 13, 1935, folder 274, box 3378, NRA; "Resolution Passed at General Meeting of Southern Pine Manufacturers," June 3, 1935, book 1, box 165, SPA; press release, May 16, 1935, book 1, box 165, SPA; Gordon, *New Deals*, 201.

59. Edgerton quoted in Tindall, *The Emergence of the New South*, 443; Carlton and Coclanis, eds., *Confronting Southern Poverty*, 65; Southern States Industrial Council, "Report on the Committee of the SSIC on Minimum Wage Recommendation and Report of the Industry Committee no. 1 (textiles)," July 5, 1939, folder 7.5.39, box 294, SPA; Tindall, *Emergence of the New South*, 536.

60. Myrdal, *An American Dilemma*, 397–98; Sitkoff, *A New Deal for Blacks*, 55; Hine, Hine, and Harrold, *The African American Odyssey*, 435. Other examples of textbooks that repeat Sitkoff's dismissal of the NRA include Kelley and Lewis, *To Make Our World Anew*, 415; Trotter, *The African American Experience*, 445; Franklin and Moss, *From Slavery to Freedom*, 395. Sitkoff's source is Leslie Fishel, who cites a "Virginia newspaper" quoted in the *New York Times*, "The Negro in the New Deal Era," 114 n. 11.

61. On the NRA and the AAA, see Finegold and Skocpol, *State and Party in America's New Deal*, and Whayne, *A New Plantation South*; Myrdal, *An American Dilemma*, 398. On prevailing wages, see Wright, *Old South, New South*, 216.

62. For a variety of black opinion on the NRA, see Eugene Kinkle Jones, "A 'New Deal' for the Negro," *Opportunity* (Apr. 1933): 105; Frank Crosswaith, "Sound Principle and Unsound Policy," *Opportunity* (Nov. 1934): 340; Loren Miller, "One Way Out—Communism," *Opportunity* (July 1934): 214. On the diversity of black intellectual reactions to the NRA, see Holloway, *Confronting the Veil*, 68–73; Ira De Augustine Reid, "Black Wages for Black Men," *Opportunity* (Mar. 1934): 73–76.

63. Sullivan, *Days of Hope*, 44; Cohen, *Making a New Deal*, 278; see also Hall et al., *Like a Family*, 303–9; Fickle, *The New South and the New Competition*, 305–14.

Chapter 5: Race, Region, and the Limits of Industrial Unionism

1. J. L. Wiggins, letter to Col. C. H. Crawford, May 16, 1935, folder 274, box 3372, NRA; J. R. Steelman, letter to Hon. H. L. Kerwin, Apr. 8, 1935, file 182-322, MCSDL.

2. Patterson, *Strikes in the United States*.

3. Jensen, *Lumber and Labor*, 191; J. R. Steelman, letter to Hon. H. L. Kerwin, Apr. 8, 1935; T. R. Simmons, letter to Hon. John D. Petras, Apr. 16, 1935, file 182-322, MCSDL.

4. Reid, *Negro Membership in American Labor Unions*; Raddock, *Portrait of an American Labor Leader*, 154. On the IAM, see Herbert Hill, *Black Labor and the American Legal System*, 209.

5. Gardner, *Built in Louisiana*, 22–25; Reid, "Lily-White Labor," 169–89; Hill, "Open Letter to Mr. William Green," *Opportunity* (Feb. 1930): 56–57.

6. E. D. Clark, letter to Hugh S. Johnson, Oct. 28, 1933; E. V. Riddle, letter to William Green, Sept. 23, 1934, Labor Complaints File, box 3371, NRA.

7. Hutchinson quoted in Galenson, *The United Brotherhood of Carpenters*, 253; see also pp. 252–77.

8. Zieger, *The CIO*, 6–21; Fink, *Progressive Intellectuals*, 214–41; Storrs, *Civilizing Capitalism.*

9. Dubofsky and Van Tine, *John L. Lewis*, 181–202; Fraser, *Labor Will Rule*, 324–48; Zieger, *The CIO*, 17.

10. T. R. Simmons, letter to John Petree, Apr. 16, 1935, file 182-322, MCSDL; Dinwiddie, "The International Woodworkers," 32–45; Brown and Davis, eds., *It Is Union and Liberty;* Galenson, *The United Brotherhood of Carpenters*, 252; Lembcke and Tattam, *One Union in Wood*, 18–46.

11. Tomlins, *The State and the Union*, 103–147; Brody, *In Labor's Cause*, 240.

12. Zieger, *The CIO*, 22–41.

13. Denning, *The Cultural Front*, 7.

14. Drake and Cayton, *Black Metropolis*, 313–14; Zieger, *The CIO*, 84; Frazer, *Labor Will Rule*, 337; Honey, *Southern Labor and Black Civil Rights*, 83.

15. Berglund, Starnes, and DeVyver, *Labor in the Industrial South*, vii, 1, 10. On Odum and the IRSS, see Tindall, *The Emergence of the New South*, 582–88.

16. Lindsay, "Women Hold Key to Unionization of Dixie," 638.

17. Lindsay, "Women Hold Key to Unionization of Dixie," 638–39.

18. Irons, *Testing the New Deal*, 30; Tippett, *When Southern Labor Stirs*, 10–15.

19. Irons, *Testing the New Deal*, 36; Van Osdell quoted in Irons, *Testing the New Deal*, 35.

20. Hall, "Disorderly Women," 367; and "Women Writers," 7, 15–16.

21. Lindsay, "Women Hold Key to Unionization of Dixie," 638; Tippett, *When Southern Labor Stirs*, 283–84; Dreiser et al., *Harlan Miners Speak*, 17; Trotter, *Coal, Class, and Color*, 63–101.

22. Foley, *Radical Representations*, 193–94; Berglund, Starnes, and DeVyver, *Labor in the Industrial South*, 17.

23. Odum and Johnson, *Negro Workaday Songs*, 1–4.

24. Griffler, *What Price Alliance*, 125; Carter, "The A.F. of L. and the Negro," 335–36.

25. William Green, letter to the editor, *Opportunity* (Dec. 1929): 381–82.

26. Irons, *Testing the New Deal;* Hall, "Disorderly Women."

27. Holloway, *Confronting the Veil*, 98–99; David Lewis, *W. E. B. Du Bois*, 250–55.

28. Solomon, *The Cry Was Unity*, 111.

29. Denning, *The Cultural Front*, 264; *The Political Plays of Langston Hughes*, 46–49; Wexley, *They Shall Not Die*, 190–91; Kelley, *Hammer and Hoe*, 159–75.

30. Hill, "Open Letter to Mr. William Green," *Opportunity* (Feb. 1930): 56–57.

31. Kelley, *Hammer and Hoe*, 122–27; Henry, *Ralph Bunche*, 43–45.

32. Granger quoted in Sitkoff, *A New Deal*, 248.

33. Kelley, *Hammer and Hoe*, 138–51; Draper, "The New Southern Labor History Revisited"; Holloway, *Confronting the Veil*, 92; Bates, *Pullman Porters*, 126–47.

34. Sullivan, *Days of Hope*, 89–92; Kelley, *Hammer and Hoe*, 123–25.

35. Denning, *Cultural Front*, 238.

36. Johnson, "The New Frontage on American Life," in Locke, ed., *The New Negro*, 294; Frazier, *The Negro Family*, 209, 355; Baker, *From Savage to Negro*, 177–80; Holloway, *Confronting the Veil*, 123–56.

37. Hemenway, *Zora Neale Hurston*, 124, 220, 243 n. 5; D'Orso, *Like Judgment Day;* Norwood, "Bogalusa Burning"; Hurston, *Every Tongue*, 257–58.

38. Preece, "The Negro Folk Cult," *Crisis* 43 (1936): 364; Wright, "Between Laughter and Tears," *New Masses* 25, no. 2 (Oct. 1937): 22, 25. Hazel Carby echoes this denigration of the South in her criticism of Hurston, *Cultures in Babylon*, 148; On Huston and

FWP, see Filene, *Romancing the Folk*, and Denning, *Cultural Front*, 132–34. On Lomax and Leadbelly, see Carby, *Race Men*, 101–9. On the significance of Popular Front literature to interracial unionism in the 1940s, see Korstad, *Civil Rights Unionism*, 226–40.

39. Korstad, *Civil Rights Unionism*, 148; Claude Williams, letter to Willard Uphaus, Sept. 26, 1936, folder 26, box 1, CW. Mark Solomon also notes that the STFU "had a paternalistic attitude toward its black members" (*The Cry Was Unity*, 294).

40. Weiss, *The National Urban League*, 285–90.

41. "Convention Action on Negro Workers," Oct. 8, 1941, box 28, series 9, WG; Weiss, *The National Urban League*, 285–90. None of the standard accounts of the 1935 convention mention the debate over racial exclusion. See, for example, Zieger, *The CIO*, 22; Dubofsky and Van Tine, *John L. Lewis*, 217–21.

42. Granger, telegraph to Lewis, Dec. 2, 1935, "CIO" file, box 3, series 2, part 1, NUL; Granger, "Industrial Unionism and the Negro," *Opportunity* (Jan. 1936): 29–30; Pfeffer, *A. Philip Randolph*, 27–29.

43. Quotes in Raddock, *Portrait of an American Labor Leader*, 154.

44. "Labor Day Celebration Monday in Bogalusa," *Franklinton Era-Leader*, Sept. 1936, 1; "Bogalusa Diamond Jubilee," *Daily News* (Bogalusa), July 2, 1989; Quick, "The History of Bogalusa."

45. Sanders Adams, letter to William Green, July 23, 1941, AFL Discrimination Survey, series 9, boxes 26, 27, 28, WG.

46. Dinwiddie, "The International Woodworkers of America," 16

47. Dinwiddie, "The International Woodworkers of America," 14–31.

48. Kelley, *Hammer and Hoe*, 191–92. Alan Draper argues that Communists succeeded at interracial organizing *because* they adopted the less radical strategies of the UWM, but he agrees with Kelley that mine unions remained weak in Alabama until the 1940s ("The New Southern Labor History Revisted").

49. Quotes in Egolf, "The Limits of Shop Floor Struggle," 204–33.

50. Zieger, *The CIO*, 74–75.

51. "Lewis Group Carries War to the A.F. of L." and "Win Increase, Ask Another," *New York Times*, Mar. 10, 1937, 1, 3; Honey, *Southern Labor and Black Civil Rights*, 82–86.

52. Schulyer, "Negro Workers Lead in Great Lakes Steel Drive," reprinted in Foner and Lewis, *Black Workers*, 469–79; Honey, *Southern Labor and Black Civil Rights*, 85–86. Schulyer would become an antiunion conservative in the 1950s, but he was a socialist in the 1930s. See Ransby, *Ella Baker*, 78–91.

53. Mason quoted in Salmond, *Miss Lucy of the CIO*, 79–80; Lumpkin, *The South in Progress*, 233; SNYC quoted in Honey, *Southern Labor and Black Civil Rights*, 165.

54. Sullivan, *Days of Hope*, 98–101; Kelley, *Hammer and Hoe*, 195–219; Korstad, *Civil Rights Unionism*, 148–49.

55. Honey, *Southern Labor and Black Civil Rights*, 136. On Koger, see Korstad, *Civil Rights Unionism*, 155–57.

Chapter 6: Black Working-Class Politics in the Postwar South

1. Cecelski, "The Home Front's Dispossessed," 37–41; "Southern Pine at War," vol. 1, box 747, SPA.

2. "Southern Pine at War"; Ben Greene interview.

3. Fickle, *The New South and the "New Competition*," 349–50; C. C. Sheppard, Statement, Apr. 14, 1943, "Statements" folder, box 167, SPA.

4. C. C. Sheppard, Statement, Apr. 14, 1943, "Statements" folder, box 167, SPA.

5. C. C. Sheppard, Statement, Apr. 14, 1943, "Statements" folder, box 167, SPA.

6. Fickle, *The New South and the "New Competition,"* 308; "Southern Pine at War," [n.d.], vol. 1, box 747, SPA; Collier,*The First Fifty Years of the Southern Pine Association,* 123.

7. "Outline of Cooperation by Southern Pine War Committee with War Department's Morale-Building Program in the Southern Lumber Industry," [n.d.], vol. 3, box 747, SPA.

8. C. C. Sheppard, Statement, Apr. 14, 1943, "Statements" folder, box 167, SPA. Loggers did not work in logging operations. They rode the carriage that directed logs through the head saw, working with the head sawyer to ensure an accurate cut. "Southern Pine Wages," July 25, 1949, folder 15, box 54, OD.

9. "Southern Pine at War"; Sheppard, Statement, Apr. 14, 1943, "Statements" folder, box 167, SPA; Fickle, *The New South and the "New Competition,"* 307.

10. Fickle, *The New South and the "New Competition,"* 306–7.

11. Carl L. White, Blames Wage-Hour Officers for Closing, letter to editor, *Arkansas Gazette* (Little Rock), June 2, 1943.

12. Clarence Stokes, letter to U.S. district attorney, May 18, 1943, frame 112, reel 11, PFUSDJ; Daniel, *The Shadow of Slavery;* Aptheker, *Afro-American History,* 191–201; Albert J. Tully, "Report of Disposition of Criminal Case File 50–1–10," Nov. 9, 1943, reel 10, frame 0141, PFUSDJ.

13. E. P. Ahern, letter to Louis Schwellenbach, Oct. 24, 1945, reel 10, frame 309, PFUSDJ.

14. Ben Greene interview; Fickle, *The New South and the "New Competition,"* 311–13.

15. SPWC, "Women Workers in South's Lumber Industry," [n.d.], box 747, SPA.

16. SPWC, "Women Workers in South's Lumber Industry," [n.d.], box 747, SPA.

17. C. C. Sheppard, Statement, Apr. 14, 1943, "Statements" folder, box 167, SPA; SPWC, "Women Workers in South's Lumber Industry," [n.d.], box 747, SPA; Fickle, *The New South and the "New Competition,"* 310.

18. SPWC, "Women Workers in South's Lumber Industry," [n.d.], box 747, SPA; Fickle, *The New South and the "New Competition,"* 315.

19. E. C. Roe, letter to J. L. Rhodes and J. T. McElveen, Aug. 5, 1941, case #196–4478, entry 14, Dispute Case Files, DLMCS.

20. Newcomb Barco, "Progress Report," Aug. 12, 1941, "Special Report," July 4 and 17, 1941, J. L. Rhodes, telegram to Mr. John R. Steelman, June 27, 1941, file 196-4478, MCSDL.

21. Patrick Means, "Special Examiner's Determination in Labor Dispute Case," Sept. 2, 1941, file 196-4478, MCSDL.

22. Dinwiddie, "The International Woodworkers of America," 45–58.

23. Honey, *Southern Labor and Black Civil Rights,* 179–90; Dinwiddie, "The International Woodworkers of America," 64–92.

24. Honey, *Southern Labor and Black Civil Rights,* 179. J. W. King, Sr., letter to Dr. John R. Steelman, Aug. 13, 1943, file 301-2997, MCSDL.

25. Paul Sanders, "Elections of Anderson and Tully Company," July 21, 1943. G. Paul Crowder, wage and hour inspector, "Interoffice Communication," Sept. 20, 1943. D. K. Jones, [Final Report], Apr. 22, 1944, file 301-2997, MCSDL; Dinwiddie, "The International Woodworkers of America," 84–87.

26. Bates, *Pullman Porters,* 148–74; Ziegler, *The CIO,* 141–90; Meier and Rudwick, *Black Detroit,* 111.

27. Halpern, "The CIO and the Limits"; Alex Lichtenstein, "'Scientific Unionism' and the 'Negro Question'"; Draper, "The New Southern Labor History Revisited"; Honey, *Southern Labor and Black Civil Rights;* Korstad and Lichtenstein, "Opportu-

nities Found and Lost"; Johnson quoted in Dalfiume, "The 'Forgotten Years,'" 100; Drake and Cayton, *Black Metropolis*, 313.

28. Nelson, "Organized Labor and the Struggle for Black Equality," 982.

29. Sugrue, *The Origins of the Urban Crisis*, 29; Nelson, "Organized Labor and the Struggle for Black Equality," 982.

30. Cy G. Lowe, letter to Louisiana Manufacturers, Sept. 13, 1945, box 316, folder 2-5, SPA; Dinwiddie, "The International Woodworkers of America," 87–92; A. F. Hinrichs, letter to Mr. Cy G. Lowe, Apr. 6, 1944, box 329, folder 2-5, SPA.

31. Korstad, *Civil Rights Unionism*, particularly 225–50.

32. "The CIO Invades Dixie," *Saturday Evening Post*, July 20, 1946, 12, 94–99.

33. "Labor Drives South," *Fortune* 34 (Nov. 1946): 134–37.

34. *Proceedings of the 10th Annual Convention of the IWA*, Edmund Ryan, letter to George Baldanzi, Oct. 26, 1946, OD. For a standard assessment of Operation Dixie, see Griffith, *The Crisis of Organized Labor*.

35. Marshall, *Labor in the South*, 151; Letwin, *The Challenge of Interracial Unionism*, 185–88.

36. Gloster Current, letter to Mr. W. J. Longmire, Sept. 10, 1954, box 3, series C, group 2, NAACP; Gandy interview.

37. Charles Peavey, "Unions," June 30, 1948, FSMCS.

38. *Proceedings of the 10th Annual Convention of the IWA*, R. Wray Alt, letter to William Smith, Oct. 26, 1946, folder 1, box 53, OD; For more on the Elizabethtown local, see William Jones, "Black Workers and the CIO's Turn."

39. "Synopsis of Incidents at Greene Brothers Lumber Company Since the Beginning of Organization to the Present Date," box 64, folder 4, OD.

40. R. Wray Alt, letter to William Botkins, Oct. 22, 1946, box 59, folder 1, OD.

41. Sitkoff, "African American Militancy," 87, "Brotherhood Week," *International Woodworker*, Feb. 24, 1948, 1. On liberals' retreat from ethnic politics in the wake of World War II, see Gerstle, *American Crucible*, 128–86.

42. Membership lists, Green [*sic*] Brothers Lumber Company, 1947, reel 5, ODM; Alvin Greene interview.

43. *Proceedings of the 10th Annual Convention of the IWA*.

44. "Strike Ends in IWA Victory," *International Woodworker*, Dec. 29, 1948.

45. "Strike Plans—Greene Brothers—Elizabethtown," July 16, 1948, reel 5, ODM.

46. Dean L. Culver, letter to William Smith, July 17, 1948, reel 5, ODM.

47. Dean L. Culver, "Transcript of Telephone Report," July 21, 1948, reel 5, ODM.

48. "Bargaining Rights at Issue: Elizabethtown Woodworkers Challenge Lumber Barons in Fight for Living Wage," *International Woodworker*, July 28, 1948, 1.

49. William Wagner Weiss, letter to Ted, Oct. 5, 1948, reel 5, ODM.

50. Orie and Louise Tyson interview; Lewis and McDowell interview.

51. William Smith, "Notes on Elizabethtown," Sept. 14, 1948, reel 5, ODM.

52. "North Carolina Locals Forging Ahead in 1950," *International Woodworker*, June 26, 1950; "Talks Highlight Union Rally Here," *Daily News* (Washington, N.C.), Sept. 1, 1951, 1; "Labor Day Celebration," *International Woodworker*, Sept. 26, 1951, 16; "PAC Meeting," *International Woodworker*, Nov. 14, 1951; *International Woodworker*, Nov. 12, 1952.

53. *International Woodworker*, July 28, 1948; Aug. 18, 1948; Dec. 24, 1948; "Labor Unions Aid Negroes in the South," *International Woodworker*, Oct. 10, 1951, 3.

54. *International Woodworker*, Oct. 10, 1951, 13; *International Woodworker*, Aug. 13, 1952.

55. "Southern Regional Conference, International Woodworkers of America," Nov.

204 *Notes to Pages 176–86*

11, 1950, box 59, folder 4, OD; Bruce Davis, letter to Franz Daniel, Nov. 9, 1950, box 59, folder 4, OD.

56. Elizabethtown Chamber of Commerce, "Elizabethtown, North Carolina: An Invitation to Industry," 1957, Local History Room, Elizabethtown Public Library.

57. Cecelski, *Along Freedom Road;* Lewis and McDowell interview; Orie and Louise Tyson interview.

58. "Labor Day," *Bogalusa News,* Aug. 30, 1940, 3; Ivan A. Magnitzky, proclamation printed in the *Bogalusa News,* Aug. 30, 1940, 3.

59. Zeiger, *Rebuilding the Pulp and Paper Workers' Union,* 151; "Many features planned for Labor Day program," *Bogalusa News,* Aug. 23, 1940, 1.

60. Northrup, *The Negro in the Paper Industry,* 30; John Oatis interview; Steven Thirstier, "To the Voters," *Bogalusa Bulletin,* Aug. 10, 1942, 4; "Magnitzky Thanks Voters," *Bogalusa Bulletin,* Aug. 31, 1942; Fairclough, *Race and Democracy.*

61. Quoted in Minchin, *The Color of Work,* 94.

62. Rickey Hill, "The Character of Black Politics"; Lance Hill, *The Deacons for Defense;* Fairclough, *Race and Democracy;* Minchin, *The Color of Work,* 94.

63. Korstad and Lichtenstein, "Opportunities Found and Lost." See also Halpern, "The CIO and the Limits"; Alex Lichtenstein, "'Scientific Unionism' and the 'Negro Question'"; Draper, "The New Southern Labor History Revisited"; Honey, *Southern Labor and Black Civil Rights.*

Conclusion: A Dream Deferred

1. Orie and Louise Tyson interview; Oatis interview; Ginn interview; Abrams interview.

2. Cross Tabulation, Race, Ownership, State (ICPSR code), in NC, AL, LA, 1960, Ruggles, Sobek, et al., *Integrated Public Use Microdata Series;* Julius A. Thomas, "The Negro in Industry and Labor," General Department File, 1941–1959, box 14, part 1, series 4, NUL; "Greene Brothers Lumber Company, Inc., Wage Scales," reel 5, ODM; Coontz, *The Way We Never Were,* 25–29, and Faludi, *Stiffed;* Coontz, *The Way We Really Are,* 36–44. Jack Temple Kirby points out that automobiles allowed many southerners to revive older traditions of splitting their work time between farming and wage work. What distinguished the 1950s from earlier periods was that industry work remained the most important source of income, while for most southerners farming was the supplemental pastime (*Rural Worlds Lost,* 353).

3. Julius A. Thomas, "The Negro in Industry and Labor," 21, General Department File, 1941–1959, box 14, part 1, series 4, NUL.

4. Cabell J. Regan, "Bladen County Development Guide," Sept. 1976, Local History Room, Elizabethtown Public Library.

5. Curry interview; Mason McGowin interview.

6. Harvey interview; Mims interview; Greenhaw, "The Fight to Survive," 11–24; Israel and Williams, "Ending the Short Stick," 16; Stein, *Running Steel, Running America,* 117.

7. On deindustrialization in the North, see Sugrue, *The Origins of the Urban Crisis.* Wright, *Old South, New South,* 250, 253.

8. Wright, afterward to *The Second Wave,* 296. See also Schulman, *From Cotton Belt to Sunbelt,* 174–205.

9. Minchin, *Hiring the Black Worker;* Schulman, *From Cotton Belt to Sunbelt,* 179–81.

10. Glazer, forward to Frazier, *The Negro Family,* vii; Lemann, *The Promised Land,* 170–76.

11. On Moynihan's proposals, see Lemann, *The Promised Land*, 174, and Reed, *Stirrings in the Jug*, 193–95.

12. Nelson Lichtenstein, *State of the Union*. On union campaigns in the contemporary South, see Charlie LeDuff, "At a Slaughterhouse, Some Things Never Die: Who Kills, Who Cuts, Who Bosses Can Depend on Race," *New York Times*, July 16, 1999; Steve Bader, "'Pre-Majority' Public Workers Union Makes Gains in North Carolina," *Labor Notes*, Sept. 2002; Stewart Yerton and Stephanie Grace, "Poll Reveals Support for Hospitality Workers," *New Orleans Times-Picayune*, July 10, 2001.

BIBLIOGRAPHY

Interviews

Interview tape and/or transcript locations:
SHC = Southern Oral History Collection, Wilson Library, University of North Carolina, Chapel Hill, N.C.
FHS = Oral History Collection of the Forest History Society, Durham, N.C.
FWP = Federal Writers Project Papers, Life Histories, Southern Historical Collection, Wilson Library, University of North Carolina, Chapel Hill, N.C.

Abrams, Ire. Interview by William P. Jones, Chapman, Ala., Jan. 12, 1998. SHC.
Bailey, William, Jr. Interview by William P. Jones, Bogalusa, La., Feb. 18, 1998. SHC.
Boyette, Evelyn. Interview by William P. Jones, Bogalusa, La., Feb. 20, 1998. Notes in possession of author.
Brumfield, Dewitt, and Leamalie Holmes. Interview by William P. Jones, Bogalusa, La., Mar. 1, 1998. SHC.
Carter, Lonnie (pseudonym). Interview by William P. Jones, Elizabethtown, N.C., May 16, 1996. Tape in possession of author.
Cartwright, Reverend Carey Miles. Interview by W. O. Saunders, Elizabeth City, N.C. [n.d.]. FWP.
Cheatham, George. Interview by William P. Jones, Georgiana, Ala., Jan. 10, 1998. SHC.
Cobb, Marie. Interview by William P. Jones, Georgiana, Ala., Jan. 11, 1998. SHC.
Curry, Fletcher. Interview by William P. Jones, Greenville, Ala., Jan. 10, 1998. SHC.
Emerson, Andrew Lee. "Andrew Jackson of Southern Labor." Interview by Covington Hall, Menton, Ala., Dec. 15, 1938. FWP.
Gandy, Reverend Roy. Interview by William P. Jones, Greenville, Ala., Jan. 10, 1998. SHC.
Ginn, Willie Everette. Interview by William P. Jones, Bogalusa, La., Feb. 28, 1998. SHC.
Greene, Alvin. Interview by William P. Jones, Elizabethtown, N.C., June 25, 1996. SHC.
Greene, Ben and Frances. Interview by William P. Jones, Elizabethtown, N.C., June 25, 1996. SHC.
Harvey, Paul. Interview by William P. Jones, Franklinton, La., Feb. 17, 1998. Notes in possession of author.
McCaffrey, Joseph E. Interview by Elwood Maunder, Atlanta, Ga., Feb. 5–6, 1964, and Georgetown, S.C., Mar. 1965. FHS.

McDowell, Adel, and Leah Betty Lewis. Interview by William P. Jones, Elizabethtown, N.C., June 5, 1996. SHC.

McGowin, Mason. Interview by William P. Jones, Chapman, Ala., Jan. 10, 1998. SHC.

Mims, Raymond. Interview by William P. Jones, Bogalusa, La., Mar. 3, 1998. SHC.

Montgomery, Mate. Interview by William P. Jones, Georgiana, Ala., Jan. 12, 1998. SHC.

Oatis, John Martin. Interview by William P. Jones, Bogalusa, La., Mar. 1, 1998. SHC.

Reeves, Talmadge, and Hogin Chapelle. Interview by William P. Jones, Franklinton, La., Feb. 16, 1998. SHC.

Rudolph, R. C. Interview by William P. Jones, Georgiana, Ala., Jan. 11, 1998. SHC.

Shaw, Mabry. "War Minded." Interview by Mary Hicks, Raleigh, N.C., Mar. 29, 1939. FWP.

Tyson, Orie and Louise. Interview by William P. Jones, Elizabethtown, N.C., Sept. 1, 1996. SHC.

Tyson, Waymond. Interview by William P. Jones, Elizabethtown, N.C., Sept. 1, 1996. SHC.

Manuscript Collections

ADIR   Alabama Department of Industrial Relations Records, SP103, Alabama Department of Archives and History, Montgomery, Ala.

ADL   Alabama Department of Labor Records, 1935–1939, 1943–, Alabama Department of Archives and History, Montgomery, Ala.

APCSF   Alabama Press Clippings Surname File, Alabama Department of Archives and History, Montgomery, Ala.

AWRR   Atlantic and Western Railroad Records, 1907–1947, Duke University Special Collections, Perkins Library, Durham, N.C.

CW   Claude Williams Papers, Archives of Labor and Urban Affairs, Wayne State University, Detroit, Mich.

FHS   Company Vertical Files, Forest History Society, Durham, N.C.

FSMCS   Field Studies in the Modern Culture of the South, Records Subseries 1.3, Southern Historical Collection, Wilson Library, University of North Carolina, Chapel Hill, N.C.

GSLC   Great Southern Lumber Company Records, Louisiana and Lower Mississippi Valley Collections, LSU Libraries, Louisiana State University, Baton Rouge, La.

KLC   Kaul Lumber Company Records, Department of Archives and Manuscripts, Linn-Henley Research Library, Birmingham Public Library, Birmingham, Ala.

MCSDL   Mediation and Conciliation Service of the U.S. Department of Labor, Dispute Case Files, 1913–1948, Record Group 280, National Archives, College Park, Md.

MMFC   Margaret Mead Film Collection, Motion Picture Collection, Library of Congress, Washington, D.C.

NAACP   National Association for the Advancement of Colored People Papers, Library of Congress, Manuscripts Division, Washington, D.C.

NRA   National Recovery Administration Records, Record Group 9, National Archives, Washington, D.C.

NUL   National Urban League Papers, Library of Congress, Manuscripts Division, Washington, D.C.

OD   Operation Dixie: The CIO Organizing Committee Papers, 1946–1953, Duke University Special Collections, Perkins Library, Durham, N.C.

ODM   Operation Dixie: The CIO Organizing Committee Papers, 1946–1953, ed. Katherine F. Martin. Sanford, N.C.: Microfilming Corp. of America, 1980

PFUSDJ Peonage Files of the U.S. Department of Justice, 1901–1945, ed. Pete Daniel. Bethesda: University Publications of America, 1989

SPA   Southern Pine Association Collection, Louisiana and Lower Mississippi Valley Collections, LSU Libraries, Louisiana State University, Baton Rouge, La.

WG   AFL President William Green Papers, George Meany Memorial Archives, Silver Springs, Md.

WPA   Works Progress Administration Manuscripts, Library of Congress, Manuscripts Division, Washington, D.C.

WTSLC   W. T. Smith Lumber Company Records, Alabama Department of Archives and History, Montgomery, Ala.

Newspapers and Magazines

Arkansas Gazette (Little Rock, Ark.)
Bogalusa Bulletin
Bogalusa Enterprise
Bogalusa News
The Crisis
Daily News (Bogalusa, La.)
Daily News (Greensboro, N.C.)
Daily News (Washington, N.C.)
Esso Oilways
Fortune
Franklinton (La.) Era-Leader
International Woodworker
Journal of Commerce (New York, N.Y.)
Lumbering Along
Nashville Banner
New Orleans Times-Picayune
New York Times
Norfolk (Va.) Ledger-Dispatch
Norfolk Virginian-Pilot
Opportunity
Saturday Evening Post
Southern Lumberman
Tri-State Builder

Books, Articles, Recordings, and Dissertations

Allen, Ruth Alice. *East Texas Lumberworkers: An Economic and Social Picture, 1870–1950.* Austin: University of Texas Press, 1961.

Aptheker, Herbert, *Afro-American History: The Modern Era.* New York: First Carol Publishing Group, 1992.

Armstrong, Thomas F. "Georgia Lumber Workers, 1880–1917: The Social Implications of Work." In *African Americans and Non-Agricultural Labor in the South 1865–1900,* ed. Donald G. Nieman. New York: Garland Publishing, Inc., 1994.

Arnesen, Eric. *Brotherhoods of Color: Black Railroad Workers and the Struggle for Equality.* Cambridge, Mass.: Harvard University Press, 2001.

———. "Up from Exclusion: Black and White Workers, Race, and the State of Labor History." *Reviews in American History* 26 (1998): 146–74.

———. *Waterfront Workers of New Orleans: Race, Class, and Politics, 1863–1923.* Urbana: University of Illinois Press, 1991.

Ayers, Edward L. *The Promise of the New South: Life after Reconstruction.* New York: Oxford University Press, 1992.

Badger, Anthony J. *The New Deal: The Depression Years, 1933–1940.* New York: Hill and Wang, 1989.

Baker, Lee D. *From Savage to Negro: Anthropology and the Construction of Race, 1896–1954.* Berkeley: University of California Press, 1998.

Barrelhouse, Blues, and Boogie Piano (1927–1930). Various artists. Blues Document LP 2033.

Barrelhouse Piano 1927–1936. Various artists. Yazoo Compact Disk B000000G7F.

Bates, Beth Tompkins. *Pullman Porters and the Rise of Protest Politics in Black America, 1925–1945.* Chapel Hill: University of North Carolina Press, 2001.

Bederman, Gail. *Manliness and Civilization: A Cultural History of Gender and Race in the United States, 1880–1917.* Chicago: University of Chicago Press, 1995.

Berglund, Abraham, George T. Starnes, and Frank T. De Vyver. *Labor in the Industrial South: A Survey of Wages and Living Conditions in Three Major Industries of the New Industrial South.* Charlottesville: University of Virginia Press, 1930.

Betts, H. S. "The Southern Pines." Washington, D.C.: U.S. Department of Agriculture, 1942.

Bond, Horace Mann. *Negro Education in Alabama: A Study in Cotton and Steel.* 1969. Reprint, Tuscaloosa: University of Alabama Press, 1994.

Bond, Horace Mann, and Julia W. Bond. *The Star Creek Papers: Washington Parish and the Lynching of Jerome Wilson,* ed. Adam Fairclough. Athens: University of Georgia Press, 1997.

Boyd, William. "The Forest Is the Future? Industrial Forestry and the Southern Pulp and Paper Complex." In *The Second Wave: Southern Industrialization from the 1940s to the 1970s,* ed. Philip Scranton. Athens: University of Georgia Press, 2001.

Brattain, Michelle. "The Pursuits of Post-exceptionalism: Race, Gender, Class, and Politics in the New Southern Labor History." In *Labor in the Modern South,* ed. Glenn T. Eskew. Athens: University of Georgia Press, 2001.

Brewer, Anthony. *Marxist Theories of Imperialism: A Critical Survey.* New York: Routledge, 1990.

Brody, David. *In Labor's Cause: Main Themes on the History of the American Worker.* New York: Oxford University Press, 1993.

———. "The Rise and Decline of Welfare Capitalism." In *Workers in Industrial America: Essays on the Twentieth-Century Struggle.* New York: Oxford University Press, 1993.

Brown, Edwin L., and Colin Davis, eds. *It Is Union and Liberty: Alabama Coal Miners and the United Autoworkers of America.* Tuscaloosa: University of Alabama Press, 1999.

Brown, Nelson Courtland. *Logging Transportation: The Principles and Methods of Log Transportation in the United States and Canada.* New York: John Wiley and Sons, Inc., 1936.

Bryant, Ralph Clement. *Logging: The Principles and General Methods of Operation in the United States.* New York: John Wiley and Sons, Inc, 1914.

Carby, Hazel V. *Cultures in Babylon: Black Britain and African America.* New York: Verso: 1999.

———. *Race Men.* Cambridge: Harvard University Press, 1998.

Cash, W. J. *The Mind of the South.* New York: Alfred A. Knopf, 1941.

Cecelski, David S. *Along Freedom Road: Hyde County, North Carolina, and the Fate of Black Schools in the South.* Chapel Hill: University of North Carolina Press, 1994.

Cecelski, David. "The Home Front's Dispossessed." *Southern Exposure* (Summer 1995): 37–41.

Cell, John W. *The Highest Stage of White Supremacy: The Origins of Segregation in South Africa and the American South.* New York: Cambridge University Press, 1982.

Cohen, Lizbeth. *Making a New Deal: Industrial Workers in Chicago, 1919–1939.* New York: Cambridge University Press, 1990.

Collier, John M. *The First Fifty Years of the Southern Pine Association, 1915–1965.* New Orleans: Southern Pine Association, 1965.

Coontz, Stephanie. *The Way We Never Were: American Families and the Nostalgia Trap.* New York: Basic Books, 1995.

———. *The Way We Really Are: Coming to Terms with America's Changing Families.* New York: Basic Books, 1997.

Cooper, Frederick. *De-colonization and African Society: The Labor Question in French and British Africa.* New York: Cambridge University Press, 1996.

Cowie, Jefferson, and Joseph Heathcott, eds. *Beyond the Ruins: The Meanings of Industrialization.* Ithaca: Cornell University Press, 2003.

Cruikshank, J. W. *North Carolina Forest Resources and Industries.* Washington: U.S. Department of Agriculture, 1944.

D'Orso, Michael. *Like Judgment Day: The Ruin and Redemption of a Town Called Rosewood.* New York: G. P. Putnam's Sons, 1996.

Dalfume, Richard M. "The 'Forgotten Years' of the Negro Revolution." *Journal of American History* 55 (June 1968): 90–106.

Daniel, Pete. *Lost Revolutions: The South in the 1950s.* Chapel Hill: University of North Carolina Press, 2000.

———. *The Shadow of Slavery: Peonage in the South, 1901–1969.* Urbana: University of Illinois Press, 1972.

Davis, Angela Y. *Blues Legacies and Black Feminism: Gertrude "Ma" Rainey, Bessie Smith, and Billie Holiday.* New York: Pantheon Books, 1998.

Davis, Francis. *The History of the Blues: The Roots, the Music, the People from Charley Patton to Robert Cray.* New York: Hyperion, 1995.

Davis, Mike. "Who Killed LA? A Political Autopsy." *New Left Review* 197 (Jan./Feb. 1993): 3–28.

Denning, Michael. *The Cultural Front: The Laboring of American Culture in the Twentieth Century.* New York: Verso: 1997.

———. "The End of Mass Culture." *International Labor and Working-Class History* 37 (Spring 1990): 4–18.

Dinwiddie, Robert Carlton. "The International Woodworkers of America and Southern Laborers, 1937–1945." Master's thesis, Georgia State University, 1980.

Dollard, John. *Caste and Class in a Southern Town.* New Haven, Conn.: Yale University Press, 1937.

Drake, St. Clair, and Horace R. Cayton. *Black Metropolis: A Study of Negro Life in a Northern City.* New York: Harper and Row, 1945.

Draper, Alan. "The New Southern Labor History Revisited: The Success of the Mine, Mill, and Smelter Workers Union in Birmingham, 1934–1938." *Journal of Southern History* 62 (Feb. 1996): 87–108.

Dreiser, Theodore, ed. *Harlan Miners Speak: Report on Terrorism in the Kentucky Coal Fields Prepared by Members of the National Committee for the Defense of Political Prisoners.* New York: Da Capo, 1970.

Drobney, Jeffrey A. *Lumbermen and Log Sawyers: Life, Labor, and Culture in the North Florida Timber Industry, 1830–1930.* Macon: Mercer University Press, 1997.

Dubofsky, Melvyn, and Warren Van Tine. *John L. Lewis: A Biography.* New York: Quadrangle, 1977.

Eagle, Bob, and Steve LaVere. "Hard Working Woman: Mississippi Matilda." *Living Blues* 8 (Mar. 1972): 7.

Edwards, Laura F. *Gendered Strife and Confusion: The Political Culture of Reconstruction.* Chapel Hill: University of North Carolina Press, 1997.

Egolf, Jeremy R. "The Limits of Shop Floor Struggle: Workers vs. the Bedaux System at Willapa Harbor Lumber Mills, 1933–1935." *Labor History* 26 (1985): 195–229.

Fairclough, Adam. *Race and Democracy: The Civil Rights Struggle in Louisiana, 1915–1972.* Athens: University of Georgia Press, 1995.

———. *To Redeem the Soul of America: The Southern Christian Leadership Conference and Martin Luther King, Jr.* Athens: University of Georgia Press, 1987.

Faludi, Susan. *Stiffed: The Betrayal of the American Man.* New York: William Morrow and Company, 1999.

Faulkner, William. *Light in August.* New York: Random House, 1990.

Fickle, James E. *The New South and the "New Competition": Trade Association Development in the Southern Pine Industry.* Urbana: University of Illinois Press, 1980.

Filene, Benjamin. *Romancing the Folk: Public Memory and American Roots Music.* Chapel Hill: University of North Carolina Press, 2000.

Finegold, Kenneth, and Theda Skocpol. *State and Party in America's New Deal.* Madison: University of Wisconsin Press, 1995.

Fink, Leon. *Progressive Intellectuals and the Dilemmas of Democratic Commitment.* Cambridge: Harvard University Press, 1997.

Fishel, Leslie H., Jr. "The Negro in the New Deal Era." *Wisconsin Magazine of History* (Winter 1964): 111–26.

Flamming, Douglas. *Creating the Modern South: Millhands and Managers in Dalton, Georgia, 1884–1984.* Chapel Hill: University of North Carolina Press, 1992.

Flynt, Wayne. *Poor but Proud: Alabama's Poor Whites.* Tuscaloosa: University of Alabama Press, 1989.

Foley, Barbara. *Radical Representations: Politics and Form in U.S. Proletarian Fiction, 1929–1941.* Durham, N.C.: Duke University Press, 1993.

Foner, Eric. *Reconstruction: America's Unfinished Revolution, 1863–1877.* New York: Harper and Row, 1988.

Foner, Philip S., and Roland L. Lewis, eds. *Black Workers: A Documentary History from Colonial Times to the Present.* Philadelphia: Temple University Press, 1989.

Franklin, John Hope, and Alfred A. Moss. *From Slavery to Freedom: A History of African Americans.* New York: McGraw-Hill, Inc., 1994.

Frazer, Steven. *Labor Will Rule: Sidney Hillman and the Rise of American Labor.* Ithaca: Cornell University Press, 1991.

Frazier, E. Franklin. *The Negro Family in the United States.* 1939. Reprinted with forward by Nathan Glazer. Chicago: University of Chicago Press, 1966.

Gaines, Kevin K. *Uplifting the Race: Black Leadership, Politics, and Culture in the Twentieth-Century.* Chapel Hill: University of North Carolina Press, 1996.

Galenson, Walter. *The United Brotherhood of Carpenters: The First Hundred Years.* Cambridge: Harvard University Press, 1983.

Gardner, Joel. *Built in Louisiana: A Social History of Louisiana Carpenters.* New Orleans: Louisiana Council of Carpenters, 1985.

Garlock, Jonathan. *Guide to Local Assemblies of the Knights of Labor.* Westport, Conn.: Greenwood Press, 1982.

Garon, Paul. *Four Women Blues: The Victor/Bluebird Recordings of Memphis Minnie, Mississippi Matilda, Kansas City Kitty, and Miss Rosie Mae Moore.* RCA Compact Disk, 07863–66719–2.

Gerstle, Gary. *American Crucible: Race and Nation in the Twentieth Century.* Princeton: Princeton University Press, 2001.

Gilmore, Glenda Elizabeth. *Gender and Jim Crow: Women and the Politics of White Supremacy in North Carolina, 1896–1920.* Chapel Hill: University of North Carolina Press, 1996.

Goodyear, Charles W. *The Bogalusa Story.* Buffalo: privately printed, 1950.

Gordon, Colin. *New Deals: Business, Labor, and Politics in America, 1920–1935.* New York: Cambridge University Press, 1994.

Green, James. "The Brotherhood of Timber Workers, 1910–1913: A Radical Response to Industrial Capitalism in the Southern U.S.A." *Past and Present* 60 (Aug. 1973): 161–200.

Greenhaw, Wayne. "The Fight to Survive in the South's Backwoods." *Southern Changes: The Journal of the Southern Regional Council* (July 1981): 11–24.

Griffith, Barbara S. *The Crisis of American Labor: Operation Dixie and the Defeat of the CIO.* Philadelphia: Temple University Press, 1988.

Griffler, Keith P. *What Price Alliance? Black Radicals Confront White Labor, 1918–1938.* New York: Garland, 1995.

Hahn, Steven. *A Nation under Our Feet: Black Political Struggles in the Rural*

South from Slavery to the Great Migration. Cambridge: Harvard University Press, 2003.

Hale, Grace Elizabeth. *Making Whiteness: The Culture of Segregation in the South, 1890–1940.* New York: Vintage Books, 1998.

Hall, Jacquelyn Dowd. "Disorderly Women: Gender and Labor Militancy in the Appalachian South." *Journal of American History* 73 (Sept. 1986): 354–82.

———. "Women Writers, the 'Southern Front,' and the Dialectical Imagination." *Journal of Southern History* 69 (Feb. 2003): 3–38.

Hall, Jacquelyn Dowd, James Leloudis, Robert Korstad, Mary Murphy, Lu Ann Jones, and Christopher B. Daly. *Like a Family: The Making of a Southern Cotton Mill World.* Chapel Hill: University of North Carolina Press, 2000.

Halpern, Rick. "The CIO and the Limits of Labor-Based Civil Rights Activism: The Case of Louisiana's Sugar Workers, 1947–1966." In *Southern Labor in Transition, 1940–1995,* ed. Robert H. Zieger. Knoxville: University of Tennessee Press, 1997.

Harrison, Daphne Duval. *Black Pearls: Blues Queens of the 1920s.* New Brunswick: Rutgers University Press, 1993.

———. "'Classic' Blues and Women Singers." In *The Blackwell Guide to Recorded Blues,* ed. Paul Oliver. Cambridge: Blackwell Publishers, 1991.

Hasse, John Edward. *Beyond Category: The Life and Genius of Duke Ellington.* New York: Simon and Schuster, 1993.

Hawley, Ellis W. *The New Deal and the Problem of Monopoly: A Study in Economic Ambivalence.* New York: Fordham University Press, 1995.

Haynes, George E., and Karl F. Phillips. *The Negro at Work during the World War and during Reconstruction: Statistics, Problems, and Policies Relating to the Greater Inclusion of Negro Wage Earners in American Industry and Agriculture.* Washington, D.C.: U.S. Department of Labor, 1921.

Hazzard-Gordon, Katrina. *Jookin': The Rise of Social Dance Formations in African-American Culture.* Philadelphia: Temple University Press, 1990.

Heide, Karl Gert zur. *Deep South Piano: The Story of Little Brother Montgomery.* London: Studio Vista, 1970.

Hemenway, Robert E. *Zora Neale Hurston: A Literarary Biography.* Urbana: University of Illinois Press, 1977.

Henry, Charles P. *Ralph Bunche: Model Negro or American Other?* New York: New York University Press, 1999.

Herring, Harriet L. "Industrial Relations in the South and the NIRA." *Social Forces* 12 (Oct. 1933): 124–31.

Higginbotham, Evelyn Brooks. "Rethinking Vernacular Culture: Black Religion and Race Records in the 1920s and 1930s." In *The House that Race Built,* ed. Wahneema Lubiano. New York: Vintage Books, 1998.

Hill, Herbert. *Black Labor and the American Labor System: Race, Work, and the Law.* Madison: University of Wisconsin Press, 1985.

Hill, Lance. *The Deacons for Defense: Armed Resistance and the Civil Rights Movement.* Chapel Hill: University of North Carolina Press, 2004.

Hill, Rickey. "The Character of Black Politics in a Small Southern Town Dominated by a Multinational Corporation: Bogalusa, Louisiana, 1965–1975." Master's thesis, Atlanta University, 1977.

Hine, Darlene Clark, William C. Hine, and Stanley Harrold. *The African American Odyssey.* Upper Saddle River, N.J.: Prentice Hall, 2003.

Holloway, Jonathan Scott. *Confronting the Veil: Abram Harris Jr., E. Franklin Frazier, and Ralph Bunche, 1919–1941*. Chapel Hill: University of North Carolina Press, 2002.

Honey, Michael K. *Southern Labor and Black Civil Rights: Organizing Memphis Workers*. Chicago: University of Illinois Press, 1993.

Horkheimer, Max, and Theodore Adorno. *Dialectic of Enlightenment*. New York: Herder and Herder, 1972.

Howard, John C. *The Negro in the Lumber Industry: The Racial Policies of American Industry, Report No. 19*. Philadelphia: University of Pennsylvania Press, 1970.

Hughes, Langston. *The Political Plays of Langston Hughes*, ed. Susan Duffy. Carbondale: Southern Illinois University Press, 2000.

Humphreys, Margaret. *Malaria: Poverty, Race, and Public Health in the United States*. Baltimore: Johns Hopkins University Press, 2001.

Hunter, Tera W. *To 'Joy My Freedom: Southern Black Women's Lives and Labors after the Civil War*. Cambridge: Harvard University Press, 1997.

Hurston, Zora Neale. *Every Tongue Got to Confess: Negro Folk-Tales from the Gulf States*. New York: Harper Collins, 2001.

———. *Mules and Men*. New York: Harper and Row, 1990.

Hutchinson, George. *The Harlem Renaissance in Black and White*. Cambridge: Belknap Press of Harvard University Press, 1995.

Irons, Janet. *Testing the New Deal: The General Textile Strike of 1934 in the American South*. Chapel Hill: University of North Carolina Press, 2000.

Isreal, Tom, and Randall Williams. "Ending the Short Stick in Mississippi's Woods." *Southern Changes: The Journal of the Southern Regional Council* (June/July 1982): 16.

Janiewski, Dolores. *Sisterhood Denied: Race, Class, and Gender in a New South Community*. Philadelphia: Temple University Press, 1985.

Jensen, Vernon H. *Lumber and Labor*. New York: J. J. Little and Ives Co., 1945.

Johnson, Charles S. *Growing Up in the Black Belt*. Washington, D.C.: American Council on Education, 1941.

Jones, Jacqueline. *The Dispossessed: America's Underclass from the Civil War to the Present*. New York: Basic Books, 1992.

———. *Labor of Love, Labor of Sorrow: Black Women, Work, and the Family, from Slavery to the Present*. New York: Basic Books, 1985.

Jones, William P. "As Good as It Gets: Three Children of Steel Remember the 'Golden Age' of American Industry." *International Labor and Working-Class History* 61 (Spring 2002): 183–87.

———. "Black Workers and the CIO's Turn toward Racial Liberalism: Operation Dixie and the North Carolina Lumber Industry, 1946–1953." *Labor History* 41 (Aug. 2000): 279–306.

———. "Cutting through Jim Crow: African American Lumber Workers in the Jim Crow South, 1919–1960." Ph.D. diss., University of North Carolina-Chapel Hill, 2000.

Kelley, Robin D. G. *Hammer and Hoe: Alabama Communists during the Great Depression*. Chapel Hill: University of North Carolina Press, 1990.

———. *Race Rebels: Culture, Politics, and the Black Working Class*. New York: Free Press, 1994.

———. "'We Are Not What We Seem': Rethinking Black Working-Class Opposition in the Jim Crow South." *Journal of American History* 80 (June 1993): 75–112.

Kelley, Robin D. G., and Earl Lewis. *To Make Our World Anew: A History of African Americans.* New York: Oxford University Press, 2000.

Kessler-Harris, Alice. *In Pursuit of Equity: Women, Men, and the Quest for Economic Citizenship in Twentieth-Century America.* New York: Oxford University Press, 2001.

Key, V. O. *Southern Politics in State and Nation.* New York: A. A. Knopf, 1949.

Kirby, Jack Temple. *Rural Worlds Lost: The American South, 1920–1960.* Baton Rouge: Louisiana State University Press, 1987.

Kluger, Richard. *Simple Justice: The History of Brown v. Board of Education and Black America's Struggle for Equality.* New York: Vintage Books, 1977.

Korstad, Robert R. *Civil Rights Unionism: Tobacco Workers and the Struggle for Democracy in the Mid-Twentieth-Century South.* Chapel Hill: University of North Carolina Press, 2003.

Korstad, Robert R., and Nelson Lichtenstein. "Opportunities Found and Lost: Labor, Radicals, and the Early Civil Rights Movement." *Journal of American History* 75 (Dec. 1988): 786–811.

Kossoris, Max D., and Frank S. McElroy. "Causes and Prevention of Accidents in Logging and Lumber Mills, 1940." *Monthly Labor Review* (Dec. 1941).

LaVere, Steven C. *Robert Johnson: The Complete Recordings.* Columbia Compact Disk 46222.

Leavel, R. H., T. R. Snavely, T. J. Woofter, W. T. B. Williams, and Francis D. Tyson. *Negro Migration in 1916–1919.* Washington, D.C.: U.S. Department of Labor, 1919.

Lemann, Nicholas. *The Promised Land: The Great Black Migration and How It Changed America.* New York: Vintage Books, 1991.

Lembcke, Jerry, and William M. Tattam. *One Union in Wood: A Political History of the International Woodworkers of America.* New York: International Publishers, 1984.

Letwin, Daniel. *The Challenge of Interracial Unionism: Alabama Coal Miners, 1878–1921.* Chapel Hill: University of North Carolina Press, 1998.

Levine, Lawrence. *Black Culture and Black Consciousness: Afro-American Folk Thought from Slavery to Freedom.* New York: Oxford University Press, 1977.

———. "The Folklore of Industrial Society." *American Historical Review* 97 (Dec. 1992): 1369–1430.

Levine, Susan. "Workers' Wives: Gender, Class, and Consumerism in the 1920s United States." *Gender and History* 3 (Spring 1991): 45–64.

Lewis, David Levering. *W. E. B. Du Bois: The Fight for Equality and the American Century, 1919–1963.* New York: Henry Holt, 2000.

Lewis, Earl. *In Their Own Interests: Race, Class, and Power in Twentieth-Century Norfolk, Virginia.* Berkeley: University of California Press, 1991.

Lewis, Ronald L. "From Peasant to Proletarian: The Migration of Southern Blacks to the Central Appalachian Coalfields." *Journal of Southern History* 55 (1989): 77–102.

———. *Transforming the Appalachian Countryside: Railroads, Deforestation, and Social Change in West Virginia, 1880–1920.* Chapel Hill: University of North Carolina Press, 1998.

Lichtenstein, Alex. "'Scientific Unionism' and the 'Negro Question'. Communists and the Transport Workers Union in Miami, 1944–1949." In *Southern Labor in Transition, 1940–1995,* ed. Robert H. Zieger. Knoxville: University of Tennessee Press, 1997.

———. *Twice the Work of Free Labor: The Political Economy of Convict Labor in the New South.* New York: Verso, 1996.

———. "Was the Emancipated Slave a Proletarian?" *Reviews in America History* 26, no. 1 (1998): 124–45.

Lichtenstein, Nelson. *State of the Union: A Century of American Labor.* Princeton: Princeton University Press, 2002.

Lindsay, Matilda. "Women Hold Key to Unionization of Dixie." *Machinists' Monthly Journal* 41 (Sept. 1929): 638–39, 684.

Lipsitz, George. *Rainbow at Midnight: Labor and Culture in the 1940s.* Urbana: University of Illinois Press, 1990.

Litwack, Leon F. *Trouble in Mind: Black Southerners in the Age of Jim Crow.* New York: Alfred A. Knopf, 1998.

Locke, Alain, ed. *The New Negro: Voices of the Harlem Renaissance.* New York: Simon and Schuster, 1997.

Lowther, Eugene J., and Roland V. Murray. "Labor Requirements in Southern Pine Lumber Production." *Monthly Labor Review* (Dec. 1946).

Lumpkin, Katharine DuPre. *The South in Progress.* New York: International Publishers, 1940.

Massey, Richard W. "A History of the Lumber Industry in Alabama and West Florida, 1880–1914." Ph.D. diss., Vanderbilt University, 1960.

Maunder, Elwood R. *James Greeley McGowin, South Alabama Lumberman: The Recollections of His Family, Interviews with N. Floyd McGowin, Earl M. McGowin, and Nicholas S. McGowin and written recollection by Estelle McGowin Larson.* Santa Cruz, Calif.: Forest History Society, 1977.

McCormick, Mac. *Robert Shaw, the Ma Grinder: Texas Barrelhouse Piano.* Arhoolie Compact Disk F1010.

Meier, August, and Elliot Rudwick. *Black Detroit and the Rise of the UAW.* New York: Oxford University Press, 1979.

Merrick, Jerry L. "History of the Great Southern Lumber Company." *Daily News* (Bogalusa), parts 1–4, Jan. 24–27, 1991.

Minchin, Timothy J. *The Color of Work: The Struggle for Civil Rights in the Southern Paper Industry, 1945–1980.* Chapel Hill: University of North Carolina Press, 2001.

———. *Hiring the Black Worker: The Racial Integration of the Southern Textile Industry, 1960–1980.* Chapel Hill: University of North Carolina Press, 1999.

Moodie, T. Dunbar, with Vivienne Ndatshe. *Going for Gold: Men, Mines, and Migration.* Berkeley: University of California Press, 1994.

Myrdal, Gunnar. *An American Dilemma: The Negro Problem and Modern Democracy.* New York: Harper and Brothers Publishers, 1944.

Myrick, Jerry L. "A History of the Great Southern Lumber Company, 1902–1938." Master's thesis, Louisiana State University, 1970.

Nelson, Bruce. "Organized Labor and the Struggle for Black Equality in Mobile during World War II." *Journal of American History* 80 (Dec. 1993): 952–88.

Northrup, Herbert R. *The Negro in the Paper Industry.* Philadelphia: University of Pennsylvania Press, 1969.

Norwood, Stephen H. "Bogalusa Burning: The War against Biracial Unionism in the Deep South, 1919." *Journal of Southern History* 63, no. 3 (Aug. 1997): 591–628.

O'Connor, Alice. *Poverty Knowledge: Social Science, Social Policy, and the Poor in Twentieth-Century U.S. History.* Princeton: Princeton University Press, 2001.

O'Neal, Jim and Amy. "Living Blues Interview: Georgia Tom Dorsey." *Living Blues* 20 (Mar. 1957): 17–34.

Odum, Howard W. *Rainbow 'round My Shoulder: The Blues Trail of Black Ulysses.* Indianapolis: Bobbs-Merrill Co, 1928.

Odum, Howard W., and Guy B. Johnson. *Negro Workaday Songs.* Chapel Hill: University of North Carolina Press, 1926.

Oliver, Paul. *Blues Fell This Morning: Meaning in the Blues.* New York: Cambridge University Press, 1990.

———. "An Introduction to the Recording of Folk Blues in the Twenties." *Jazz Review* 2 (Feb. 1959): 20–25.

Orleck, Annelise. *Common Sense and a Little Fire: Women and Working-Class Politics in the United States, 1900–1965.* Chapel Hill: University of North Carolina Press, 1995.

Ovington, Mary White. "Bogalusa." *Liberator* (Jan. 1920): 31–33.

Patterson, Florence. *Strikes in the United States, 1880–1936.* Washington, D.C.: U.S. Department of Labor, 1938.

Pfeffer, Paula F. *A. Philip Randolph: Pioneer of the Civil Rights Movement.* Baton Rouge: Louisiana State University Press, 1990.

Proceedings of the 10th Annual Constitutional Convention of the International Woodworkers of America-CIO, Canadian Congress of Labor, 1946.

Proceedings of the 11th Annual Constitutional Convention of the International Woodworkers of America-CIO, Canadian Congress of Labor, 1947.

Proceedings of the 12th Annual Constitutional Convention of the International Woodworkers of America-CIO, Canadian Congress of Labor, 1948.

Proceedings of the 13th Annual Constitutional Convention of the International Woodworkers of America-CIO, Canadian Congress of Labor, 1949.

Proceedings of the 16th Annual Constitutional Convention of the International Woodworkers of America-CIO, Canadian Congress of Labor, 1950.

Proceedings of the 17th Annual Constitutional Convention of the International Woodworkers of America-CIO, Canadian Congress of Labor, 1951.

Proceedings of the 18th and 19th Annual Constitutional Convention of the International Woodworkers of America-CIO, Canadian Congress of Labor, 1952–53.

Proceedings of the 20th Annual Constitutional Convention of the International Woodworkers of America-AFL-CIO, Canadian Congress of Labor, 1954.

Putnam, Lara. *The Company They Kept: Migrants and the Politics of Gender in Caribbean Costa Rica, 1870–1960.* Chapel Hill: University of North Carolina Press, 2002.

Quick, Amy. "The History of Bogalusa, the 'Magic City' of Louisiana." Ph.D. diss., Louisiana State University, 1942.

Rachleff, Peter J. *Black Labor in the South: Richmond, Virginia, 1865–1890.* Philadelphia: Temple University Press, 1984.

Raddock, Maxwell C. *Portrait of an American Labor Leader. William L. Hutcheson.* New York: American Institute of Social Science, Inc., 1955.

Randolph, John. "A Pioneer Race Recorder." *Jazz Journal* 10 (Feb. 1957): 11.

Ransby, Barbara. *Ella Baker and the Black Freedom Movement: A Radical Democratic Vision.* Chapel Hill: University of North Carolina Press, 2003.

Reed, Adolph, Jr. "Parting the Waters." *Nation* (Nov. 23, 1992): 633–41.

———. *Stirrings in the Jug: Black Politics in the Post-Segregation Era.* Minneapolis: University of Minnesota Press, 1999.

———. *W. E. B. Du Bois and American Political Thought: Fabianism and the Color Line.* New York: Oxford University Press, 1997.

Reich, Steven A. "The Making of a Southern Sawmill World: Race, Class, and Rural Transformation in the Piney Woods of East Texas, 1830–1930." Ph.D. diss., Northwestern University, 1998.

Reid, Ira De Augustine. *Negro Membership in American Labor Unions.* New York: National Urban League, 1930.

Reidy, Joseph P. *From Slavery to Agrarian Capitalism in the Cotton Plantation South: Central Georgia, 1800–1880.* Chapel Hill: University of North Carolina Press, 1992.

Robbins, William G. *Lumberjacks and Legislators: Political Economy of the U.S. Lumber Industry, 1890–1941.* College Station: Texas A&M University Press, 1982.

Robinson, Elzadie. *Elzadie Robinson, 1926–1929.* Document LP 588.

Roediger, David. "Gaining a Hearing for Black-White Unity: Covington Hall and the Complexities of Race, Gender, and Class." In *Towards the Abolition of Whiteness: Essays on Race, Politics, and Working Class History.* New York: Verso, 1994.

Rose, Tricia. *Black Noise: Rap Music and Black Culture in Contemporary America.* Hanover, N.H.: University Press of New England, 1994.

Rosengarten, Theodore. *All God's Dangers: The Life of Nate Shaw.* New York: Avon Books, 1974.

Rowe, Mike. "Piano Blues and Boogie-Woogie." In *The Blackwell Guide to Recorded Blues,* ed. Paul Oliver. Cambridge: Blackwell Publishers, 1991.

Rubin, Morton. *Plantation County.* New Haven, Conn.: College and University Press, 1951.

Ruck, Rob. *Sandlot Seasons: Sport in Black Pittsburgh.* Urbana: University of Illinois Press, 1993.

Ruggles, Steven, Matthew Sobek, et al. *Integrated Public Use Microdata Series: Version 2.0.* Minneapolis: Historical Census Projects, University of Minnesota, 1997.

Russell, Jacqueline H. "A Historical Study of the Development of the Bogalusa School System, 1907–1967." Ph.D. diss., University of Southern Mississippi, 1968.

Rustin, Bayard. "From Protest to Politics: The Future of the Civil Rights Movement." *Commentary* (Feb. 1965): 25–31.

Sawaya, Charles Phillip. "The Employment Effects of Minimum Wage Regulation in the Southern Pine Lumber Industry." Ph.D. diss., Indiana University, 1958.

Schulman, Bruce J. *From Cotton Belt to Sunbelt: Federal Policy, Economic De-*

velopment, and the Transformation of the South, 1938–1980. Durham, N.C.: Duke University Press, 1994.

Scott, Daryl Michael. *Contempt and Pity: Social Policy and the Image of the Damaged Black Psyche, 1880–1996.* Chapel Hill: University of North Carolina Press, 1997.

Scott, James C. *Domination and the Arts of Resistance: Hidden Transcripts.* New Haven, Conn.: Yale University Press, 1990.

Scott, Joan W. "Experience." In *Feminists Theorize the Political,* ed. Judith Butler and Joan W. Scott. New York: Routledge, 1992.

Seligman, Herbert J. *The Negro Faces America.* New York: Harper and Brothers Publishers, 1920.

Shapiro, Michael J. "Politicizing Ulysses: Rationalistic, Critical, and Genealogical Commentaries." *Political Theory* 17, no. 1 (Feb. 1989): 9–32.

Simon, Bryant. *A Fabric of Defeat: The Politics of South Carolina Millhands, 1910–1948.* Chapel Hill: University of North Carolina Press, 1998.

Singal, Joseph Daniel. *The War Within: From Victorian to Modernist Thought in the South, 1919–1945.* Chapel Hill: University of North Carolina Press, 1982.

Sitkoff, Harvard. "African American Militancy in the World War II South: Another Perspective." In *Remaking Dixie: The Impact of World War II on the American South,* ed. Neil R. McMillan. Jackson: University Press of Mississippi, 1997.

———. *A New Deal for Blacks: The Emergence of Civil Rights as a National Issue: The Depression Decade.* New York: Oxford University Press, 1978.

Sitton, Thad, and James Conrad. *Nameless Towns: Texas Sawmill Communities, 1880–1942.* Austin: University of Texas Press, 1998.

Solomon, Mark. *The Cry Was Unity: Communists and African Americans, 1917–1936.* Jackson: University Press of Mississippi, 1998.

Sosna, Morton. *In Search of the Silent South: Southern Liberals and the Race Issue.* New York: Columbia University Press, 1977.

Spero, Sterling D., and Abram L. Harris. *The Black Worker.* New York: Atheneum, 1972.

Stanley, Amy Dru. *From Bondage to Contract: Wage Labor, Marriage, and the Market in the Age of Slave Emancipation.* New York: Cambridge University Press, 1998.

Stein, Judith. *Running Steel, Running America: Race, Economic Policy, and the Decline of Liberalism.* Chapel Hill: University of North Carolina Press, 1998.

Storrs, Landon R. Y. *Civilizing Capitalism: The National Consumers' League, Women's Activism, and Labor Standards in the New Deal Era.* Chapel Hill: University of North Carolina Press, 2000.

Sugrue, Thomas J. *The Origins of the Urban Crisis: Race and Inequality in Postwar Detroit.* Princeton: Princeton University Press, 1996.

Sullivan, Patricia. *Days of Hope: Race and Democracy in the New Deal Era.* Chapel Hill: University of North Carolina Press, 1996.

Sullivan, William H. "World's Greatest Lumber Plant." *Logical Point* 1, no. 2 (Sept. 1910): 31–35.

Thodes, Charlotte. *Labor and Lumber.* New York: International Publishers, 1931.

Tindall, George. *The Emergence of the New South, 1913–1945.* Baton Rouge: Louisiana State University Press, 1967.

Tippett, Thomas. *When Southern Labor Stirs*. New York. J. Cape and H. Smith, 1931.

Tolnay, Stewart E. *The Bottom Rung: African American Family Life on Southern Farms*. Urbana: University of Illinois Press, 1999.

Tomlins, Christopher L. *The State and the Unions: Labor Relations, Law, and the Organized Labor Movement in America, 1880–1960*. New York: Cambridge University Press, 1985.

Trotter, Joe William, Jr. *The African American Experience*, vol. 2. New York: Houghton Mifflin, 2001.

———. *Black Milwaukee: The Making of an Industrial Proletariat, 1915–45*. Urbana: University of Illinois Press, 1985.

———. *Coal, Class, and Color: Blacks in Southern West Virginia, 1915–1932*. Urbana: University of Illinois Press, 1990.

Turner, Lorenzo Dow. *Africanisms in the Gullah Dialect*. Columbia: University of South Carolina Press, 2002.

U.S. Bureau of the Census. *Negroes in the United States, 1920–32*. 1932.

U.S. Department of Labor. "Wages and Hours of Labor in the Lumber Industry in the United States, 1930." *Bulletin of the U.S. Bureau of Labor Statistics* no. 560 (Mar. 1932): 1–25.

———. "Wages and Hours of Labor in the Lumber Industry in the United States, 1932." *Bulletin of the U.S. Bureau of Labor Statistics* no. 586 (Aug. 1933): 1–25.

———. "Wages in the Basic Lumber Industry, 1944." *Bulletin of the U.S. Bureau of Labor Statistics* no. 854: 1–13.

———. "Work Injuries in the United States during 1945." *Monthly Labor Review* (Sept. 1946): 1–11.

Waldrep, G. C. *Southern Workers and the Search for Community: Spartanburg County, South Carolina*. Chapel Hill: University of North Carolina Press, 2000.

Washington, Forrester B. "Recreational Facilities for the Negro." *Annals of the American Academy of Political and Social Sciences* 140 (Nov. 1928): 272–82.

Weems, Robert E., Jr. *Desegregating the Dollar: African American Consumerism in the Twentieth Century*. New York: New York University Press, 1998.

Weiss, Nancy J. *The National Urban League, 1910–1940*. New York: Oxford University Press, 1974.

Wexley, John. *They Shall Not Die: A Play*. New York: A. A. Knopf, 1934.

Whayne, Jeannie M. *A New Plantation South: Land, Labor, and Federal Favor in Twentieth-Century Arkansas*. Charlottesville: University Press of Virginia, 1996.

Wilson, William Julius. *The Truly Disadvantaged: The Inner City, the Underclass, and Public Policy*. Chicago: University of Chicago Press, 1987.

Wolcott, Victoria W. *Remaking Respectability: African American Women in Interwar Detroit*. Chapel Hill: University of North Carolina Press, 2001.

Wolters, Raymond. *Negroes and the Great Depression: The Problem of Economic Recovery*. Westport, Conn.: Greenwood Publishing Corporation, 1970.

Woodson, Carter G. *The Rural Negro*. New York: Russell and Russell, 1930.

Woodward, C. Vann. *Origins of the New South*. New York: Alfred A. Knopf, 1951.

Wright, Gavin. Afterword to *The Second Wave: Southern Industrialization from the 1940s to the 1970s*, ed. Philip Scranton. Athens: University of Georgia Press, 2001.

Wright, Gavin. *Old South, New South: Revolutions in the Southern Economy since the Civil War.* New York: Basic Books, 1985.

Zieger, Robert H. *The CIO: 1935–1955.* Chapel Hill: University of North Carolina Press, 1995.

———. *Rebuilding the Pulp and Paper Workers' Union: 1933–1941.* Knoxville: University of Tennessee Press, 1984.

———. "Textile Workers and the Historians." In *Organized Labor in the Twentieth-Century South,* ed. Robert H. Zieger. Knoxville: University of Tennessee Press, 1991.

INDEX

Brown, Jesse, 36–37
Brown, R. B., 113
Brown Bombers, Chicago, 77
Brumfield, Dewitt, 52
Bunche, Ralph, 139–40
Butler County, Ala. *See* W. T. Smith
  Lumber Company

Campanella, Roy, 77
Cape Fear River, 40
Carby, Hazel, 4, 200n38
carpenters union. *See* United Brother-
  hood of Carpenters and Joiners
Carter, Elmer, 136, 138
Carter, Lonnie, 55, 89–90, 95, 109,
  181
Cartwright, Rev. Cary Miles, 69
Cash, W. J.: *Mind of the South,* 5
Cassiday, E. R., 85, 145
Cayton, Horace, 131, 163
Chapman, Ala. *See* W. T. Smith Lum-
  ber Company
Cheatham, George, 54–55, 168
Christian, Lee, 161
Christianity. *See* religion
Christmas, Joe, 46
churches, in mill towns, 8, 61–62, 75.
  See also religion
Civilian Conservation Corps, 30, 39–
  40, 78
Civil Rights Act (1964), 115
civil rights movement, 12, 124, 173,
  178–80, 184, 187; in Ala., 168; in
  La., 176–79; in N.C., 176. *See also*
  black working class: civil rights or-
  ganizations and
civil rights unionism, 152, 168–76
Civil War, 1, 15
Cleveland Lumber Company, 165
Cobb, Marie, 78, 84
Cobb, Ned, 8, 19
Cohen, Lizbeth, 124, 165
college admission policies. *See* higher
  education, access for African Americans
Colly Swamp, N.C., 40, 93
commercial music, 61–65, 80–81, 87
Commission on Interracial Cooperation, 106

Committee for Industrial Organization, 130. *See also* Congress of Industrial Organizations
Communist Party: African Americans
  and, 137–38, 149–50; lumber workers and, 130, 146–50, 161; racial
  analysis of, 107, 135, 156; textile
  workers and, 133–34. *See also* anti-
  communism; International Labor
  Defense; National Textile Workers
  Union; Trade Union Unity League
Congress of Industrial Organizations
  (CIO), 11, 126–27, 165, 167; civil
  rights organizations and, 163; formation of, 130–32, 144–50; interracial unionism and, 151, 159–76; Political Action Committee, 172. *See
  also* Food, Tobacco, and Allied
  Workers of America; International
  Ladies' Garment Workers Union;
  International Longshoremen's Association; International Woodworkers of America; Mine, Mill, and
  Smelter Workers Union; Operation
  Dixie; Steel Workers Organizing
  Committee; United Cannery, Agricultural, Packing and Allied Workers of America; United Mine Workers of America; United
  Packinghouse Workers of America;
  United Textile Workers of America
conservation, 29–31, 37, 117
Consumption, commercial: African
  American culture and, 9–11, 63,
  78–79; federal government and,
  109, 114; wage employment and, 7,
  181
convict labor, 21, 24, 157
Cook, Staley, 93
Cooper, Frederick, 190n14
Cotton, Reverend, 171, 181
craft unions. *See* unions: craft
craft workers, 92, 95. *See also* unions:
  craft
Crisis, The, 123, 142
Crosby, L. O., 99, 119
Crown Zellerbach Corporation, 178–
  79, 184
Cruikshank, J. W., 40

Worker City, Company Town: Iron and Cotton-Worker Protest in Troy and
Cohoes, New York, 1855–84   *Daniel J. Walkowitz*
Life, Work, and Rebellion in the Coal Fields: The Southern West Virginia
Miners, 1880–1922   *David Alan Corbin*
Women and American Socialism, 1870–1920   *Mari Jo Buhle*
Lives of Their Own: Blacks, Italians, and Poles in Pittsburgh, 1900–1960
John Bodnar, Roger Simon, and Michael P. Weber
Working-Class America: Essays on Labor, Community, and American
Society   *Edited by Michael H. Frisch and Daniel J. Walkowitz*
Eugene V. Debs: Citizen and Socialist   *Nick Salvatore*
American Labor and Immigration History, 1877–1920s: Recent European
Research   *Edited by Dirk Hoerder*
Workingmen's Democracy: The Knights of Labor and American
Politics   *Leon Fink*
The Electrical Workers: A History of Labor at General Electric and
Westinghouse, 1923–60   *Ronald W. Schatz*
The Mechanics of Baltimore: Workers and Politics in the Age of
Revolution, 1763–1812   *Charles G. Steffen*
The Practice of Solidarity: American Hat Finishers in the Nineteenth
Century   *David Bensman*
The Labor History Reader   *Edited by Daniel J. Leab*
Solidarity and Fragmentation: Working People and Class Consciousness in
Detroit, 1875–1900   *Richard Oestreicher*
Counter Cultures: Saleswomen, Managers, and Customers in American
Department Stores, 1890–1940   *Susan Porter Benson*
The New England Working Class and the New Labor
History   *Edited by Herbert G. Gutman and Donald H. Bell*
Labor Leaders in America   *Edited by Melvyn Dubofsky
and Warren Van Tine*
Barons of Labor: The San Francisco Building Trades and Union Power in
the Progressive Era   *Michael Kazin*
Gender at Work: The Dynamics of Job Segregation by Sex during World
War II   *Ruth Milkman*
Once a Cigar Maker: Men, Women, and Work Culture in American Cigar
Factories, 1900–1919   *Patricia A. Cooper*
A Generation of Boomers: The Pattern of Railroad Labor Conflict in
Nineteenth-Century America   *Shelton Stromquist*
Work and Community in the Jungle: Chicago's Packinghouse Workers,
1894–1922   *James R. Barrett*
Workers, Managers, and Welfare Capitalism: The Shoeworkers and
Tanners of Endicott Johnson, 1890–1950   *Gerald Zahavi*

WILLIAM P. JONES is assistant professor
of history at the University of Wisconsin,
Milwaukee.

The University of Illinois Press
is a founding member of the
Association of American University Presses.

Composed in 9.5/12.5 Trump Mediaeval
by Celia Shapland
for the University of Illinois Press
Manufactured by Thomson-Shore, Inc.

University of Illinois Press
1325 South Oak Street
Champaign, IL 61820-6903
www.press.uillinois.edu